CW00539775

A PEOPLE'S TRAGEDY

A PEOPLE'S TRAGEDY

Studies in Reformation

EAMON DUFFY

BLOOMSBURY CONTINUUM
LONDON · OXFORD · NEW YORK · NEW DELHI · SYDNEY

BLOOMSBURY CONTINUUM
Bloomsbury Publishing Plc
50 Bedford Square, London, WC1B 3DP, UK

BLOOMSBURY, BLOOMSBURY CONTINUUM and the Diana logo are trademarks
of Bloomsbury Publishing Plc

First published in Great Britain 2020

Copyright © Eamon Duffy, 2020

Eamon Duffy has asserted his right under the Copyright, Designs and Patents Act, 1988,
to be identified as Author of this work

All rights reserved. No part of this publication may be reproduced or transmitted in any form or
by any means, electronic or mechanical, including photocopying, recording, or any information
storage or retrieval system, without prior permission in writing from the publishers

Bloomsbury Publishing Plc does not have any control over, or responsibility for, any third-party
websites referred to or in this book. All internet addresses given in this book were correct at the
time of going to press. The author and publisher regret any inconvenience caused if addresses have
changed or sites have ceased to exist, but can accept no responsibility for any such changes

A catalogue record for this book is available from the British Library

Library of Congress Cataloguing-in-Publication data has been applied for

ISBN: HB: 978-1-4729-8385-5; ePDF: 978-1-4729-8387-9; ePub: 978-1-4729-8386-2

2 4 6 8 10 9 7 5 3 1

Typeset by Deanta Global Publishing Services, Chennai, India
Printed and bound in Great Britain by CPI Group (UK) Ltd, Croydon CR0 4YY

To find out more about our authors and books visit www.bloomsbury.com
and sign up for our newsletters

For 'tony
with love

Contents

List of Illustrations

Introduction

On 5 November every year tens of thousands of visitors descend on the small Sussex town of Lewes for one of the last major manifestations of a tradition that was once a shaping force of British national identity. In the wintry darkness up to 30 torchlight processions, led by brass bands and thundering kettledrums, trail through the narrow streets, the flames illuminating exotically costumed paraders – pirates, Tudor townsfolk, skull-faced zombies and even, for some reason, feather-crowned Zulu warriors. The processions climax in a gigantic firework display and a bonfire, on which human effigies (which in 2019 included Boris Johnson and Nigel Farage) are immolated to the sound of jeers and cheers.

The Lewes Guy Fawkes celebrations are now a complex folk event encoding a multitude of meanings, in which elements of local, national and international popular culture and issues of current concern jostle tourist-board promotion and local patriotism. But the event itself originated in deadly religious divisions, because 5 November was the anniversary of the Gunpowder Plot, the abortive attempt by a group of disgruntled Roman Catholic conspirators to blow up King James I and his Parliament and place a Catholic ruler on the English throne. In 1606 an annual commemoration was instituted to keep alive the memory of this foiled atrocity, and a special service was added to the Book of Common Prayer for the purpose. Over the next two centuries further 'deliverances' from popery were included in the commemorations, notably the deposing of the Catholic King James II in favour of his son-in-law

William of Orange and the replacement in 1714 of the religiously unreliable Stuart dynasty by the staunchly Protestant Hanoverians. Guy Fawkes night became a ferocious and fiery annual celebration of 'the deliverance of our Church and Nation from Popish tyranny and arbitrary power'. Well into the nineteenth century the effigies burned on bonfires up and down the country included not merely the Catholic plotter Guy Fawkes but also, more often than not, the reigning Pope, in an aggressive collective re-affirmation of Protestant national identity. And at Lewes the celebrations were given additional fervour because the bonfires served also to commemorate the brutal execution by burning alive of 17 local Protestants during the reign of the Catholic Queen Mary.

If one strand in English national consciousness has been a carefully fostered folk memory of the nation's narrow escapes from tyrannical Catholic domination under Elizabeth I and her Stuart successors, another equally important element has been the myth of Good King Harry, the titanic figure of Henry VIII, who in the 1530s severed England's 900-year-old links with the papacy, declared his kingdom 'an empire unto itself' and created a national Church subordinated to the monarchy. The new Church was not at first 'Protestant', and while Henry lived it retained the medieval Mass almost unchanged. But Henry's Reformation involved far more than a switch from papal to royal jurisdiction. Henry put an end to the immemorial and resonantly symbolic practice of pilgrimage, and with it the multitude of major and minor shrines that had criss-crossed England with a network of pilgrim routes that constituted a sacred landscape, literally grounding the people's sense of the sacred. Henry also suppressed all English and Welsh houses of monks and nuns. Early Tudor monastic communities could be sleepy, over-comfortable institutions, and some were openly corrupt. But monasticism had been central to the health of Christendom for more than a millennium, at its best an inspiring witness to the radical demands of the Gospel and a perennial source of religious zeal and moral and institutional reform. Female religious communities had offered women a dignified form of life in which their identity and value were not constituted by their role as some man's daughter or wife. The outlawing of this venerable and versatile form of religious expression for the next three centuries was an impoverishment at least as profound as any entailed by the revolt against the papacy.

Until a generation or so ago, the historiography of the English Reformation made little of such losses. The break with Rome was widely understood as a necessary liberation into national autonomy – the 'prequel' to modernity or imperial greatness – and the suppression of monasticism was viewed as an overdue escape from rank superstition. Major late medieval religious institutions – pilgrimage, the priesthood, monks and nuns, confraternities and guilds, indulgences – were viewed unsympathetically and little studied, and the late medieval Church itself was seen as an ailing institution, whose unpopularity with the men and women of early Tudor England explained their rapid and eager adoption of Protestantism.

In recent years there has been welcome change in this situation. Historians are newly sensitive to the vigour and popularity of many hitherto ignored and unstudied aspects of late medieval Christianity, expressed most obviously in massive lay investment in the rebuilding and lavish furnishing for Catholic worship of many of the parish churches of Plantagenet and early Tudor England. There has also been a growing awareness of the existence of widespread discontent with and resistance to the Reformation process, which is now understood as a long labour, not a rapid and popular push-over. The study of minority religious communities, Protestant and Catholic, who refused conformity to the national Church has moved from a denominational niche interest to the historical mainstream.

The studies that make up this book are intended as contributions to this recovery of such rich and hitherto neglected aspects of English religion, from the fifteenth century to the seventeenth. Several essays in the first half of the book consider central aspects of late medieval religion – pilgrimages and monasticism – and their suppression at the Reformation; others examine resistance to that Reformation – political resistance in the story of the last great armed rebellion against the Tudor Crown in the north of England in 1569, and intellectual and spiritual resistance in an exploration of the novel religious studies adopted in the English seminaries founded abroad in Catholic Europe to roll back the triumph of Protestantism at home. In the second half of the book I turn to consider how the Reformation, European as well as English, has been understood and written about, starting with the mostly unsympathetic ways in which Catholic writers through four centuries have understood – or misunderstood – Martin Luther. Other essays examine the assumptions and prejudices that have shaped treatments of the Tudor Reformation and the religion it displaced by major historians in the nineteenth and twentieth centuries. Finally, the last essay in the book considers the changing ways in which that religious revolution has been turned into entertaining fiction, culminating in the TV adaptation of Hilary Mantel's gripping trilogy on the rise and fall of Henry VIII's political and religious fixer, Thomas Cromwell. The bookshop shelves nowadays groan with a multitude of books, factual and fictional, about Tudor England: in adding to their number, I hope this collection will enhance understanding and appreciation of both Tudor fact and Tudor fiction.

PART ONE

Studies in Reformation

Cathedral Pilgrimage:
The Late Middle Ages

In 1986 work to strengthen the south-east tower pier in Worcester Cathedral uncovered a shallow late medieval grave containing the skeleton of a man who had died in his sixties and who had been buried in a lined woollen tunic and thigh-length walking boots. By his side was a stout metal-shod wooden staff, once painted bright red, and a cockle shell, the conventional sign of a medieval pilgrim, pierced and probably once attached to his staff or hat. The boots had been almost new when they were slit along their lengths to dress the corpse; the metal spike that shod the staff showed little sign of wear. The state of the skeleton's knee, hip and right arm joints, by contrast, suggested that he had walked long and far wielding a staff, and the dead man's funeral arrangements were clearly designed to emphasize his identity as a pilgrim.[1]

The subject of this mysterious but resonantly symbolic burial on the edge of the monastic enclosure in a prestigious site within the cathedral was presumably a well-to-do citizen of the city. The great building in which he was laid to rest itself housed the shrines of two saintly Anglo-Saxon bishops, Oswald and Wulfstan, and a famous wonder-working statue of the Virgin, all of which were objects of pilgrimage in the 1490s. Yet the state of the Worcester pilgrim's skeleton suggests that he had wandered far from the cathedral and his native city in search of holiness. His burial is a reminder that the cathedral shrines of late medieval England formed one strand in a complex web of sacred sites that had ramifications throughout Christian Europe, and beyond. The desire to go on pilgrimage might take medieval English people to venerate relics or a notable image in the next village, to the mother church of their diocese, to a national shrine such as Walsingham or Canterbury or to one of the great international pilgrimage destinations of Jerusalem or Rome, Cologne or Santiago de Compostela.

The pilgrim accoutrements of the Worcester burial may have been intended as a memorial of some such pilgrimages made in the past, or a more generalized symbolic representation of life conceived as a journey towards heaven. But it may equally have been a confession of a vow of pilgrimage unfulfilled at the time of the Worcester pilgrim's death. Such confessions were often made in the wills of devout men and women in the later Middle Ages, such as the Somerset gentleman James Hadley, who, on the very eve of the break with Rome, confessed that 'I have beyne negligent to visit holy places and in going of pilgrimage', and sought to make amends with a series of bequests to local and national shrines.[2]

Pretty well every fifteenth-century will collection would yield examples of testators anxious about the completion of pilgrimages promised but unfulfilled in their lifetimes, such as Richard Suttone of Oxbrough in Norfolk in 1451, who provided for a surrogate to put into effect 'my vows, which I made to divers saints in times of necessity'.[3] Another Suffolk testator, Thomas Peckerell of Rickinghall Superior, provided for a pilgrim to go on his behalf to the image of the Trinity in Norwich Cathedral, to St Etheldreda's shrine in Ely, to St Edmund's shrine in Bury and to the Holy House at Walsingham, but also to lesser shrines in Lowestoft and Thorpe St Peter: significantly, all these shrines were local to East Anglia.[4] In fact, the specified destinations in most such fifteenth-century lists were predominantly to local and lesser pilgrimage sites, in many cases of recent establishment, and they overwhelmingly outnumber cathedral shrines such as Canterbury and national shrines like Walsingham. And when testators did look further than their own localities, they might more often than not think in international terms, rather than sending their surrogates to one or other of the English great churches. If the 2,300 Sudbury archdeaconry wills made between the 1440s and the 1470s and calendared by Peter Northeast are anything to go by, only a handful of late fifteenth-century Suffolk testators sent surrogates to Walsingham or Canterbury, whereas 19 made elaborate and costly provision for a professional pilgrim, in most cases specifically a priest, to go to Rome and stay there for up to a year, for the health of the testator's soul.

The pilgrimage destinations mentioned in such wills therefore alert us to the embedding of cathedral pilgrimage in a much broader landscape of holiness. In 1501 the Devon landowner Sir John Wadham, who had himself made the pilgrimage to Jerusalem in the 1470s, made a will requesting 'sum honest man to go for me on pilgrimage to St Jamys, to Haills, to Master John Schorne, to Walsingham, to Canterburye, to the rode of Northdore at Pawlis, to our Ladye of pewe, to king Harrye, to our Lady of Bowe, to Saint Brownewill, to Byshoppe Lacy'. Wadham's pilgrim was thus to go on his behalf to the shrine of St James in Compostela, to the Holy Blood of Hailes in Gloucestershire, to the shrines of the uncanonized saints Master John Schorne and Henry VI (by 1501 both at Windsor), to the image of the Virgin in Bow church and to the miraculous Rood of the North Door in St Paul's Cathedral (both in London), to Becket's shrine in Canterbury Cathedral and, nearer at hand, to the shrines of two local Devon saints: the eighth-century cleric Beornwald, venerated in the north transept of Bampton parish church, and Bishop Edmund Lacy, whose grave in Exeter Cathedral had become the focus of pilgrimage and healings immediately after his death in 1455, a *cultus* evidently still active in 1503.[5]

Pilgrimage to the great churches of late medieval England was therefore one strand in an intricate network of pilgrimage sites and routes that made up England's complex landscape of the sacred. That's not to suggest that there was nothing distinctive about pilgrimage to cathedral saints. The twelfth and thirteenth centuries witnessed a striking acceleration of pilgrimage observances within

England's great churches, as the example of Becket established the pattern of the saintly bishop as the most eagerly desired of patrons. Thomas's murder in his own cathedral in 1170 sent shock waves through Europe, and his extraordinarily rapid canonization just three years later established him as the definitive pattern of sanctity for his age. Within a decade of his death his feast day was being celebrated, his relics circulated, his image venerated and churches and oratories dedicated to him, from the Mediterranean to the Baltic. The translation of his relics to a magnificent new shrine in 1220, and the establishment of the 'Jubilee of St Thomas', celebrated every 50 years, clinched his primacy in the calendar of English saints.[6]

Thomas was unique in his threefold claims to sanctity – as martyr for the liberties of the Church, as convert from an extravagant secular career to an austerely ascetical life as holy bishop and, not least, as an exceptionally prolific thaumaturge (more than 700 miracles were attributed to him by the time of his canonization in 1173). No other episcopal saint would quite match all that, but in the centuries that followed many English cathedral churches had a go. Holy bishops had, of course, been venerated since antiquity, but the popularity of Thomas's cult unquestionably promoted the fashion for holy bishops. Indeed, the sudden miraculous flow of sweet-scented oil from the tomb of William of York in 1223 looks like a direct riposte by the mother church of the Northern Province to the spectacular translation of Becket's body to a new shrine in 1220. The miraculous oil would remain prominent in St William's *cultus*, and pilgrims drawing healing oil from spigots in the shrine were vividly portrayed in the early fifteenth-century window in the minster's north-east transept depicting St William's life and miracles.[7]

Unless they already had their own established major patron, like St Etheldreda at Ely, cathedrals without a sainted bishop sought to acquire one, and episcopal saints multiplied – between 1173 and 1320 eight English bishops achieved canonization, and new or refurbished cults of holy bishops were added to the established cults of Chad (Lichfield), Erkenwald (London), Cuthbert

(Durham) and Wilfred (Ripon, not of course in the twelfth century a cathedral) – Hugh of Lincoln (d. 1200, canonized 1220), William of York (d. 1154, canonized 1227), Richard of Chichester (d. 1253, canonized 1262) and Thomas Cantilupe at Hereford (d. 1282, canonized 1320).[8] As well as these new saints, some older shrines and cults were clearly given new impetus by Becket's celebrity. At Worcester the relics of Bishop Wulfstan (d. 1095) were translated into a new shrine in 1198 and a book of miracles begun in preparation for his canonization, achieved in 1203.[9] Bishops noted for a holy life were buried in tombs that manifestly aspired to the status of a shrine, such as the canopied tomb of Bishop Walter Grey (d. 1255) in York Minster.[10] Unofficial episcopal cults flourished, such as the fifteenth-century cults around the tomb of the executed Archbishop Richard Scrope in York Minster (d. 1405) or, later in the century, that of Bishop Edmund Lacy in Exeter. Most such cults were probably relatively short-lived. Miracles were reported at his tomb soon after the death of Bishop Walter Suffield of Norwich, a notable benefactor of the poor, and for 40 years pilgrim offerings at his tomb made a substantial contribution to the finances of the cathedral: thereafter, pilgrim numbers declined steeply, and by 1404 the annual offerings at his tomb amounted to just a single penny.[11]

'Saint' Walter's *cultus* remained unofficial, and there were many abortive or delayed campaigns to place such cults on an official basis and hence perpetuate them by securing formal papal endorsement. There were five unsuccessful attempts by successive bishops and chapters of Lincoln between 1254 and 1307 to secure the canonization of Robert Grosseteste,[12] and the long-drawn-out cause of Osmund of Salisbury, initiated in 1228, came to tardy fruition with his canonization as late as 1456.[13] But even after the establishment of papal monopoly on the process of canonization, the shrines of some uncanonized saints might command enduring devotion. Two early sixteenth-century inventories allow us to glimpse the precious metal ex-votos fixed to the tomb of Archbishop Scrope in York Minster, concrete expressions of the gratitude of those who attributed healing or help to his intercession: miniature

figures of men and women, replicas of individual body parts –
arms, legs and feet, breasts, eyes, teeth, heads and hearts – as well as
implements of hurt and deliverance – arrows, hooks and anchors,
and a whole fleet of silver ships, great and small.[14]

Despite its accumulation of ex-votos, still accreting in 1509,
Scrope's tomb in the choir of York Minster was a grave, not a purpose-
built shrine. But a distinctive form of cathedral shrine did emerge
in England in the course of the thirteenth and fourteenth centuries.
This was characteristically a richly decorated raised rectangular
marble base, surmounted by an open pillared superstructure which
allowed kneeling pilgrims to reach or lean into the monument, on
top of which was placed the *feretrum* or jewelled coffin containing
the bones or body of the saint. In great shrines such as Canterbury,
York and Durham the raised *feretrum* was concealed by an elaborate
wood, metal and fabric canopy, which could be raised by pulley
to reveal the *feretrum* itself. At Durham the ropes of the raisable
canopy were decorated with six silver bells, whose chiming as the
mechanism was activated summoned pilgrims elsewhere in the
cathedral to Cuthbert's *feretrum* as it was exposed for veneration.[15]

Most saints were initially venerated at the site of their burial,
which was often in the sanctuary, near the high altar. But in the
course of the thirteenth and fourteenth centuries many of the
major saints of English cathedral and other great churches were
translated to grander shrines in more prominent positions. Even
before his canonization Thomas Cantilupe's body was translated by
his successor, Bishop Swinfield, from his grave in the Lady Chapel
at Hereford to an elaborate new shrine in the north transept in
1287, a relocation that was crucial in kick-starting his cult.[16] But
many of the principal shrines of cathedral and other great churches
were relocated or elaborated in the ancient position for a patronal
saint, east of the high altar, in enclosures or chapels extended or
newly constructed for the purpose. Edward the Confessor's elevated
shrine east of the high altar at Westminster was constructed in
1269, St Richard of Chichester's shine in his former cathedral in
1274, St Hugh's at Lincoln in 1280, St David's in his cathedral in
or soon after 1280, St William's at York in 1284, St Erkenwald's at

St Paul's in 1326 and St Werbergh's at Chester around 1340, while Cuthbert's shrine in Durham was lavishly reconstructed, at a cost of 200 pounds of silver, in 1370.[17]

It was a process that would continue into the late Middle Ages: St William of York's shrine was remade in 1471 and a new and grander shrine for St Swithin created at Winchester in 1476. At Salisbury the newly canonized Osmund's old-fashioned 'foramina' tomb – a table-height flat-topped structure with porthole-like openings below to allow pilgrims to touch the coffin – was replaced between 1473 and 1493 by a newly constructed high shrine supporting a silver feretory, located centrally in the Trinity Chapel to the east of the high altar.[18] In many churches a consequence of this placement was that the shrine became obscured or entirely concealed from view by increasingly elaborate screenwork behind the high altar, as was the case at both Winchester and Durham.[19] Such translations might therefore create problems of sight and access, perhaps especially in monastic cathedrals, where the erection of elaborate screens, doors and lockable enclosures was often specifically designed to ensure the integrity and privacy of the monastic liturgy, with the collateral effect, intended or otherwise, of restricting lay access to the saint. The extreme case here was Durham, where women were excluded altogether from approaching the shrine of St Cuthbert, or indeed from entering the main body of the nave, but concerns about the conflicting claims of the monastic *clausura*, and devotional access for female pilgrims, was an issue in other monastic cathedrals, for example in early fourteenth-century Ely.[20]

There were more mundane reasons as well for tight security and restricted access at a shrine, not least concern about the theft of the valuables deposited there as ex-votos. The early fifteenth-century Canterbury Customary directed the official responsible for locking the shrine doors for the lunch hour to 'close or bolt the doors of the shrine and [...] with some attacking or defensive instrument make [...] a careful search in every dark place and suspect corner in which [there might be] anything stolen by a pernicious trick, where, God forbid, a thief could lie hidden, or in which any stray or rabid dog could secretly conceal itself'.[21] And though any pilgrim might

approach a shrine when it was open, privileged and more complete
access was often restricted to social and religious elites. At Durham,
'when any man of honour or worshippe were disposed to make
there praiers to god and to Sainte Cuthbert: or to offer anything
to his sacred shrine', the custodian of the shrine was summoned to
unlock it and order the cover to be drawn up:

> And when they had maid there praiers and dyd offer any thing
> to yt, yf yt weare either gould sylver or jewels, streighte way it
> was hounge on the shrine. And if yt weyre any other thinge, as
> unicorne horne, Eliphant Tooth, or such like thinge then yt was
> hounge within the fereture at the end of the shrine, and when
> they had made there praiers, the Clarke did let downe the cover
> therof and did locke yt at every corner.[22]

When Erasmus and John Colet visited Canterbury, armed with a
letter of introduction from Archbishop Warham, the prior himself
showed them the choicest relics and treasures of the shrine and
'pointed out each jewel by touching it with a white rod'.[23]

Difficulty of access might itself form part of the mystique of
pilgrimage. The movement from the open and accessible space of a
cathedral nave to penetration of the locked enclosure of the shrine
was itself a recapitulation of the act of pilgrimage, heightening the
devotional impact of arrival at the longed-for presence of the saint.
The ringing of the bell as the doors at Canterbury were unlocked
summoning pilgrims to the early morning Mass of St Thomas,[24]
like the jangling of the bells attached to the canopy on St Cuthbert's
shrine, was a call to an encounter with the holy, made all the more
powerful by the sense of entering a secluded inner sanctum. And
that sense of movement within the cathedral as itself a kind of
pilgrimage was heightened by the fact that, in all cathedrals, arrival
at the principal shrine was almost always the climax of a progress
through or past other altars, images and shrines, at which the
pilgrim was encouraged to pause, pray and make an offering. This
was especially so at Canterbury, with pilgrim stations at St Thomas's
original burial place in the crypt, at the scene of the martyrdom, at

the so-called Corona, where Thomas's head relic was displayed, and at the main shrine itself. Canterbury was not alone in displaying the saint's head separately from his body: Ripon, Salisbury, Chichester, Lincoln, York, Worcester, Hereford and Lichfield all enshrined the heads of their major saints for veneration separately from their bodies, eliciting additional offerings, in a different part of the building.[25] A concern to intensify devotional impact, however, was probably more important than any mercenary concern, for head-shrines, which were often life-size and richly jewelled, constituted a particularly potent representation of the living presence of the saint. The mitred head-shrine of St Osmund, commissioned in 1457 in the wake of the canonization from a goldsmith named 'John the Jew', was of silver-gilt, studded with precious stones, and cost a stupendous £52 1s. 8½d.[26]

But all cathedrals contained many altars, many relics and many notable images, and particularly on major feasts and special 'pardon days', when most pilgrims came to the shrines, there must have been established itineraries around the cathedrals to channel pilgrims around safely and in manageable numbers. Such altars and images might exercise an imaginative hold greater even than that of the principal shrine – at St Paul's in London the Rood of the North Door was more famous and probably more popular than the shrine of St Erkenwald.[27] Durham was dominated by the presence of St Cuthbert, but the south aisle of the cathedral also housed the 'marveylous lyvelye and bewtifull Image of the picture of our Ladie so called the Lady of boultone', a large-scale *vierge ouvrante* which opened to reveal a carved and gilded Trinity ensemble, including the splendid crucifix used for the ceremony of 'Creeping to the Cross' on Good Friday. This image of Our Lady of Bolton had its own *cultus* and was solemnly displayed on feast days, 'that every man might se pictured within her, the father, the sonne and the holy ghost'.[28] Her altar was in a part of the cathedral closed to women, but by the late Middle Ages the angle between the north door and the entrance to the Galilee Chapel at the west end of the cathedral housed altars supporting two of the most popular devotional images with late medieval English laypeople: a statue of St Saviour on a pillar bracket and, opposite it, the altar of Our Lady of Pity, 'carrying our saviour on her knee as he was taiken from the crosse, verey lamentable to behoulde'.[29] And from 1370 the bones of St Bede were separately venerated in a portable gilded feretory on a raised shrine in the Galilee Chapel. Bede's feretory was carried in procession into the town on high days and holy days and, unlike Cuthbert's shrine, was accessible to women as well as men all the year round: for these reasons alone it will have had its own devotional following.[30]

Durham had many other relics, the most notable ranked in tiers round the *feretrum* of St Cuthbert in reliquaries that included arm, head and chest reliquaries, and even a silver-gilt stag which contained a relic of St John the Baptist.[31] But most were kept in cupboards or 'almeries' by St Cuthbert's shrine, which were opened whenever the canopy over the shrine was raised, 'that every man that came thither at that time might see the holy reliques therein [...] accounted to bee the most sumptuous and richest jewells in all this land'.[32] There were similar arrangements at many cathedrals – the reliquary chest by the shrine of St Richard in Chichester measured eight feet by twenty, and included a door for the display of relics and a slit for pilgrim offerings.[33] Canterbury probably held the largest cathedral relic collection – the standard edition of an early fourteenth-century inventory of the cathedral relics runs to 14 closely printed pages: in addition to the body of St Thomas, the list includes the entire bodies (skeletons) of Sts Alphege, Wilfrid, Anselm, Aelfric, Blaise, Audoen, Salvius, Wigan and (allegedly) Swithin, enshrined in chests on beams in the sanctuary. In the relic cupboards there were head-shrines of Blaise, Fursy and Austroberte, arm shrines of eleven major saints, including Blaise, Hugh of Lincoln and Richard of Chichester, scores of partial body relics from the blood of St Edmund to a finger of St Francis, as well as assorted Holy Land relics – wood from the True Cross, Veronica's veil and Aaron's rod.[34] The solemn display of these relics, many of them in their own elaborately jewelled reliquaries, must have contributed significantly to the pilgrims' sense of being admitted into the presence of the assembled company of heaven, and of direct access to multiple sources of healing and blessing.

The cod-Chaucerian *Tale of Beryn* offers a plausible vignette of the experience of an average group of mid-fifteenth-century pilgrims to St Thomas's shrine at Canterbury. Travelling in company, the pilgrims (lodging in one of the many inns and pilgrim hostels catering for pilgrims – there were said to be more than 90 such hostels in late medieval Glastonbury, many of them owned by or leased from the monastery) – made their way early in the morning to the cathedral 'to make hir offringes,/ Righte as hir devocioune was, of sylver broch and rynges'. As they entered the church, a monk, 'as the maner is', sprinkled them with holy water. Once inside, the pilgrims made immediately 'towards the holy shrine/ To do that they were com fore, and after for to dyne'.[35]

But the splendour of the building, a fundamental part of the experience of pilgrimage to a cathedral, was evidently liable to deflect the worldly minded. 'Lewd sots' such as the Pardoner and Miller might gawp at the stained glass, making wild guesses at the scenes depicted and paying at least as much attention to the armorial escutcheons as to the edifying religious scenes. 'Like lewde gotes', they

> Pyred fast and poured highe oppon the glase,
> Counterfeting gentilmen, the armes for to blase,
> Diskyveryng fast the peyntour, and for the story mourned.

But eventually the company of pilgrims, still 'goglyng with hir hedes' at the splendour around them,

> Kneled adown tofore the shryne, and hertlich hir bedes
> They preyd to Seynt Thomas, in such wise as they couth.
> And sith the holy relikes ech man with his mowth
> Kissed, as a goodly monke the names told and taught.
> And sith to other places of holynes they raughte
> And were in hir devocioun tyl service were al doon,
> And sith they drowgh to dynerward, as it drew to noon.

Then, as manere and custom is, signes there they boughte,
For men of contre shuld know whom they had soughte.
Ech man set his sylver in such thing as they liked.
[...] the Miller had i-piked
His bosom ful of signes of Caunterbury broches [...]
They set hir signes oppon hir hedes, and som oppon hir capp,
And sith to the dynerward they gan for to stapp.[36]

In its broad outline this sequence – an awed progress to the central shrine through the magnificent building and its sometimes baffling iconography, the veneration there of the saint, the kissing of the displayed relics, named and explained by one of the shrine custodians, then a progress round the rest of the building to 'other places of holiness', all this against the background of the singing of the cathedral liturgy, and finally, when 'service were al doon' (which might include attendance at Mass by the pilgrim), departure to buy souvenir badges, 'as manere and custom is', to fix on their hats so that the folks back home would know where they had been – will have been replicated at every cathedral and major monastic shrine. The grandeur, complex space, multiple sacred sites and elaborate iconography of a great church must have made pilgrimage to a cathedral or large monastic church qualitatively different from the more familiar experience of visiting a favoured image or relic in more modest local sanctuaries. And the musical elaboration of cathedral and monastic liturgy in fourteenth- and fifteenth-century England, where the daily Lady Mass was often accompanied by both plainsong and elaborate polyphony, will certainly have had an impact on pilgrims, as it must have been intended to do. In late medieval Canterbury a special choir, including boys' voices, adult male cantors and a secular master of music, whose duties included the composition of polyphony, was established to enrich the daily Lady Mass. We do not know how many non-elite pilgrims, if any, attended the Lady Mass, but since it was celebrated at the east end of the cathedral they can hardly have avoided hearing and being impressed by its music.[37]

Some other details of pilgrim experience remain surprisingly obscure. Very few pilgrims can have left a shrine without buying at least one souvenir badge or ampulla for holy water or holy oil.[38] But we have very little information about exactly who made these familiar and ubiquitous objects, how and where they were sold and who reaped the profits. Every great church must have had an attendant army of candle, rosary, holy-picture and metal-badge sellers at pardon times. The vast numbers of wax candles deposited at the shrine of St Thomas were certainly collected up, recycled and resold by the shrine authorities themselves, but whether the vendors of other holy accoutrements worked freelance or on licence, and whether shrines sometimes, always or never benefited directly from sales, is far from clear. We know of at least one (surely rare) example of a shrine where badges were given away free. At the great fenland shrine of St Guthlac, at Crowland Abbey near Peterborough, it had become customary by the fifteenth century to give every pilgrim to the annual St Bartholomew's day pilgrimage in August a souvenir shaped like a miniature fletcher's knife, the instrument of Bartholomew's martyrdom. In the 1470s Abbot John de Wisbech ended this custom, as being too great a drain on the monastery's finances.[39]

The puzzlement of the pilgrims in the prologue to the tale of Beryn about the meaning of the Canterbury windows cannot have been rare, but most shrines made serious efforts to inform pilgrims about the history and miracles of their saints. On major pilgrimage days shrine staff routinely preached to successive groups of pilgrims, recounting the saint's miracles and identifying the more notable relics and ex-votos. Windows illustrating the saint's life and miracles, like the Becket windows at Canterbury, the St William window in the north-east transept at York or the lost Cuthbert window in the Chapel of Nine Altars in Durham, could be supplemented at the shrine itself by panel paintings with explanatory text, like those that survive in the Society of Antiquaries from the shrine of St Etheldreda: such images provided visual cues and illustrations for shrine staff addressing pilgrims.[40] Wooden, paper or brass tablets, on which verse or prose retellings of the shrine legend were inscribed, might be posted for the benefit of the literate, or to be read aloud by the custodians. Late fifteenth-century examples from the shrine at Glastonbury, and from the small Norfolk shrine of St Walstan of Bawburgh, survived the Reformation.[41] These verse legends were all derived ultimately from the example of John Lydgate's sumptuously illustrated retelling of the legend of St Edmund, composed to mark the visit of Henry VI to the shrine at Bury in 1443. With the advent of print, verse legends of this kind, widely differing in length and sophistication, were published by Richard Pynson for several major monastic shrines – St Werbergh in Chester and St Joseph of Arimathea at Glastonbury, the Holy Blood at Hailes and the Holy House at Walsingham – but no cathedral shrine seems to have ventured in this populist direction.[42]

The prologue to the tale of Beryn offers a satirical picture of some not very devout pilgrims discharging a conventional religious duty. The miracle stories collected at the shrines themselves provide many more intimate details of pilgrim behaviour, and remind us that for many pilgrims the shrine was a place of agonized hope for release from disease or misfortune. Few late medieval shrines produced healings in such numbers as twelfth- and thirteenth-century Canterbury or Hereford at the outset of the celebrity of Thomas Becket and Thomas Cantilupe, though the miracle book prepared for Henry VI's canonization contains over 150 miracles.[43] But if wonders were reported in smaller numbers and lesser frequency, expectations about miracles, and the behaviour of pilgrims in quest of healing or help, remained remarkably consistent through the medieval period. The cluster of 33 miracles collected at Salisbury in 1423 and 1424 to advance the canonization of St Osmund offers an illuminating snapshot of the conventions and expectations operative at cathedral shrines in the fifteenth century.[44] As might be expected, many of those giving testimony had some formal association with Salisbury cathedral, and no fewer than 16 of the 45 witnesses or recipients of favours were clergy currently or formerly attached to it, while a further two were Franciscan friars based in the city. Two of the miracles were connected with the village of Larkstoke, where the parish priest (one of the witnesses) had formerly been on the cathedral staff. The reported miracles were spread over a 40-year period, and included examples that could be matched from any medieval miracle collection: of children resurrected after drowning in rivers or wells, or healed after being impaled at home on an unguarded spit or when running with a knife or a sharpened stick ('as is the way with little boys when they play'), of a young girl brained by a metal quoit, a man blinded by thorns while hedging, another clubbed by a neighbour while mediating in an altercation during a 'friendly' match of rounders, of another stabbed during a quarrel, another dragged by the stirrup of a bolting horse, and two restored during divine service after years of madness.

The Salisbury miracle accounts themselves are terse and formulaic, as one would expect in a document prepared for submission to the papal chancery, but they leave no doubt about the centrality of physical proximity to the shrine to most of the stories. Though some of the miracles happened outside Salisbury, in answer to simple invocation of the saint, most involved a promised or actual visit to St Osmund's tomb. Sir Steven Botwell, a cathedral vicar, was restored to pristine health from a lifelong affliction of gout by kneeling and praying at the tomb.[45] The infant son of William Westmoor, drowned in the town stream, was restored to life when he was carried to the shrine in his shroud and laid down upon it.[46] Sir Thomas Adekyn, cathedral vicar for 50 years, was cured of a crippling cramp which left him using a crutch by sleeping three nights at the tomb.[47] George Louthorp, canon treasurer, was restored to health and cured of dumbness when his friend John Dygon, Bachelor of Law, 'secretly and devoutly' visited the shrine on his behalf.[48] And both the lunatics described in the collection were cured in the same way, by prolonged contact with the tomb. John Beminster was led there, shackled in chains, during the singing of the Lady Mass and placed with his head and manacled hands 'in foramine eiusdem tumbe', in one of the openings of the tomb: during the singing of the Agnus Dei his shackles fell away and he was restored to his right mind. Another madman, 'crazy Tom', was similarly led to the tomb and his chained hands placed 'in foraminibus eiusdem sepulcri', while his friends invoked God and St Osmund – once again the manacles fell away as he was healed.[49]

If the miracles reported in fifteenth-century Salisbury would have seemed familiar at any shrine at any point in the previous 400 years, so would the conventions of intercession and thanksgiving reported in the testimonies. When John Hoggys, servant of Canon Richard Wyche, fell ill, Hoggys's master and his chaplain laid two silver pennies on Hoggys's body and vowed to take them to the shrine.[50] When William Roper's servant (and subsequently wife) Matilda lost the use of a withered right leg, she was measured for a candle the length and breadth of her body and vowed to take it to the shrine.[51] And the ex-votos left by those favoured with miracles were equally conventional. John Swift, a Salisbury dyer, whose ruin was averted by the restoration of a vat of woad that had curdled and gone bad, had a model of the vat made in wax and took it to the tomb.[52] When John Lloyd of Durrington recovered after being stabbed by his neighbour Robert Clerk, the two men took the dagger to the shrine and together laid it on the tomb.[53] And St Osmund himself behaved in ways that would not have been out of place in the *miracula* of Becket or Cantilupe two centuries earlier. When Thomas Adekyn slept at the tomb seeking healing for a withered leg, St Osmund appeared in a dream on the third night, drew the bone out of his leg and healed him.[54] When Canon Ralph Selby lay ill in London, a voice in the night told him to go to Osmund's shrine.[55] When John Combe lay on his bed of pain after having his shoulder smashed with a club, a man clad in a white robe like a surplice but brighter than lightning appeared and told him to take a wax image with his wounds marked on it to the tomb.[56] Thomas Rylee, a clerk at the point of death and choking from a tertian ague, invoked Osmund three times: the saint appeared and cleared the obstruction by thrusting his crozier into his throat.[57]

A figure of 33 miracles spread over 40 years suggests a modest but by no means moribund cult. The fact that everyone involved in these fifteenth-century miracles of St Osmund was either associated with the cathedral or lived within the city or its rural hinterland suggests that Osmund's appeal was regional rather than national. But other fifteenth-century cathedral shrines still had the power to attract pilgrims from much further afield. The chance survival of a much emended note on the back of a draft letter about the state of the cathedral bell-tower at Durham offers a vivid glimpse of that power in action.[58] Just before Candlemas 1445 (and therefore in the depth of winter) a 'gentilman of debynshir, distrait in his mynd, haffyng gret and mesrable seknesse in hys body', was led by friends at eight in the morning 'to the feretre of the confessor'. In his right hand he carried a penny which had been vowed to St Cuthbert, and he called out continually, 'Cuthbert, Cuthbert, Cuthbert'. Eventually he offered the penny, but 'Wyth out [devotion] or prayer as he was a fou wyth owt discrecioun and resoun'. In his madness and bodily distress he had to be held down, 'grapytt with ther hands' till two o'clock in the afternoon, when he was once more brought to the shrine and fell into an uneasy sleep on an improvised bed, 'sor wexit and gaff mony gret grones and syghes'. A priest sprinkled him with holy water, but as soon as the water touched his clothes he sprang up 'as he war wexhid wyth on wykytt spratt and wold a passyd fro the feretre, bot he was holdyn styll there agayn his wyll'. Once more he fell into an exhausted sleep; when he awoke almost two hours later, he had been restored to his right mind and freed from all bodily illness. As he told the onlookers, 'in his slepp came to hym an byshopp, the fayrest man that ere he saw, and towchyd hym in the places off his body and at the last wher his most suor was he gropytt hym be the hertt, and wytht that toyk away all his pa[yn] and seknesse off body and mynd.'

A miracle this spectacular was clearly a rare and significant event. On the following Sunday, 'be for the grettest audience off pepuoll that evr was seen in that kyrk', including official witnesses, 'mony notable persones off prestes and laymen sworn and examynd', the Devonshire gentleman stood in the pulpit, declared the details of the miracle '[a]nd swar ther to uppon a booke' that 'all this was trow and noght feynd, for this gret myracle was gyffen [by] all mighte god [a]nd his gloriose confessor Saynct Cuthbert', eliciting 'grett thankynge and lewyng off all the pepull gedyrt att thatt tyme'. The account of the events at Candlemas 1445 was clearly drafted with an eye to publicizing the benefits on offer at Cuthbert's shrine, as its opening lines make clear: 'Be it known to all [that the] prayer and merytes off the gloriouse confessour Saynt Cuthbert Whos body by restyth incour[rupt] hath shewyd on gratt mircle late tyme passyd, in the fest of Kandylmesse last.' For even so famous and venerable a shrine as that of St Cuthbert needed constant reassertion.

In that process of promotion, cathedral shrines had the advantage over all others that the patronal celebrations in the mother church of the diocese were embedded in the diocesan calendar, in theory at least observed in every parish in the diocese, thus keeping the claims of the shrine alive in the minds of the laity. But the appeal of a cathedral shrine to the laity could not be taken for granted, as emerges from the efforts of the bishops and the Dean and Chapter of St Paul's to promote the cult of St Erkenwald in the fourteenth-century diocese of London. Between 1314 and 1326 the canons of St Paul built an elaborate new high shrine, and Erkenwald's relics were translated into a new *feretrum* at Candlemas 1326. Significantly, the translation took place at night because of fear of mass hysteria among the crowds of devotees. In 1339 three goldsmiths were set to work on the shrine for a whole year. Despite this, offerings were apparently meagre both in London and in the diocese at large. In 1386 Bishop Robert Braybrook complained that the four major patronal festivals of the cathedral – the two feasts of the conversion and the commemoration of St Paul and the two feasts of the translation and commemoration of Erkenwald – '*ubique per nostras Civitatem et diocesin quasi ab omnibus prophenari*' ('were prophaned by almost everybody everywhere throughout our city and diocese'). Over the next 20 years Erkenwald's cult was steadily promoted within cathedral and diocese. Braybrook required all the parish clergy of London to take part, vested in copes, in the cathedral processions for the saint's feast days, and there is evidence of a stream of gifts to the shrine, newly fenced in with an elaborate metal railing, from London clergy and the wealthy city laity. In 1407 the dean, Thomas de Evere, bequeathed £100 to buy city property, to maintain lights before the shrine, and to pay the stipend of a chaplain for the St Erkenwald guild, which was now functioning within the cathedral, itself perhaps a sign of growing lay involvement in the cult. The commissioning of the late fourteenth-century alliterative Middle English poem *St Erkenwald* may have been part of this promotion of the cult.

There seems to have been a special connection between the cult of St Erkenwald and the London legal profession, and in 1431 Erkenwald's Translation, on 14 November, was proclaimed as one of the four principal feasts kept annually at Lincoln's Inn. It is not obvious what to make of the fact that there are no recorded lay bequests to Erkenwald's shrine after 1404.[59]

A century on, officials at Lincoln seem to have been successful in renewing lay devotion to St Hugh's head on the very eve of the Reformation. A striking feature of a recent survey of 1,500 Lincolnshire wills made in the 30 years prior to the break with Rome was the sudden appearance of a rash of hitherto unprecedented bequests to the shrine of 'the blessyd hed off holy St Hugh of Lincoln' – there were 30 of these bequests, none made before 1522 and two-thirds of them between 1532 and 1534. Though it is possible that John Longland, Lincoln's conservative bishop from 1520, had a hand in the matter, I'm inclined to associate this sudden outbreak of lay devotion to St Hugh's head with the activity of the energetic Henry Lytherland, prebendary of Lincoln from 1520. Lytherland became cathedral treasurer in 1535; he was the chapter's most outspoken critic of the Henrician Reformation, and a vigorous opponent of the Royal Supremacy, who resisted the removal of venerated images, and urged his parishioners in Newark to continue to pray for the dead. He was eventually executed in 1538 for his support of the Pilgrimage of Grace. But whoever was responsible, the surge in lay bequests to the head shrine of St Hugh must represent a response to deliberate promotion by the cathedral itself.[60]

Rich and poor came on pilgrimage, the very poorest being entitled to claim alms, food and even shelter at the shrine. But every pilgrim who knelt at a shrine was expected to make an offering. For those seeking or giving thanks for specific favours, these might take the form of representational ex-votos like those we have encountered at the shrines of Osmund, Richard Scrope and St Cuthbert, or in the form of candles moulded round wicks measured to the length of the suppliant's body. Like these 'trindles', ex-votos were most commonly made of wax, but the well-to-do might have them cast in precious metal, and these more costly offerings would be given pride of place near or on the feretory. But from the early Middle Ages the usual offering in the collecting boxes or 'pyxes' that stood at every shrine was a pilgrim's penny: pilgrims vowing a pilgrimage often bent the silver penny they intended to offer, as a pledge of their commitment. On the assumption that one penny represents one pilgrim, Ben Nilsen has analysed the surviving figures of receipts from shrine offerings from seven great churches – Canterbury, Durham, Hereford, Ely, Lincoln, Norwich and Westminster Abbey – in an attempt to trace the rise and fall of the popularity of the shrines.[61] It is admittedly a crude measure. Even in the best-documented cathedrals financial records are incomplete and hard to interpret. We know a fair amount about the ebb and flow of the money offerings at some of these major cathedral shrines in general but are much less certain how closely the figures for offerings in the shrine pyxes accurately reflect the rise and fall of the individual cults themselves. But so far as the figures for offerings can be trusted, the general profile of pilgrimage to cathedrals and great churches seems to have been one of boom in the thirteenth century, relative subsidence in the first half of the fourteenth century, revival and a second boom in the decades after the Black Death, and from 1420 or so a very slow gradual decline down to the Reformation. In other words, and appropriately enough, the overlapping lifetimes of Geoffrey Chaucer and Margery Kempe almost exactly cover the boom time of late medieval offerings at cathedral shrines.

The most spectacular example of this pattern is the cult of St Thomas at Canterbury: in 1220, when St Thomas's relics were translated into his new shrine, offerings reached the astonishing figure of £702, the largest recorded for any medieval English pilgrim site. There were 240 pennies to the pound, so on the assumption that each penny represents one pilgrim, this would suggest that 168,480 pilgrims came to Canterbury that year. Just 30 years later, in 1252, however, offerings had plummeted to an implausibly small £57 15s. They had climbed back up to £260 by 1300, and though offerings fluctuated significantly, they remained high throughout the first half of the fourteenth century. The Black Death produced a further surge, despite the drastically reduced population, and offerings in 1350 reached their highest point since 1220, at £667. In the Jubilee of 1419–20 offerings reached a fifteenth-century high of £360. Thereafter record-keeping becomes scrappy, but the figures we have suggest that income declined slowly but steadily, and by the 1530s may have been only a tenth of the 1420 figure.[62]

Making allowance for local variations, a similar general pattern of gentle decline from the boom period between the Black Death and about 1420 seems to be implied by the surviving records from other great churches. But it must be emphasized that we have no idea whether this accurately reflects an actual decline in pilgrim numbers. The assumption that all pilgrims offered a penny is itself by no means certain: in the later Middle Ages many may have offered a candle rather than a coin and so have eluded the historian's ability to count them. Certainly other more impressionistic sources suggest that there was no general waning of interest in pilgrimage in these years. As we have seen, the wills of the late medieval laity offer glimpses of a thriving pilgrimage ecology, in which the great shrines were complemented, but perhaps also competed with, by the rise and fall of a multitude of lesser local shrines. If numbers to the great shrines were indeed declining, it may well be because in an age in which expressions of local religion were multiplying, the benefits of pilgrimage were still valued but considered to be attainable at less cost and inconvenience by a visit to an image or relic shrine closer at hand.[63] And the continuing investment of late medieval monastic communities, cathedral chapters and episcopal patrons in the lavish renewal and refurbishing of shrines such as those of Osmund at Salisbury, William at York or Swithin at Winchester, while certainly intended to enhance the shrines' attraction, does not suggest any malaise or lack of confidence in pilgrimage as an institution.

In the late Middle Ages the acquisition of new and more lavish indulgences was an increasingly important aspect of the process of rebooting and reviving the attraction of shrines. Every shrine, great and small, sought to draw pilgrims by securing indulgences, and some of the most striking surges in pilgrim numbers and shrine income can be associated with such indulgences, as in the case of the Jubilee Indulgence at Canterbury in 1420. More generally, pilgrims travelled to shrines in large numbers mainly on specific annual 'pardon days' when such indulgences were to be gained, normally in the summer, when travel was easiest, though the surviving financial records on which we depend for estimated numbers only occasionally enable us to document the impact of such indulgences with certainty. At Canterbury the largest crowds attended at Easter, Whitsun, the feast of the Translation of St Thomas at the end of the first week in July and at Michaelmas: the feretrans were excused all monastic offices and other duties for an entire week at those seasons, 'so that they can freely attend to the shrine and the people flocking to it'.[64]

The situation in fourteenth-century Norwich illustrates the importance of indulgences as motives for pilgrimage. Norwich was one of the unlucky cathedrals that never managed to acquire the whole body of a major saint. The nearest it came was the repellently anti-Semitic cult of William of Norwich, a teenage boy allegedly murdered by the Norwich Jewish community at Easter 1144, and after a series of translations eventually enshrined at the north end of the cathedral rood screen. The cult was only sporadically popular, for much of the later Middle Ages drawing small numbers of pilgrims from the city and its hinterland. A refurbishment of the shrine in 1305 led to a surge of interest, and annual offerings leapt from just 9d. in 1304 to £1 1s. 8½d. in the year after the refurbishment. But by 1342 offerings had dwindled to a new low of 4d. per annum. There was a dramatic change in the uncanonized 'Saint' William's fortunes in 1376, when the Norwich Peltiers guild adopted 'the holy Innocent and digne martyr' as their patron (William had been an apprentice skinner) and instituted an annual guild procession, led picturesquely by 'a knave child, innocent, tokening of the glorious martyr'. Offerings surged, and a St William scholars' guild was established at King's Lynn the same year. But again the impact was short-lived: within a generation annual offerings at the shrine had dwindled once more to pence rather than pounds.[65]

Norwich therefore had to rely on the attraction of multiple relics, altars and images rather than a single shrine, and on the pull of special indulgences, to attract pilgrims. In 1278 the monastic community created a 'reliquary arch' in the north aisle of the presbytery, and eventually a separate relic chapel, on the ceiling of which were painted images of the saints whose relics were displayed there – the apostles Peter, Paul and Andrew, early Christian martyrs real and legendary, such as Laurence, Margaret and Catherine, and English saints such as Edmund and Richard of Chichester. All or most of these relics are likely to have been small bone fragments, or contact relics like chain filings or pieces of cloth, but the concentrated display nevertheless attracted substantial lay interest – between 1296 and 1315 annual offerings to them ranged between £6 and £14. Once again, however, pilgrimage to the relics evidently flagged as the novelty wore off, and income from them dwindled.[66]

Far more significant in attracting pilgrims were the papal indulgences the cathedral secured from time to time for its visitors. The Trinity altar in Norwich, presumably supporting an appropriate image, was an established pilgrimage site,[67] and in 1398 Pope Boniface IX granted the coveted 'Portiuncula' plenary indulgence (originally granted only to pilgrims to Assisi on the anniversary in October of St Francis's death) to all those who visited that and the other two principal altars of Norwich Cathedral on its patronal feast of the Trinity. An indication of the expected surge in numbers is the provision of the papal bull granting the indulgence for eight priests to be hired to hear pilgrims' confessions. The impact did not disappoint. In 1400, when details first appear in the sacrist's accounts, offerings at the Trinity altars amounted to £85, as opposed to £33 for the rest of the year. Offerings dropped to £55 3s. 8d. the following year, and the Pope subsequently rescinded all his grants of indulgences made before 1402, putting an end to what had clearly been a significant attraction to Norwich pilgrims.[68] But there seems little doubt that by the end of the Middle Ages a special indulgence of this kind was probably the single most important way in which custodians could promote their shrine, and cathedrals probably routinely employed criers and pardoners to publicize the spiritual benefits on offer to pilgrims at 'pardon' times.[69]

With the mention of indulgences we arrive at the age of Reformation, and the end of cathedral pilgrimage in England. Whether or not those pilgrimages were experiencing a gentle decline in the century before their destruction, nothing about them can have given any inkling of the cataclysmic changes in the English Crown's religious policy that would put an abrupt end to pilgrimage altogether in the late 1530s. In September 1538 one of the most famous and most popular shrines in Europe was stripped of its valuables: St Thomas's relics were burned and scattered, the very mention of his name in prayer was outlawed and the shrine itself dismantled and its fabric and treasures dragged away in 26 heavily laden carts.[70] The desecration of England's greatest cathedral shrine was merely the most spectacular and shocking episode in a campaign that vilified the whole institution of pilgrimage as a conspiracy to palm on to a gullible public what the royal commission for the destruction of St Hugh's shrine at Lincoln described as 'dyverse feuyned reliquys and juellys wherewith all the simple people be moche deceyvyd'.[71] A glance through the relic lists of any medieval cathedral shrine leaves no room for doubt that these Henrician holocausts did indeed sweep away much that was tawdry, bogus and exploitative. But along with the fantasy and commercialization, one of the most vital and persistent institutions of medieval Christianity was snuffed out, some of the greatest names in English history mocked and dishonoured, and a resonant symbol of hope and healing banished from the great buildings that had sheltered it for half a millennium. Who can doubt that the English imagination was the poorer for it?

2

The Dissolution of Ely Priory

On 18 November 1539 Prior Robert Steward led his sub-prior and 22 other monks in signing the deed of surrender of the monastery of Ely into the hands of Henry VIII.[1] In doing so, they brought to an end a monastic tradition that stretched back to the seventh century. That tradition had been sustained at Ely by the presence of the shrine of the Anglo-Saxon princess Aethylthryth, a former queen of Northumbria who, despite two marriages, had managed to remain a virgin and had taken the veil at the hands of St Wilfred with the reluctant permission of her second husband, and who established a community of monks and nuns on this island in the fenland which had apparently been part of her marriage dowry.[2] Aethylthryth, whom we know as St Etheldreda, established a family dynasty of sanctity: after her death from the plague she was succeeded as abbess by her elder sister Saxbearh, who in turn was succeeded by her daughter Eormenhild, widow of the king of Mercia, who in turn was succeeded as abbess by her daughter Werburh. The relics of Etheldreda's younger sister Withburga would also end up at Ely: this gaggle of royal nuns would later be venerated as saints alongside the matriarch of the holy dynasty, Etheldreda, in shrines around hers behind the high altar.[3]

The cult of Etheldreda and her sisters and nieces would survive the destruction of her community by Danish invasion a century after her death, the refoundation of the abbey in the late tenth

century and initial Norman suspicion both of Saxon saints and
of Ely's special prominence as a centre of Saxon resistance to the
conquest – Hereward the Wake and all that.⁴ Finally it would
survive the transformation of the community from independent
abbey into a cathedral priory in the early twelfth century, when the
community at last came under episcopal oversight. It was housed
in one of the largest and most magnificent buildings in medieval
Europe, a church that, like Durham Cathedral, was created by
Norman churchmen to honour the cult of a Saxon patron saint.

For a century or so after its refoundation Ely housed a relatively
large community of up to 70 or more monks, a record it would never
again equal: numbers declined to around 40 for much of the rest of
the Middle Ages, and in the wake of the Black Death dropped to 28.⁵
Creatively, the community's glory days were in the early fourteenth
century, when the priory was blessed with a cluster of remarkable
monks who transformed the building and, in the process, both
intensified and broadened its spiritual life. The key figure here was
the sub-prior and subsequently sacrist, Alan of Walsingham, who laid
the foundation stone of the wonderful Lady Chapel, once vibrant
with coloured glass and painted sculpture. Alan of Walsingham was
also the driving force behind the creation of the glorious Octagon
which replaced the central tower after its collapse just a matter of
months after the laying of the foundation stone of the Lady Chapel.⁶

So it's not surprising that the Lady Chapel took 30 years to
complete. Ely was late in creating a separate Lady Chapel – and
distinctive in placing that chapel not to the east of the choir and
high altar, as in most other cathedrals, but, as at Peterborough, on
the north side of the cathedral building and separate from it. The
chapel was linked to the choir by a covered wooden gallery for
the monks and by a walkway from the angle of the north transept
for laypeople and pilgrims. The placing of the Lady Chapel was
determined by the existence of monastic buildings to the east of
the choir, but may also have been influenced by the position of the
Holy House on the north side of the priory church at Walsingham.⁷

As that suggests, the cult of the Virgin Mary was one of the
most vital aspects of medieval religion, bringing a dimension of

beauty, tenderness and femininity into the religious experience of both clergy and laypeople that had been comparatively lacking in the Christianity of the first millennium. From the twelfth century onwards it became more and more important, nourished, of course, by the handful of New Testament appearances of the mother of Jesus but also by allegorical interpretations of key passages in the Hebrew scriptures, such as Psalm 45, or a range of passages from the wisdom books. Of almost equal importance was one of the earliest Christian texts outside the canon of scripture, the 'proto-Gospel of St James', which is the source of the cluster of charming legends about Mary's birth and childhood and about the infancy miracles of Jesus which dominate medieval preaching and storytelling about the Virgin. All this gave rise to collections of miracles attributed to Mary, endlessly retold and elaborated in the hugely popular medieval miracle books that circulated in their hundreds all over Europe. They seem in fact to have originated in England, where they had been assembled from a range of earlier sources in eleventh- and twelfth-century English Benedictine monasteries. And it is obvious enough why a great monastic church would give a special place to the cult of Mary – her virginity was the supreme model for monastic celibacy, and her attentive reception of the Gospel, treasuring all these things in her heart, was the model for the contemplative life of the monk.[8]

But the cult of the Virgin was equally appealing to laypeople, because it provided a mothering, tender and approachable aspect of the mystery of the Incarnation, very different in feel from the often stern and frightening portrayal of Christ Pantocrator and Judge which had been so prominent in the iconography of the first thousand years. The miracles of Mary are full of stories in which the mother of God steps in to rescue sinners from the consequences of their sins, such as the weighing of souls, and many of these stories were once vividly sculpted on the walls of the Lady Chapel: their ruins can still be deciphered.[9]

Devotion to Mary ramified throughout the liturgy of the medieval Church, and we know it was prominent in medieval Ely: as early as 1258 the bishop felt obliged to forbid the custom of distributing candles free of charge for the procession at Candlemas to the crowds who attended the liturgy that day, because it was costing the community 700 lb. of wax each time, an indication of the huge numbers of laypeople turning up for what was, relatively speaking, one of the lesser Marian feast days.[10] Here in this Lady Chapel, as in most other great churches, the thirteenth and fourteenth centuries saw an increasingly elaborate use of polyphonic music to beautify the daily Lady Mass and the various evening services at which anthems to the Virgin were sung. Monks sang at these services in the Lady Chapel, but so did eight choirboys – *pueri in choro* – and the monks also hired professional lay singers to augment the musical resources there, a sure indication of the elaborate polyphonic music used in Ely's liturgy, and equally an indication of the presence of laypeople at those services.[11]

And it wasn't just the music of the Mass that was elaborated and eagerly attended by laypeople. Vespers of the Virgin would have been sung with elaborate settings of texts such as the Magnificat. And, perhaps even more importantly, all over Europe in the fourteenth and fifteenth centuries the custom of singing an anthem in honour of Mary after Compline, the last service of the day, became one of the most popular of all religious observances: laypeople came to these evening services in large numbers, to pray by candlelight and listen to the music, and in towns of any size well-to-do laypeople often pooled money to pay professional musicians and to provide organs to accompany these anthems, which were usually sung before the main image of the Virgin in the church, often preceded by an elaborate procession.[12]

Clearly, all this presented problems in a monastic cathedral, where there was a constant concern about lay access interrupting the devotional life of the monks. For much of the earlier Middle Ages the townspeople of Ely had to use a nave altar on the west side of the great stone screen, or *pulpitum*, for their parish services. In the course of the fourteenth century this was found to be unsatisfactory for everyone – the monastic chanting interrupted parish masses, while the bustle surrounding the parish services interrupted the monastic liturgy – and eventually a lean-to church was created outside the cathedral at the north-west end to accommodate the parish.[13]

The presence of women in the cathedral was a particular distraction: the cathedral's relic collection, for example, was displayed in a chapel in the south choir aisle, and the monks in the end had to put up a screen between that aisle and the choir where they sang the office so that they wouldn't be distracted by the sight of women going to venerate the relics. In 1300 Bishop Ralph of Walpole even tried to ban women from the choir altogether, and therefore from the shrine of St Etheldreda.[14] That prohibition can't have lasted, because pilgrimage to the shrine of Etheldreda flourished up to the eve of the Reformation, and many of those pilgrims were women. To judge by the receipts from pilgrims made at the shrine, pilgrim numbers seem to have peaked in the early fifteenth century: in 1408–9 offerings to St Etheldreda amounted to £94 9s. 10d. Since the usual offering at a shrine was a penny, and there were 240 pennies to a pound, that suggests that 23,000 pilgrims came to Ely that year. That was probably a record, but up till the very eve of the dissolution of monastery and shrine annual receipts were between £30 and £40, suggesting pilgrim numbers of up to 10,000 a year.[15] Another £10 a year was raised by the sale of little coloured woven necklaces of silk, known as St Audrey's chains, and probably especially favoured by women pilgrims. And pilgrim numbers in the early sixteenth century included pilgrims to the grave of Bishop Alcock, who was venerated as a saint after his death, though his cult had dwindled away by the time of the dissolution.[16]

Pilgrims to St Etheldreda certainly also visited the Lady Chapel, whose brightly painted and sculpted cycle of scenes from the life and miracles of Our Lady was the greatest of its kind anywhere in England, indeed in Europe. To preserve a separation, the monks entered the chapel via the gallery walk already mentioned, through a door in the sanctuary of the chapel, separated from laypeople by a wooden screen with two doors; the laity entered by a larger door further west. The narrative cycle of the carvings started at that laypeople's door and unfolded clockwise round the chapel telling the story of the Virgin's life and then a selection of her miracles, with the scenes illustrating the three major Marian festivals – Annunciation, Visitation and Assumption – spaced evenly round:

Annunciation facing Assumption across the chapel, with the Visitation half-way between, in the west wall. The scenes in the monks' part of the chapel have disappeared around the altar, but those nearest the monks' door illustrated stories of erring clerics and nuns, reminders to the monks of the demands of their calling.[17]

The community that surrendered to the Crown in November 1539 was at a low ebb in terms of numbers, smaller even than the depleted monastery had been in the wake of the Black Death: just 22 monks joined their prior and sub-prior in signing away a millennium of Christian history in return for their pensions. But the priory on the eve of the dissolution was not otherwise notably decadent or in decline. Tudor visitation records at Ely list no crime much worse than supplying the servants with weak beer. On the other hand, early Tudor Benedictine monasticism was no one's idea of the ascetic life: the monks' domestic needs were catered for by a large staff of lay servants – bell-ringers, altar clerks, kitchen staff, bakers, doorkeepers, barber, brewers, tailor, schoolmaster for the almonry school, launderer and stable-boys – all of them clad in green livery. Some of the monks kept pet dogs, and the major obedientiaries – that is, the monks with special responsibilities such as the sacrist, chamberlain, almoner, hospitaller – kept their own kitchens and their own small household of servants. But we know of at least two members of the community in the generations immediately before the dissolution who read and collected spiritual literature, one of whom tried his vocation in the stricter monastery at Syon on the Thames before deciding that this was too demanding and returning to the gentler observance of Ely. And the cathedral was regularly sending small numbers of men, probably on average a couple a year, to study at Cambridge. This may not sound many, but in fact for a small to medium-size community it represents a large investment of manpower and money. We get occasional glimpses of some of the costs involved – for example, the monastic historian Joan Greatrex has drawn attention to an order for 266 rabbits from the monastery's warrens at Lakenheath to be eaten at the inception feast of one of the fourteenth-century Ely monks, Roger of Norwich. That appears to have been an exceptional blowout – more typical was the gift of two eels for the inception feast of another monk, the gift of the precentor. To a greater extent than other houses in the region, most of the Ely monks were local men, drawn from the families of monastic tenants across East Anglia: of the total of just under 550 monks whose names we know, 24 came from Ely itself, 13 from Swaffham, 9 from Wells (including the last prior, Robert Steward), 7 each from Ramsey, Sutton, Wisbech and Walsingham, and 6 each from Lakenheath, Ixworth, Soham, Cambridge and Thetford. This strong regional identity must have helped promote community harmony, and down to the end of its life Ely Priory was attracting postulants: at the visitation of 1534 there were ten novices, a sure sign of health for a relatively small community.[18]

More than half the Ely monks at university appear to have studied law rather than theology, an unusually high number, so theology doesn't seem to have been a priority in the community. And unlike some other Benedictine houses, such as Westminster Abbey, where Prior Benson at the dissolution had definite Protestant sympathies, there's no indication that any Ely monk welcomed the Reformation: one of the monks, John Skelsyn, studying at Buckingham College in the early 1530s, did own a collection of pamphlets by Luther, but Luther's books were in wide circulation in the university and anyone in Cambridge interested in theology or current affairs in those years will have been keeping an eye on what was going on in Germany. Reading Luther was no necessary indication that one agreed with him. Five of Prior Steward's books have survived, and they were all blamelessly conventional medieval manuscripts.[19]

The end of monastic life in England, and in Ely, was a juggernaut that gathered speed and weight rapidly in the late 1530s. The passing of the Act of Supremacy in 1534 opened the way for King Henry to set about asset-stripping the Church. The king's first minister, Thomas Cromwell, had his eye on the revenues and possessions of the bishops, but the monasteries were an easier and more vulnerable target. To begin with, at least, Henry's motive was not exclusively financial. Even devoutly Catholic humanist writers such as Erasmus and Thomas More had satirized the monasteries as centres of worldly luxury and theological reaction, and there were plenty of small monastic communities whose members enjoyed revenues originally intended to sustain two or three times as many monks or nuns. There was plenty of precedent for dissolving ailing or uneconomic monastic communities and diverting their resources to some more obviously worthy cause – Cardinal Wolsey had done so to fund his collegiate foundations in Ipswich and Oxford, and Cromwell had acted for the cardinal in these transactions. The saintly Bishop Alcock of Ely had dissolved the convent of St Radegund in Cambridge and used its revenues and buildings to found Jesus College, and his friend the even more saintly John Fisher acted as his executor in doing so. And as events would show, there were hordes of opportunistic aristocracy and gentry who, whatever their religious beliefs or lack of them, were only too eager to support the royal attack on the monasteries, in the hope that crumbs from the royal table, in the form of monastic land or buildings, would come their way.[20]

So in July 1535 the Crown sent commissioners through the country to pick off the smaller monasteries and nunneries and confiscate their possessions. The ostensible reason was twofold: to stamp out scandalous corruption – sexual, financial and theological – and to rationalize institutions that were too small or too poor to be viable. The visitors were instructed to find and publicize notable examples of sexual depravity, financial mismanagement or pious fraud such as bogus miracles at shrines, in order to justify the confiscations. The Act for the Dissolution of the Lesser Monasteries that formalized all this in February 1536 opened with a denunciation of the 'manifest sin, vicious, carnal and abominable living' allegedly rife in these small communities, and suggested that any good monks and nuns made homeless by the act but anxious to continue in religious life could relocate to one of the 'great and solemn monasteries of this realm, wherein, thanks be to God, religion is right well kept and observed'.[21] But Protestant voices denouncing all monasteries whatever as centres of superstitious devotion to the saints or belief in purgatory now became bolder, and Crown endorsement of these Protestant sentiments came in the Royal Injunctions of August 1536, which forbade the clergy to 'set forth and extol any images, relics or miracles for any superstition or lucre, nor allure the people by any enticements to the pilgrimage of any saint'.[22]

Reaction in the north of England was swift, and catastrophic. The dissolution of hundreds of religious houses there was one of the main triggers for the terrifying rebellion known significantly and defiantly as the Pilgrimage of Grace, which began in Lincolnshire in late September and rapidly spread across all the northern counties: up to one third of the country was involved in one way or another, and the rebellion came within a whisker of toppling Henry's regime.[23] The Pilgrimage was eventually defused and its leaders executed, but it had helped convince Henry that the monasteries were fortresses for resistance to his authority. In February 1537 he told the Duke of Norfolk that 'All these troubles have ensued by the solicitation and traitorous conspiracy of the monks'.[24] Even now, there doesn't seem to have been a master plan for the destruction of monasticism altogether, and there were even some new foundations. But the king's need for support for the supremacy meant that Protestant opinion was becoming more outspoken at court, and his need for money, not least to cover the expenses of suppressing the Pilgrimage of Grace, made him eager for spoil. Over the next two years momentum would grow for the suppression of all religious houses with no exceptions. Abbots and priors all over the country saw what was coming and began to sell off monastic property to prevent it falling forfeit to the Crown; to halt this, Cromwell circulated a blandly reassuring letter claiming that the king had no designs on any of the greater monasteries, despite the rumours being put about by 'malicious and cankered hearts' and insisting that only houses that made a voluntary and free surrender would be dissolved. The 1539 Act for the Dissolution of Abbeys which sealed the fate of the greater houses insisted that the monasteries had been surrendered by 'divers and sundry' abbots and abbesses, priors and prioresses, 'of their own free and voluntary minds [...] without constraint, coaction or compulsion'.[25]

The writing was now on the wall for all shrines, in East Anglia as elsewhere. Cromwell's visitors were at Bury St Edmunds towards the end of February dismantling the greatest shrine in the region, and for good measure gleefully pillaged the abbey of 5,000 marks in gold plus 'a rich cross with emeralds and stones of great value'. They told Cromwell that Ely was next on their list, but they were deterred from proceeding there by the news that two monks in the priory there had recently died of plague, and there were many other deaths from plague in the city itself.[26] Meanwhile, the regime's hostility to pilgrimage became more explicit. In September, England's greatest shrine, of St Thomas at Canterbury, was destroyed, Becket's bones allegedly burned as those of a traitor, and cartloads of precious metal and jewels hauled off to the royal treasury.[27] In October a new set of injunctions denounced 'the most detestable offence of idolatry' especially in 'wandering to Pilgrimages, offering of money, candles, or tapers to images and relics', ordered all images to which such offerings had been made to be taken down and forbade the lighting of candles at any shrine.[28]

The attack on the shrines was not the only signpost to Ely's imminent demise. On 2 May 1538 the other great East Anglian cathedral priory, Norwich, was formally dissolved and reconstituted as a secular cathedral. Norwich was almost unique among English cathedrals in housing no major saint's shrine, and the transition from monastic to secular cathedral there seems to have been relatively painless: the prior became dean, and the twenty-one monks, plus one other, John Salisbury (a protégé of Cromwell's, drafted in from outside and probably the only member of the new foundation with reforming sympathies), became prebendaries and canons. In due course between 1540 and 1542 seven other cathedral priories, including Ely, would become secular cathedrals, though in most of these cases there would be a more explicit reforming agenda at work.[29]

The following year, 1539, would see the end of most of the major monasteries of eastern England: November and December would be the cruellest months. November was particular bloody, with the public executions of three Benedictine abbots who, though they had all at some point accepted the Royal Supremacy, had resisted the dissolution of their houses – the abbots of Glastonbury and Reading were executed on 13 November and the abbot of Colchester on the 31st.[30] If all this was designed *pour encourager les autres* it certainly worked. Ely surrendered on 18 November, Ramsey on 22 November, Peterborough on 29 November, Thorney on 1 December, Croyland on 4 December and Spalding on 8 December. Ely would remain in a limbo state for almost two years, neither a priory nor a formally constituted cathedral of the new foundation, but 'the King's house'. During this interim period, Steward was left in charge, with 14 of his former monks to help him maintain service in the quire. Henry insisted that all former monks must cease wearing the monastic habit immediately on the dissolution of their houses, so the Ely clergy must have adopted the dress of secular priests, but since it is what they knew, presumably they went on singing the Benedictine offices; however, we have no information on that score. The cathedral's anomalous status came to an end in September 1541, when it was reconstituted as a cathedral of the New Foundation. Unsurprisingly, former prior Steward was appointed as first dean, and his 14 remaining former monks became prebendaries, canons and vicars choral. This strong ex-monastic presence certainly ensured a strong religious conservatism in the new cathedral, but that will have been tempered by the prebendaries and other staff appointed in 1541 by Bishop Goodrich, who drafted in some notable figures from Cambridge University to shift the institution in a Protestant direction, of whom the best-known were Richard Cox, who eventually became the first Elizabethan bishop of Ely, and Matthew Parker, Elizabeth I's archbishop of Canterbury.[31]

As that suggests, Bishop Goodrich was the key figure in the Protestantizing of the cathedral. An exact contemporary and friend of Thomas Cranmer at Jesus College, Cambridge, he had attracted the king's favour by his role in the team of writers justifying the divorce of Catherine of Aragon, and he was appointed bishop of Ely in 1534, almost certainly at Cranmer's suggestion, as part of the push to create an episcopate favourable to the Supremacy and the break with Rome. Goodrich held advanced Protestant views on the Eucharist and was eager to purge the Church of all vestiges of popery in the later 1530s.[32] We don't have any information about exactly when St Etheldreda's shrine was destroyed, but I think we can be fairly sure that Goodrich would have seen to it that it was dismantled promptly in the wake of the destruction of Becket's shrine at Canterbury in September 1538, or perhaps even earlier, in the wake of the destruction of St Edmund's shrine at Bury the previous February. By the same token, we don't know exactly when the magnificent sculptures of the Lady Chapel were battered to dust: various dates have been offered, as late as 1547 or maybe in the autumn of 1541. That date has been suggested because in October that year Goodrich issued a set of injunctions ordering his clergy to search out and destroy

> all Images & Bones of suche as the Kyng's people resorted and offered unto' and 'the Ornaments, Writtings, Tables, Monument of Myracles or Pylgrymage, Shryne, Coveryng of Shryne appertaining to the saide Images and Bones.'[33]

But those injunctions were in fact issued in every diocese in 1541, in the wake of a letter from Henry complaining about the failure of many parishes to obey the injunctions of 1538 – Henry had been infuriated on his progress into Yorkshire that year by the evidence of religious conservatism in the form of the cult of the saints he found everywhere. It is highly unlikely that Goodrich would have tolerated any such foot-dragging in his own cathedral, so I think it overwhelmingly likely that the Lady Chapel was purged of its imagery at the same time as the destruction of St Etheldreda's shrine, in late 1538 or early in 1539.[34]

So Goodrich's episcopate saw the destruction of the externals of Catholicism at Ely. But transforming the cathedral into a flagship Protestant institution was another matter and would never be entirely satisfactorily accomplished. With the accession of Queen Mary, the five committed Protestant prebendaries would be deprived and replaced by equally committed Catholics, of which the most notable were John Boxall, archdeacon of Ely and dean of Peterborough, secretary of state to the queen and a leading writer for the Catholic cause,[35] and John Young, Master of Pembroke, the 'bitter and relentless' enemy of the European Protestant reformer Martin Bucer and a leading figure in the resistance to Protestantism in Edwardine Cambridge, and in the restoration of Catholicism in

the university under Queen Mary.[36] Bishop Goodrich, luckily for
him, died in post in 1554 before his Protestant opinions could lead
him to the stake, like his friend Thomas Cranmer. He was replaced
by Thomas Thirlby, another friend of Cranmer's, who had served as
a diplomat under Henry and Edward but whose private opinions
were certainly Catholic. Thirlby was to be a reluctant participant
in Cranmer's disgrading and ritual defrocking before his burning.[37]
But their friendship did not affect Thirlby's beliefs: on Elizabeth's
accession he resolutely refused the Oath of Supremacy, and led
resistance to the Protestant settlement in the House of Lords. He
would die a prisoner of Archbishop Parker's in 1570.

On Dean Steward's death in 1557 he was replaced by another
university grandee, Andrew Perne, Master of Peterhouse. Perne was
an immensely learned theologian who had flirted with Protestantism
in Edward's reign, but he had cheerfully conformed under Mary and
as vice-chancellor presided at the burning of the bones in Cambridge
market-place of Martin Bucer, with whom Perne had once been on
friendly terms. Perne conformed yet again on Elizabeth's accession,
and when the university in 1560 staged a ceremony to restore Bucer's
good name, Perne, once again vice-chancellor, shamelessly presided.
But Perne was certainly a crypto-Catholic: he believed strongly that
the Church's tradition was superior to mere scripture, and is said to
have advised a woman who asked him which was the true Church
that, while it was safe to *live* as a member of the reformed Church
of England, it was a bad idea to *die* in it. He remained dean till his
death in 1589, having become in his own lifetime a byword for a
religious turncoat – to 'perne' became a verb meaning to spin like
a weathercock. And given his advice to his female enquirer, it is
perhaps a fitting irony that he died very suddenly while on a visit to
his friend Archbishop Whitgift in Lambeth Palace.[38]

Richard Cox, the first Elizabethan bishop of Ely, would do all he
could to move the cathedral and diocese in a radically Protestant
direction, appointing committed Protestants to the prebendal stalls
as the old monk prebendaries died off, but he didn't care for Ely
itself – he called it 'that unsavory isle with turves and dried up lodes'
and, like most committed reformers, he didn't in any case really see

the value of cathedrals. He told Edmund Grindal that he hoped cathedral churches would be brought to 'some better form, touchinge exercise of learninge, whose exercyse now is only in singinge and very little in edifyinge'.[39] Despite these sentiments, it was Cox who brought to Ely as master of the choristers the composer Christopher Tye. Tye's career had begun as a chorister at King's College, but in Edward's reign he had probably sung in the chapel royal and served as music tutor to the young king, with whom he was on friendly terms. Though Tye had composed great music for the Catholic liturgy, and his Mass setting *Euge bone* may have been sung at the reception of Cardinal Pole as papal legate under Mary, he was certainly a convinced Protestant. He was ordained priest by Bishop Cox in 1561 and resigned his cathedral post. It is a testament to the confused and shifting religious loyalties in the cathedrals in the 1560s that he was replaced by his son-in-law Robert White, who, like Tallis and Byrd, was a devout Catholic who was nevertheless to spend his career in the service of the new Church. Till his arrival in Ely, White had sung in the choir of Trinity College, Cambridge. Trinity College was a Marian foundation and, under its master, John Christopherson, bishop of Chichester and Queen Mary's confessor, had been a flagship institution in the restoration of Catholicism in Cambridge. White remained in post in Ely for only four years, departing for Chester Cathedral in 1566, and he ended his career as organist and master of the choristers at Westminster Abbey.[40] So for the first six years of Elizabeth's reign the music of the liturgy in this great church was in the hands first of a devout Protestant and then an equally devout Catholic, both of whom composed notable music for both Catholic and Protestant worship.

The religious ambiguity of the personnel of early Elizabethan Ely, halting in one way or another between Catholicism and Protestantism, was by no means unique: the Catholic William Byrd was master of the choristers at Lincoln, and at another former cathedral priory, Durham, the master of the choristers till 1576, John Brimley, had been in post since the mid-1530s and the last days of the monastic cathedral. Old habits die hard. During the Rebellion of the Northern Earls in 1569 the entire musical establishment of

Durham Cathedral – all the vicars choral and minor canons – were formally reconciled to the Catholic Church, and Brimley himself schooled the choirboys once more in the music for the Mass. Those Catholic echoes would not last, though at Durham they were persistent: the last prebendary who had been a monk at Durham survived in post into the 1590s.[41] All the former monk prebendaries at Ely had died 20 years earlier, but the very idea of a cathedral was in any case an anomaly in a reformed Church. Those great buildings had been created for processional liturgy, for soaring polyphony and plainsong, for the beauty of holiness; the vast unheated spaces of Ely's nave and choir were ill suited to reformed worship, conceived essentially as listening to sermons and singing communal psalmody. Addressing himself to members of the House of Commons in 1572, the puritan John Field put cathedrals and their worships high among the list of 'Popish abuses yet remaining in the English Church'.

> We should be too long to tell your honours of cathedral churches, the dens aforesaid of all loitering lubbers, where master dean, master vicedean, master canons or prebendaries [...] master treasurer, otherwise called Judas the pursebearer, the chief chanter, singingmen, special favourers of religion, squeaking choristers, organ players, gospellers, pistellers, pensioners, readers, vergers etc. live in great idleness and have their abiding. If you would know whence all these came, we can easily answer you, that they came from the pope, as out of the Trojan horse's belly, to the destruction of God's kingdom. The church of God never knew them, neither doth any reformed church in the world know them.[42]

Field was not altogether wrong in suspecting the cathedrals as redoubts of a very different kind of religion from his stark worship of the Word, and under Elizabeth's successor, James I, it was in the cathedrals, under Catholic-minded deans and bishops such as Lancelot Andrewes and William Laud, that the ideal of the beauty of holiness would revive among English Protestants, and so Anglicanism would be born. But that, as they say, is another story.

3

1569: A People's Tragedy?

At four o'clock in the afternoon of 14 November 1569 a party of 60 or so horsemen, clothed in plate armour and armed with spears, arquebuses and daggers, rode the five miles from the Earl of Westmorland's stronghold at Brancepath into Durham, trooped up the Bailey to Palace Green and entered the cathedral. They were led by the two premier noblemen of the north of England, Charles, Earl of Westmorland, and Thomas, Earl of Northumberland, and included some of the leading gentry of Durham and North Yorkshire. Inside the cathedral they gathered up, ripped in pieces and burned the English service books and bibles, and 'defaced [...] and broke in pieces' the communion table. They then assembled the citizens, in the name of the queen forbade the celebration of any Protestant services in the cathedral or city churches and set up a watch committee of 24 local men to enforce this order. An hour later the earls were gone, on their way towards Richmond, via Darlington, to raise Yorkshire against the Elizabethan religious settlement.[1]

This carefully staged incident inaugurated the last serious rebellion against the Tudor Crown. Badly planned by an ill-matched consortium of northern nobles and gentry, whose leaky conspiracy was soon known to the government, the revolt was triggered prematurely when Elizabeth summoned the two earls to explain themselves at court. It was to prove both short-lived and futile: there was no coherent plan of campaign, the hoped-for support from Scotland and the men of Lancashire and Cheshire failed to materialize and, though over a thousand of the rebels came from the region round Richmond, the earls lingered too long attempting to raise the rest of the North Riding. Crucially, they failed to liberate Mary, Queen of Scots, whom the regime hastily moved south under guard to Coventry, to prevent the earls from reaching her. They had seized and occupied Hartlepool, to provide a base for a hoped-for Spanish expeditionary force, but, like so many other of the rebel expectations, no such force ever materialized.

It used to be thought that the bulk of the rebel army consisted of clients and tenants of the two earls, more or less reluctantly supporting their lords. In fact, Northumberland signally failed even to try to mobilize his tenantry, and fewer than 20 per cent of the rebel army had direct dependencies or links to any of the rebel leaders: in Richmond, where enthusiasm for the rebel cause was strong, 16 of the 48 known rebels were in fact members of the town oligarchy, substantial and independent members of the community who had served as aldermen, bailiffs or school governors.[2] The leader of the royalist forces in Durham, the lord lieutenant, Sir George Bowes, at first claimed that plebeian support for the earls was either bought or coerced, 'first by faire speech, and after by offers of money, and lastlye by threats of burnings and spoilings': he reported that when one of the rebel leaders, Sir John Swinburne, caused Mass to be celebrated at Darlington on 16 November, he 'with a staff drove before him the poor folks, to hasten them to hear the same'.[3] But it was soon evident that this radically underestimated popular sympathy for the rebellion. Few of the rebels needed much coercion, and by late November Bowes was reporting that 'dayly the people flee from theys parts to the Erles'. The president of the Council of the North, the Earl of Sussex, cooped up in York in a county full of rebel sympathizers, told William Cecil on 20 November that 'He is a rare burde, that, by one meanes or another, hathe not some of his with the two earles, or in his harte wisheth not well to the cause they pretend'. Another royalist activist, Sir Ralph Sadler, told Cecil that 'There are not ten gentlemen in this country that favour [the queen's] proceedings in the cause of religion', while 'the common people are ignorant, superstitious, and altogether blinded with the old popish doctrine, and therefore so favour the cause which the rebels make the colour of their rebellion, that, though their persons be here with us, their hearts are with them'. Even gentry who came forward to help suppress the rebellion could not be trusted, especially those who were papists, 'for if the father come to us with X men, his son gooeth to the rebels with XX'.[4] Bowes learned this lesson the hard way: besieged by the rebel forces in Barnard Castle in early December, and with supplies of food and drink failing, his own troops 'did daily, by great numbers, leape over the walls to go to the rebells'. Mutiny grew, and in a single day 226 of Bowes's men 'leaped over the walles, and openyd the gaytes, and went to the enemy'. Though 35 of them broke necks, legs or arms in doing so, Bowes was forced to surrender the castle, but was granted safe conduct for himself and his 400 remaining troops.

Despite all that, almost exactly one month after its outbreak, the rebel army, which had numbered at least 6,000 men – between 1,500 and 2,000 of them mounted gentlemen and yeomen, comparatively well armed – was melting away in confusion, and the earls themselves were in retreat towards Hexham, and then to Scotland, seeking in vain for support from Mary's allies there. There had been very few fatalities during the rebellion itself, most of the damage being to property and livestock, but its collapse was followed by the most savage reprisals of even that bloody Tudor century. As provost marshal, Bowes oversaw summary executions under martial law in every town and village in Yorkshire and Durham that had supplied men, money or moral comfort for the rebel cause, and the Earl of Sussex's avenging royalist troops looted their way northwards, impounding horses, slaughtering cattle, plundering barns and storerooms and leaving the region to face the worst of a bitterly snow-bound winter stripped of cash, victuals and animal fodder. A lot of the plunder was opportunistic and dismayed the royalist generals themselves, who wanted control of the captured resources, because there was more to the savage, officially enforced retribution than outrage at rebellion: Elizabeth saw the revolt as an opportunity to replenish the royal finances and directed that any of the rebels with significant property should not be dealt with under martial law but formally tried for treason, since the property of convicted traitors was forfeit directly to the Crown. The consequent trials, executions and confiscations stretched on into the following spring. In all, somewhere in the region of 700 men, most of them small yeomen, artisans or farmworkers and labourers, were ordered by the queen to be hanged, though in all probability the actual death toll was smaller.[5] Whatever the number, *pour encourager les autres*, bodies were left to rot on the gallows at each public execution site, as a grim reminder of the cost of rebellion. The earls themselves never returned home. Westmorland escaped to the Spanish Netherlands and a hand-to-mouth career as an impoverished soldier of fortune and Spanish pensioner; Northumberland, betrayed by supposed Scottish allies, ended up in the custody of James Douglas, Earl of Morton, later regent of Scotland, who sold him to the English government for £2,000. Northumberland had, of course, already been attainted by Parliament, and he was executed without trial on the Pavement at York in August 1572.

Till relatively recently, historians have been inclined to explain the rebellion in essentially secular terms, as the last gasp of northern feudalism, an attempt by northern grandees, resentful of their own exclusion from the corridors of power and the domination of the Elizabethan court by upstart new men like Cecil, to mobilize their tenants and clients to oust Elizabeth and replace her with Mary, Queen of Scots. Mary, by the autumn of 1569 a prisoner under close guard in Tutbury Castle in Staffordshire, was in Catholic eyes not only the rightful successor to Elizabeth but had a better claim to the throne, because of both her legitimate Tudor blood and her religion – unlike Elizabeth, she was neither a bastard nor a heretic. She was indeed central to the conspiracy, though the earls didn't in fact agree on what they wanted from her: Westmorland was the Duke of Norfolk's brother-in-law and an ardent supporter of a marriage between Mary and the duke. But Norfolk was a Protestant, and Northumberland distrusted him almost as much as Elizabeth did: rather unrealistically, he favoured instead a marriage between

Mary and King Philip of Spain, ensuring a Catholic succession reminiscent of the glory days of Mary Tudor.

And it is increasingly accepted that the desire to restore Catholicism was the most important single motive for the rebels. The earls themselves spelled that out in a proclamation the day after the seizure of Durham Cathedral: having protested that they intended no hurt to the queen, they declared that

> for as much as the order of things in the churche and matters of religyon are presently sett furthe and usyd contrary to the auncyent and Catholick fayth: therefore there purposes and meanynges are, to redewce all the said cawsses in relygyon to the ancyent customs and usages before used, wherin they desyre all good people to take their partes.

Subsequent proclamations reiterated the aim of the rebellion to 'amend and redress' the triumph of 'a new found religion and heresie, contrary to God's word', and events would demonstrate that that aim exercised a powerful attraction to the common people of the region.[6]

That was a specially powerful appeal in northern England, where the Elizabethan Church had few sincere supporters, and where traditionalist religious attitudes and practices were winked at or positively encouraged by many of the parish clergy, most of whom had themselves served in Mary Tudor's Catholic Church. The diocese of Durham, in particular, had been ruled till 1559 by Cuthbert Tunstall, a Henrician conformist but formerly the friend of Erasmus, More and Fisher. Despite his acceptance of the Royal Supremacy, Tunstall's deep-seated Catholic convictions ensured that Protestantism had made few inroads in his diocese and, under Edward VI, led to his imprisonment and the suppression of the bishopric itself. Reinstated during the Marian restoration, Tunstall came to see the Royal Supremacy as an instrument of heresy, and to Elizabeth's dismay he refused conformity to her religious settlement, thereby depriving her of a much-needed symbol of continuity and legitimacy.

Tunstall's deprivation and death in 1559, however, meant that he could be replaced by a vehement Protestant activist, James Pilkington, while the new dean of the cathedral, William

Whittingham, was even more radical, a puritan who, like Pilkington, had fled to the continent in Queen Mary's reign, became one of the principal translators of the Geneva Bible and received Presbyterian ordination – Whittingham was never episcopally ordained. Bishop and dean, radicalized by European exile, set about turning cathedral and diocese into Protestant strongholds, importing committed reformers such as the brothers Thomas and Ralph Lever, both of them also former Zurich exiles under Mary, to replace ousted conservative prebendaries, most of whom had been former monks. Though five of those former monks survived among the 12 prebendaries, through the 1560s a rigorous Protestant regime was enforced in the cathedral. Pilkington and Whittingham's campaign extended into the wider diocese: many of these new cathedral clergy also held key parish appointments, and most of them also made preaching circuits to other parishes, where their abrasive reforming zeal frequently antagonized. In the cathedral itself Whittingham's conspicuous campaign against so-called superstition caused outrage, as perhaps it was meant to do. In addition to smashing stained glass and defacing a venerated statue of St Cuthbert, he removed the two fine white marble holy water stoups from the cathedral, and redeployed them for scrubbing vegetables and washing pots in his own kitchen: his French wife, as a conservative contemporary lamented, 'in the notable contempt and disgrace of all auncyent & goodly Reliques',[7] was reputed to have supervised the burning of St Cuthbert's banner, an ancient battle standard that was one of the most revered local treasures. But lamentations over such attacks on ancient pieties cut little ice with the dean, the bishop or their supporters: 'Our poor papists weep to see our churches so bare', Pilkington gleefully reported, since 'there is nothing in them to make curtsy too, neither saints nor yet their old little god'.[8]

Bishops of Durham had often been drafted in from outside the region to act as a counterweight for the Crown against the entrenched power of great local landowners. By contrast, the monastic cathedral had been deeply embedded in Durham society, most of its monks being drawn from middle-ranking local families: those involvements ensured that it had been perceived as a relatively benign landlord and employer. The new Protestant prebendaries, however, were almost all drawn from outside the region and were of a higher social status than the monks and first generation in the chapter. They were also married men, eager to provide for their families by maximizing cathedral revenues, just as Bishop Pilkington was eager to protect the temporalities of his see and to exploit valuable resources such as coal-mines. In the mid-1560s, therefore, the bishop and the Protestant prebendaries were frequently involved in acrimonious lawsuits against tenants in arrears and other local vested interests, including those of the Earl of Westmorland. Inevitability, this cocktail of abrasive attacks on ancient pieties and financial acquisitiveness proved toxic, deepening dislike of and resistance to the new religion.

A revealing example of the resulting animosities flared up at Sedgefield in November 1567, two years before the rebellion. The vicar of Sedgefield was Robert Swift, hawkishly Protestant chancellor of the diocese, like Dean Whittingham a refuser of the surplice and one of Bishop Pilkington's hand-picked team of zealous reformers, parachuted into this highly conservative community to promote Protestantism. Unsurprisingly, Swift encountered resistance in his own parish: in 1562 Pilkington had ordered that all communion tables should be removed from the chancels, to avoid association with the altars on which the sacrifice of the Mass had been offered, and that they should be placed instead in the body of the church, pointing east and west, not north–south as the altars had been. Like many conservative communities, Sedgefield ignored this new arrangement, and Swift's diocesan duties meant he was often absent, serving the parish via a curate, so it was not till September 1567 that for once 'being personallie present in the parishe church', Swift oversaw the removal of the table into the nave and placed round it 'certeyn formes or desks' for the communicants. The parish was not co-operative. On 7 November the Sedgefield churchwardens 'after diverse contemptuouse words [...] did forceableye, contemptuouslie and rashelie take up and remove the said table, formes or desks', and denounced Swift 'as a hinderer and no furtherer of God's service'.[9] There were similar confrontations elsewhere in 1567 and 1568, for example at Barnard Castle, where the four churchwardens, with the backing of the town bailiff and some of the town council, protested against their radical Protestant vicar, Thomas Clarke, by barricading themselves into the church on a Saturday evening, so that service could not be held the next morning. The wardens ended up being hauled into the assize court, but the bailiff, Thomas Rolandson, continued their campaign by presenting the vicar before the high commission in York for puritanism: Pilkington was forced to defuse the situation by moving Clarke to a vicarage in Berwick.[10]

The Sedgefield wardens undoubtedly spoke for most of the parish in denouncing Swift: opposition to him would rumble on, and in the following year the parish witnessed a series of confrontations provoked by a conservative parishioner, Brian Headlam, who showed his contempt for the new worship by talking loudly during services, abusing the curate and refusing to remove his hat. The wardens, though probably sharing Headlam's views, attempted to fine him for these offences, and on his refusal one of them, Thomas Watkin, presented him in the diocesan courts, which were of course presided over by none other than Swift. But all this was probably the manifestation of a family falling out, rather than a sign of a parish divided between Catholic and Protestant. Watkin and Headlam were in fact brothers-in-law, having married a pair of sisters, and Headlam reproached Watkin for a breach of parish solidarity in acting against him: 'you have done to me as never was done to any of Sedgefield parish, for ever one of us has born with another.' Another of Headlam's accusers was the churchwarden Roland Hinkson, but, as we shall see, he was a notorious Catholic, and despite their apparent differences, all three men joined the rebellion: Hinkson and Headlam would jointly play the most prominent roles in the destruction of Protestant books and the restoration of Catholic worship in Sedgefield, along with more than 50 other parishioners who had eventually to sue for clemency for their part in the rebellion.[11]

Inevitably, conspicuously active Protestant clergy, most of whom wisely fled south to safety at the first rumours of rebellion, were immediate and obvious targets. Bernard Gilpin left his 'golden rectory' at Haughton for refuge in Oxford: he returned in late December to find that the rebels had made 'wast of all, selling the corne, consuming

the fatted ware, and basely making havocke of all those things which
Mr. Gilpin had provided for pious and honest vses'. That pattern
of destruction and plunder was repeated wherever reformers had
made themselves obnoxious, and in Durham Dean Whittingham's
house, library and barns were robbed and gutted; the houses and
property of Protestant gentry were also common targets. And with
greater symbolic resonance the public destruction of emblems of
the Elizabethan religious settlement, begun by the earls in Durham
Cathedral, was from the outset a crucial part of the theatre of rebellion:
as Bowes reported to Cecil just five days into the revolt, 'These Earles
hathe, and dothe, everie where, burne the service bokes and bible: and
breake the communion tables.'[12] The leaders of the rebellion certainly
enforced the destruction of Protestant service books and communion
tables wherever the revolt had spread, and some of those involved may
have done so reluctantly. Robert Gilson, churchwarden of St Giles
in Durham, claimed that the parish clerk of St Giles had told him
the church books had been burned at the other city churches of St
Nicholas and St Oswald, and that they should bring out their books
for burning 'or else their houses would be ripped'.

But there is abundant evidence of local officials and co-operative
parishioners who needed no threats or urging. A crowd of 40 St
Giles parishioners gathered outside Gilson's door to watch the Book
of Common Prayer, the Bible, the homilies, two metrical psalters
and John Jewel's *Apology of the Church of England* go up in smoke.[13]
At Sedgefield, Brian Headlam took the initiative, ordering the
churchwarden Roland Hinkson to 'send up the church books, and he
might burn the books byfore he went to Darlington'. Hinkson later
claimed that he had been constrained by orders given 'in the Quenes
name and the earles', but several parishioners testified that 'his tong
was hiest' at the burning, and that while the books were burning
before a crowd at the cross by the town gate, Hinkson had poked the
flames with his staff, declaring 'See where the homilies fleith to the
devyll'. John Newton, the parish clerk, who handed the books over to
Hinkson, claimed he had substituted a book of his own for the Bible,
and some of the women of the parish claimed they had tried to rescue
the Bible from the bonfire, but 'the said Roland wold not lett them

have any', but scattered the pages with his staff. Some of the women gathered up stray pages for their children to play with.[14]

Alongside the destruction of the equipment of Protestant worship went the restoration of the ritual furniture of Catholicism. There is an issue about timing here. Most accounts of the rebellion state or imply that the earls restored the Mass in the cathedral on 14 November and that the restoration of Catholic worship in the parishes followed soon after. But although Mass was undoubtedly celebrated in Darlington on 16 November, at the prompting of John Swinburne, the subsequent prosecutions of Durham Cathedral officials and of churchwardens and parishioners for participation in the restoration of Catholic worship relate to incidents alleged to have taken place between 30 November and 14 December. Significantly, 30 November was St Andrew's day, a date laden with symbolism, for it was on St Andrew's day 1554, 15 years earlier, that Cardinal Pole had solemnly reconciled the kingdom to the Holy See, absolving parliament and the nation from the sin of schism. Pole's legatine synod had established 30 November as an annual commemoration of the return of England to Catholic unity. There were in any case practical reasons why the restoration of Catholic worship was delayed till then: for most of the last two weeks of November the rebel forces had been in Yorkshire, but on 30 November Sir Ralph Sadler reported that 'the rebells are returned into the Bishoprick', and it was from this point onwards that Catholic observance in the city and diocese began to be enforced.[15]

The moving spirit in Durham itself seems to have been Cuthbert Neville, assisted by the priest William Holmes, who orchestrated a campaign of re-Catholicization from their base in the castle on Palace Green. None of the local clergy were, of course, able to celebrate Mass, since all were excommunicate schismatics. The St Andrew's day Mass in the cathedral was celebrated by Robert Pearson, one of four clergy in the earl's entourage who between them seem to have presided at all the cathedral Masses. In the days that followed, Catholic choir offices were revived in the cathedral, in which some of the prebendaries, most notably the former monk George Cliffe, participated, along with the choir and minor canons. The Earl of Northumberland returned to Durham on Saturday, 3 December, and on Sunday

morning High Mass was sung in his presence in the cathedral before
an immense crowd. Another of the earl's priests, William Holmes,
who had faculties to absolve from the sin of schism, preached against
the Elizabethan settlement and reminded the congregation that
they had all been living in schism for eleven years. He commanded
anyone who did not wish to be reconciled to the Holy See to leave
the building, ordered the remaining congregation – which seems to
have been almost everyone – to kneel, and solemnly absolved them
from the sin of schism in the name of Pope Pius V.[16]

This absolution did not, however, enable the local clergy
to resume Catholic ministrations. Another of the priests
accompanying the earls, Sir John Pearson, told a group of the
minor canons, who had been present and knelt for absolution with
the rest, that they 'colde enjoy no lyvinge, nor doo any service'
till they had all been individually reconciled. They therefore
sought out Holmes, by this time based at Staindrop (perhaps at
Raby Castle), where they repudiated the Elizabethan settlement
and made a formal submission to the Catholic Church. Holmes
was then 'content to admit them as deacons to minister in the
Churche, but not to celebrat.'[17] The rest of the minor canons were
required to go through the same process of individual renunciation
of schism and formal reconciliation as were all the clergy of the
town churches. The process was not always straightforward. Oliver
Ash, curate of St Giles, had evidently once been a monk or friar,
and in addition to the sin of schism in ministering the heretical
rites of the Elizabethan Church, he was technically an apostate
from religious life, a sin whose absolution was reserved to the
Holy See. When he approached Holmes for reconciliation and
authority to resume Catholic ministry at St Giles, Holmes, who
had presumably received his faculties to reconcile schismatics from
the papal emissary Nicholas Morton, told him that, 'for as much
as this examinate had been a religious man, he coulde not absolve
hym, sainge that he […] was excommunicate, and so shulde be for
hym […] unto he had further auctoritie'.[18] Some of the Durham
city clergy seem to have officiated at the daily offices and in minor
sacramental rites such as the blessing of bread and holy water, but

none of them seems to have been allowed to celebrate Mass, and all the Durham city masses mentioned in the court proceedings after the rebellion were celebrated by priests from the earl's entourage.

Here Counter-Reformation rigour came face to face with a more malleable traditionalism, a reminder that the rebellion itself was a manifestation of a newly militant Catholicism informed by Counter-Reformation ideology. Northumberland himself had been reconciled to the Church in 1567 by an itinerant priest named Copley, one of a group of Marian clergy who had refused conformity and who remained at large in the region attempting to convert traditionalists from timid conformity to open recusancy. Copley was one of the priests who provided the earls, the Nevilles, the Nortons, John Swinburne and other rebel leaders with theological expertise on the question of whether or not Elizabeth was excommunicate and therefore deposed, and it may have been he who had introduced the earl to the Counter-Reformation treatises by the Louvainists Thomas Harding, Nicholas Sander and Thomas Stapleton which had helped to harden Percy's resolve.[19] As a result of those consultations, the earls did petition Pius V to excommunicate Elizabeth, but by the time he did so, the rebellion had come and gone, and the corpses of those who had rallied to the earls' call were already food for crows and kites.

Most of the clergy reconciled by Holmes would conform once again in the face of the savage retribution that followed the collapse of the rebellion. But for some, perhaps most, absolution from schism must at the time have seemed a watershed. One of the minor canons who went to Staindrop to seek absolution from William Holmes was Sir John Browne, who was also the curate of Witton Gilbert. In the first flush of his reconciliation Browne made himself conspicuous by serving Holmes's Masses in the cathedral, and at Witton Gilbert he burned his boats by telling his parishioners that although, whenever using the prayer book and homilies, he had 'left furth' anything he thought might harm them, nevertheless,

I have thes eleven yeares taught you the wrong way in such learninge as is against my own soule and yours bothe, and I am sorry and aske God mercie therfore, and yow my parishioners, and do here renounce my living before you all: and wherever you meit me, in town or field, taike me for a strainger and none of your curate.[20]

Holmes may have made some such declaration a condition of absolution: Richard Chaumber, a husbandman of Wyndelston, testified that 'being in his parish church, he hard Sir Edward the priest say openly in the pulpit that he hadd taught then with wrong'.[21] However that may have been, John Browne evidently did leave Witton Gilbert, but his repudiation of Protestant conformity did not survive the rebellion: a year later he was serving as curate at Chester-le-Street, though in trouble in the diocesan court for celebrating the communion with Mass wafers.[22]

The full extent of lay enthusiasm for the restoration of Catholic worship is hard to assess, because the direct evidence comes from testimony given after the suppression of the rebellion, when everyone concerned was eager to protest that they had acted under coercion. Coercion there certainly was. The restoration of altars in the city churches was overseen by the alderman.[23] Robert Hutcheson was one of the masons who set up two Catholic altars in Durham Cathedral: he testified, convincingly, that he done so 'at commandement of Mr Cuthbert Nevell, which sent for Henry Younger and this examinate to the castell, and kept them therein one dungeon, bycause they refused to deale or meddle with settinge up of any aultars, and, for that he threatened them still to continew ther, the said Robert and Henry did at last consent'. Younger confirmed that what he had done was 'sore against hys will', and only after they had been 'in prison fast in the castell two day and one night'. One of the labourers who helped with the altars was John Oliver, and he too testified that Cuthbert Neville had commanded him 'upon pain and hanging'. And according to Hutcheson, the work was supervised and materials provided by the priest from the Neville parish of Brancepath, 'the which priest was the overseer of all their working, furst and last'.[24]

Robert Hutcheson had been a teenager when Elizabeth came to the throne, and may well have been a Protestant by conviction: his declaration to the Church court that he prayed God that he might 'never see the masse again' does not sound like camouflage. If so, he was a rare bird in early Elizabethan Durham, and even those fearful or uncertain about the short-lived Catholic restoration might nevertheless display strong conservative sympathies. On 6 December William Watson, the parish clerk of St Nicholas, was summoned by four of the earl's men to help bury Hans Faucon, goldsmith, with Catholic rites. When he arrived at the church, William Holmes was preparing to celebrate the requiem Mass. Holmes asked Watson if he had been reconciled, 'or wold be or noo': Watson refused, 'bycause it was against his consciens and the Quene's lawes'. Yet, as he himself admitted, 'he tarried masse ther, and helped the said Holmes on with his mess clothes [...] bowed ther downe of his knees, but knoked nott, and he toke holy water'. Watson insisted that 'he dyd ytt for feir', but the same mixture of reservation about wholehearted commitment to the Catholic restoration, combined with participation in some Catholic rites, characterized the behaviour of Watson's vicar, William Headlam: coming to the church on Saturday, 10 December, he found one of the earl's clergy, Sir Robert Pearson, saying Mass, 'whereat he was not contentyd, and tarried not, but went his waies'. Headlam insisted he had attended no other Mass, yet he also admitted to having himself blessed holy water and holy bread, read the lesson in Latin at Matins and Vespers and eventually, 'after moche persuasion', had agreed to be reconciled by Holmes.[25]

And there is abundant evidence of the positive enthusiasm of many of those involved in dismantling the paraphernalia of Protestant worship and restoring that used in the Mass. At Auckland St Andrew, one of the local gentry, John Lilburne of Childon, 'rent the byble in pieces [...] and further toke 2 boords of the communion table [...] and throw them under fott'. At Auckland St Helen, William Cooke, a labourer who had been in the rebel army, 'strove with other soldiers about the tering of the books [...] whereof he [...] tere part of them with his hands and teith'. At Sedgefield, where Brian Headlam had ordered the reconstruction of the altar, the whole parish 'mett to gyther and consultyd to fett in the aulter stone and hallywater stone'. The high altar mensa had been hidden in a local field, Gibsons

Garth, and a crowd of parishioners, variously reported as numbering 30 or 80, harnessed themselves in pairs to drag the stone from its hiding place to the church and set the altar up again. Women as well as men were involved, and there and in several other parishes women would be prosecuted for having carried sand, clay or lime cement to help rebuild the altars. Every parish had also been ordered to replace the holy water stoups: almost everywhere they too had been hidden rather than destroyed, and once again support for their restoration was obviously widespread. Most of those questioned in the Church courts in 1570 confessed to having taken holy water when the stones went up again, like the crowd at St Giles's church in Durham who gathered when the holy water stoup was restored, 'and ther was water put in the stone, wherwith the folk sprinkelde themselves therwith'.[26] A similar crowd flocked to the restored holy water stoup at St Oswald's, 'and men sprinkled the same upon them'.[27]

Holy water was not the only sacramental that reappeared in December 1569: open praying with rosary beads became another mark of complicity. Thomas Wayinman, a yeoman who sold and carried 8d. worth of stone to St Margaret's, Durham, to rebuild the altar, where he was promised there would be Mass next morning, was obviously no mere mercenary: he confessed to having 'occupied ten gawdies or beads in the Church', and to have eaten a piece of blessed bread given to him by a neighbour 'which he now remembers was his own wife'.[28] Elizabeth Watson came to the cathedral to see the Mass on St Andrew's day, 'but the throng of people was so much that she could nott, and so sett downe in the low end of the same church and said her prayers [...] She saith she used hir beads.' Agnes Nixon was at the same Mass 'by the commandyd of the officers', but if that information was intended to imply reluctance, her actions betrayed her, for she too 'used her beads', evidently much prized, since in March 1570 she confessed to Robert Swift's unsympathetic court that 'she hath her beads still, of currell, which she saith she occupyeth nott'. Alice Wilkinson, a 36-year-old widow, confessed that she had attended Mass at St Nicholas, Durham, and 'willinglye used suche reverencd jestur therunto', and she had also 'occupied her gaudes, as many thowsand dyd'.[29]

Most of the population of Durham seem to have attended the Mass in the cathedral on St Andrew's day and on the following Sunday, when William Holmes solemnly absolved the vast congregation from the sin of schism. Particularly alarming to the authorities was the fact that, although the former monk George Cliffe was the only prebendary known to have attended, almost all the minor canons and all the lay clerks were present on both occasions, and received absolution along with the rest of the congregation, and most of them took part in the Latin choir offices, Masses and processions celebrated in the cathedral in the weeks that followed. Inevitably, after the collapse of the rebellion they would all claim to have acted unwillingly, under compulsion, and almost to a man they claimed that, though present when Holmes pronounced absolution, they could not hear him either because 'he had so small a voice' or because of the 'great prease of the people', and only knelt because they thought he was simply reciting a prayer. But these protestations must be taken with a pinch of salt. One of the minor canons, the former religious Oliver Ash, to whom Holmes had refused absolution, was in the cathedral to hear Holmes preach, and celebrate Mass, on Sunday, 4 December. When the sacring bell rang at the consecration, he looked towards the altar hoping to see the elevation of the host, a sure sign of his conservative religious beliefs, but he was too far away. So instead, he looked up into the choir loft, where the cathedral organist and master of the choristers, John Brimley, was 'and smyled at hym'.[30] Brimley, a layman, had been the last cantor of the monastic Priory, and became the first Master of the Choristers of the refounded Cathedral. He had retained his post under all the religious changes in the intervening decades, and settings for the Henrician and Edwardine liturgy by him survive. But with the help of one of the minor canons he had cheerfully taught the boys to sing the Mass and Latin offices. He too would, of course, excuse his part in the restored Catholic services on a plea of compulsion.[31] But that smile exchanged between choirmaster and ex-monk during the elevation of the host, the climax of a Mass at which the entire congregation had just been solemnly absolved from schism and reconciled to Rome, tells a quite different story: men forced to participate in religious rites repugnant to them do not share the complicity of a smile.

With the retreat of the earls northwards from Durham on 17 December came retribution swift, savage and summary. The queen wanted to know exactly who was to blame:

> who were the principall persons that accompanied the Erles in ther owtragiowse doings at Duresm: what number of men they were at that tyme, how the townsmen allowed or misliked of ther doinges, whether any resistance was made against them [...] and who were ther counsellours and drawers on.[32]

She wanted the well-to-do among them to be tried for treason; the rank and file would not be granted the luxury of a trial. So Sussex told Cecil on 28 December that he was en route to Durham,

> to take order for such of the common people as shall be exequuted by the martial law: emongs whom I mean to exequut specially, constables and other officers that have seduced the people [...] to rebell: and such other as have been most busye to further those matters, so as ther shal be no towne that hath sent some to the rebells, or otherwyse ayded them, but some of the worsts disposed shallbe exequuted for example.[33]

A week later he sent Cecil the list of those hanged in County Durham: they included in Durham City the alderman Master Sruther and 30 citizens, 40 constables and 30 serving men of 'the meaner sorte and worst disposition taken prisonyrs, countrymen [i.e., villagers] appointed to be exequited in every towne where they dwell 172, of those who did leape over the walles at Barny Castle, 20'. In total he had executed 80 people in Durham city, 41 at Darlington, 20 at Barnard Castle and 172 in other towns and villages in the county. He added that 'the like executions shall be done' at Richmond, Allerton, Topcliffe and Thirsk, for the North Riding, and at Ripon, Boroughbridge, Wetherby and Tadcaster, for the West Riding, and beside the executions in the larger towns 'ther shal be no towne wher any men went owt of the towne to serve the Earls [...] but one man or more, as the bignes of the towne is, shall be exequuted for example, in the principall place of that towne'. The whole grisly process was highly systematic. Bowes, aware that many of the rebels had gone into hiding, billeted troops in the Darlington area to lie in wait and make sudden raids to arrest culprits once they had crept home again. The carnage dragged on to the end of January, but already by 4 January even Bishop Pilkington was stunned by the sheer scale of the retribution: he told Cecil, 'The cuntre is in grete mysery: and as the Sheriff writes, he can not doe justice bi anie number of juries of such as be untouched in this rebellion [...] The number off offenders is so grete, that few innocent ar left to trie the guiltie.'[34]

Alongside the horror of the executions, the spoiling of the country by royalist troops added to the misery: Sussex told Cecil on New Year's Day that troops had seized all the lands, goods leases and cattle between Newcastle and Doncaster, and ransacked the people 'in such miserable sort, and made such open and common spoil, as the like I think was never harde of, putting no difference between the goode and the bad'.[35] Sussex was concerned that this unauthorized spoil had cost the Crown £10,000 in revenue. Despite his relentless pursuit of the rebels, Bowes, himself a man of the region, seems to have felt some compassion for those innocents suffering collateral damage from the punitive measures. He told Sussex that he had ordered those responsible for confiscations of the property of those executed under martial law 'that they showlde deale favourable with the wyfes and children, so as they might not only have cause to complane, but to be satisfyed'. From widows of the executed with many children nothing was to be taken, and 'worshipful neighbours' in charge of the process had been ordered to 'favour the poor'.[36]

By 23 January 1570 Bowes had completed his bloody circuit through Durham, Richmond, Allerton, Cleveland, Ripon and Wetherby 'for sifting of theys rebells by martiall law', and reported that he had hanged more than 600, 'so that now the auctors of thys rebellyon ys cursscd of everye syde; and sure the people are in marvelous feare, so that I trust there shall never suche thing happen in these partes agayn'.[37] It was time to call a halt to the slaughter. In early February, Sir Thomas Gargrave, a loyalist member of the Council of the North, advised Cecil to confine further proceedings to 'some select number [...] of the least and meane sorted, and chefely the papists' to be attainted, 'and all the rest I would wish to be pardoned, except certen chosyn persons that be abrode: for in myn opynyon, the pore husbandman and meane subjecte (yf he be not a grett papyste) wyll become good subjectes'.[38] In Durham, Robert Swift would pursue the clergy and parishioners not punished by martial law as rebels through the consistory court as sinners: they would all be forced to perform humiliating penance and confess to having 'by speciall motion of the divell' 'madly meaning to overethrowe the knowledge of God among men, and to bring horrible damnation upon our selves and others'.[39] The altar stones and holy water stoups resurrected in December were by January once more buried in dunghills and sandpits or smashed into pieces under official supervision. At Sedgefield a group of children followed Roland Hinkson as he dragged the holy water stoup to a midden, where he hid it under a pile of straw. They reported that he spoke to the stone as he buried it: 'Dominus vobiscum', he said.

Papistry would, of course, remain a potent force in the north, and Catholic leaders and Elizabethan courtiers alike would continue to hope or fear that the Catholic sympathies of both the northern gentry and 'the meaner sort' could be all too easily harnessed against the Protestant Crown. To his dying day, or at any rate till the failure of the Armada, William Allen harboured the illusion that a Spanish force landing in the north of England would be welcomed with open arms and would trigger a near-universal repudiation of the Elizabethan settlement, and he schemed to bring about that happy outcome. But Bowes and Gargrave were right: the 1569 rebellion exposed a widespread northern nostalgia for the old religion, and briefly stirred thousands to resist a Protestantism that many of them perceived as an alien and oppressive import. But it also demonstrated that the residual Catholicism of the region lacked the leadership, focus and determination to stand against the regime. Only one priest was executed in the wake of the rebellion, a Master Plumtree, 'an Old Queen Mary's priest' who, it was said, 'had mercy offered him, in case he would go to church, which he refused to do'.[40] To a man, the Durham clergy who had been reconciled to Rome conformed once more to Elizabeth's Church. The polemicists of Louvain might formulate resistance theory, and Pius V might call on all good Catholics to reject the rule of a Protestant harlot's daughter: in the 1570s and 1580s recusancy would demand of Catholics a tougher and more demanding commitment, in which the memory of the 'martyred' Earl of Northumberland himself would be co-opted. But the call for an end to mere nostalgia, and a vocation if necessary to resistance, even to death, was one that few would have the courage to embrace.

The memory of great events is often recorded in monuments, but the tragedy that engulfed the North-East in 1569, leaving hundreds of the nameless dead to hang and rot, found no memorial. None of the rebels executed in the wake of 1569 is commemorated in the Cathedral where their Rising began. Only the marginal figure of a Cathedral musician has a tomb inscription there, and one that obscures rather than recalls the tumultuous events of that terrible winter. A ledger stone in the centre of the floor of Durham's Galilee Chapel marks the grave of John Brimley, Cathedral choirmaster for more than forty years. Despite having accepted the pope's absolution from William Holmes, played the organ for Catholic services, led the singing of Salves to Our Lady, and trained his choirboys to accompany the rebel Masses, Brimley died in his bed seven years later, still Master of the Choristers of a Cathedral once more dedicated to protestant worship. Evidently Brimley's plea that 'he is sory for the same, and that he dyd yt by compulcion' was considered adequate exculpation. And the visitor pausing to decipher the charming inscription on the tombstone of this man who had led the Cathedral's music from the days of the monks till the days of puritan Dean Whittingham, might be forgiven for finding in it only a symbol of harmonious continuities, rather than an erasure of memory, veiling the murderous political and religious animosities that brought such savage reprisals on the people of Elizabethan Durham and Yorkshire – and in which John Brimley too had played his part.

> John Brimley's Body here doth ly,
> Who praysed God with hand and voice:
> By music's heavenlie harmonie
> Dull myndes he maid in God rejoice.
> His soul into the heavens is lyft,
> To prayse Him still that gave the gyft.[41]

4

Douai, Rheims and the Counter-Reformation

Douai College, the most important English Counter-Reformation institution, opened its doors on Michaelmas day 1568. The Council of Trent had ended just five years earlier, and it's often been said that Douai was the first Tridentine seminary.[1] There is a grain of truth in that claim: Trent's 23rd session, in July 1563, had made Cardinal Pole's plan for the establishment of English diocesan clergy training colleges the basis for Trent's momentous Canon 18 on diocesan seminaries, but even in Italy its actual implementation took decades, and in southern Italy and many parts of Europe it would take centuries. So although probably not the first, Douai was certainly one of the earliest attempts to turn the council's paper plan into concrete reality. But the differences between Douai College and other early modern European seminary foundations are at least as significant as any similarities. I want to argue here that the urgent need to confront the Elizabethan settlement at home profoundly shaped the formation on offer in the English college, at any rate in its first generation, and rendered William Allen's enterprise distinctive, perhaps even unique, in Counter-Reformation Europe.

The first thing to remark about Douai College is that it would never have existed at all if Philip II had not chosen a quiet town in Artois as the location for a new militantly Catholic university. Douai, chosen by Philip for its staunch loyalty to the old religion, was strategically located near the border with France, and so was well placed to counter the spread of Protestantism into the Walloon- and French-speaking Low Countries. Philip intended his new foundation to complement the older foundation at Leuven, the intellectual bulwark of Catholicism for the Flemish- and Dutch-speaking Netherlands. The establishment of the new university in 1562, expressly 'pour l'augmentation de la Sante foi et religion catholique, [et l'] extirpation des heresies pullulantes',[2] was part of a general shake-up and reordering of the Church in the Habsburg Netherlands whose most startling aspect was the creation of 14 new dioceses out of the existing four Dutch sees in 1559, in order to energize and equip Dutch and Belgian Catholics for the struggle with militant Calvinism.[3]

Notoriously, for the English exile community established in Leuven, the brain drain created by the need to staff the University of Douai was a godsend, an instant job opportunity that the pool of English academics displaced by Elizabeth's succession were eager to seize. Douai's first chancellor was Richard Smyth, formerly regius professor of divinity at Oxford, hitherto a lecturer at Leuven, who cannily published an astonishing cluster of high-profile anti-Protestant theological works in 1562, just as King Philip's search committees were recruiting senior staff. And over the next few years English and Welsh exiles would feature prominently in the new university's professoriate: Owen Lewis, Cardinal Borromeo's future vicar-general and then bishop of the Neapolitan see of Cassano, would hold the chair of canon law and later serve as rector of the university; William Allen himself was to be professor first of catechetics and then of dogmatic and controversial theology; and, most distinguished of all, Thomas Stapleton would teach at Douai for two decades before becoming professor of scripture at Leuven, and his best-selling Gospel commentaries, as we shall see, would shape parish preaching across Counter-Reformation Europe well into the seventeenth century.[4]

It was out of the eagerly pro-active Counter-Reformation ethos of Douai University that the English college emerged. William Allen,

36 years old in the year of Douai College's foundation and formerly a fellow of Oriel College and principal of St Mary's Hall, Oxford, was a Lancashire man who, with his tutor and friend Morgan Philips, had been a significant figure in the defence of Catholicism in Edward's reign and its restoration in Marian Oxford. In 1561 he joined the exodus of Catholic Oxonians to the Low Countries, one of the dozens of out-of-work dons who established themselves precariously in Leuven, many of them living communally in two houses, nicknamed Oxford and Cambridge. Allen soon had to return to England because of ill health, and on his recovery took up work among the gentry of the Lancashire Fylde, but he left England for good in 1567, returning to Leuven, where he formed a momentous friendship with an influential canon lawyer, Jean de Vendeville.

Vendeville, born in Lille in 1527, would end his life as bishop of Tournai, but at the time he and Allen met he was a married layman and a member of the Grand Council of Malines. He was an ardent admirer of the Jesuits, deeply dismayed by the ascendancy that Calvinism had established in neighbouring Tournai. His spiritual director was Martin Rythovius, formerly chancellor of the University of Leuven, who in 1559 became first bishop of Ypres, one of Philip II's 14 newly created dioceses. Vendeville's relationship with Rythovius was close and affectionate, and Vendeville's influence on his spiritual director was evidently at least as great as the bishop's influence on him. Vendeville was a passionate advocate of the importance of education as a weapon of the Counter-Reformation, campaigning even before Trent for the establishment of seminaries to train clergy, and he was the author of an academic memorial which played a crucial role in persuading Philip II to establish Douai University.[5] Rythovius attended the Tridentine session that enacted the seminary legislation, and certainly shared Vendeville's enthusiasm for colleges and seminaries as bulwarks against the Reformation. In 1565 Rythovius, as bishop of Ypres, established a diocesan seminary of his own at Ypres, one of the earliest implementations anywhere of the Tridentine decree.

In 1567, two years after returning to Leuven, Allen travelled on pilgrimage to Rome, in company with Morgan Philips and with Vendeville, who had recently been appointed regius professor of canon law at Douai. Vendeville's journey to Rome was to persuade Pope Pius V to establish seminaries for mission clergy to convert and Latinize the Greek and Maronite Christians of the Near East. But 1567 was a bad year for any client of Philip II to seek a favourable hearing from Pope Pius V, a choleric man currently enraged by what he took to be Philip II's half-hearted handling of Calvinist rebellion in the Netherlands and his refusal to invade Geneva en route to sort out the Dutch Calvinists, so Vendeville never managed to secure a papal audience. But on the long homeward journey he discussed his aborted scheme with Allen. Never a man to pass up a possible benefaction, Allen persuaded Vendeville to transfer his enthusiasm from the remote project of the conversion of the Greek East to the more attainable recovery of the British west. Vendeville's project of a missionary seminary dedicated to the reclamation of schismatic and heretical Christians for the Roman obedience bore fruit the following year in the establishment of a similar enterprise, aimed now at England and Wales.

Allen's own thinking at this stage may still have been shaped by the English exiles' experience in Leuven. 'Our first purpose', as he later reminded Vendeville, had been to establish a single college in which the scattered scholarly exiles might study 'more profitably than apart', to secure a continuity of clerical and theological training, so that there would be theologically competent Catholic clergy on hand for the good times ('were they neere, were they far of') when England returned to Catholic communion, and, finally, to provide an orthodox alternative to Oxford and Cambridge, thereby snatching young souls 'from the jaws of death'. But Vendeville clearly felt from the outset that Douai College itself would have an explicit missionary dimension, for in 1568 he told the Spanish authorities in the Netherlands that the students were to be specially trained in religious controversy and, after a two-year preparation, sent back to England to promote the Catholic cause 'even at the peril of their lives'.[6]

However that may be, from its inception Douai College was certainly an institution orientated towards England, intended, in Gregory Martin's words, 'to doe our contry good' and specifically dedicated to religious debate: the mindset of its staff and students was consciously confrontational. Founded in part as an academic home for clergy displaced from university and cathedral posts by men they despised as 'heretic jesters',[7] its senior personnel had all been participants in the Marian campaign to purge Oxford and England of Protestantism, and their leaders were all protagonists in the polemical literary fight-back against the Elizabethan settlement, which was getting belatedly into its stride in the mid-1560s. Just as significantly, they were also men acutely conscious of the precariousness of their own refugee status in the Low Countries, as the waves of violent Reformation lapped at their doors.

A key figure here was the most distinguished early resident of the new college, Thomas Stapleton, whose controversial writings and scriptural commentaries would earn him a reputation and an influence in Counter-Reformation Europe to rival that of Robert Bellarmine. Before migrating to Douai, Stapleton had been part of the British expatriate community in Leuven, and he had been present in Antwerp during the iconoclastic fury that had gutted the cathedral and churches there on 19 and 20 August 1566. The experience left an indelible memory of 'the horrible and outragious sacrileges of that night' and a conviction that such atrocities were the inevitably malign fruit of the Reformation, 'an eternal document of the ghospellike zele of this sacred brotherhood'.[8]

This sense of embattlement was accentuated by the fact that the recusant community in Douai in the late 1560s and 1570s included not only the growing number of clerical students and staff of the English college but also a stream of other Catholic exiles displaced from Elizabeth's England. Just 18 months after the college's foundation that stream would be swollen by northerners in flight in the aftermath of the Rebellion of the Northern Earls in 1569, and the Elizabethan regime's ferociously punitive response. And to clinch the general sense of precariousness, in 1578 the college itself would be obliged by a rising tide of anti-Spanish feeling in Artois to relocate to Rheims, a second exile that would precipitate further financial and existential crises for the college, and which was to last for 15 years.

Unsurprisingly, therefore, a fundamental aim of teaching in the college was to instil into its students a vivid horror of the evils of Protestantism. As Allen explained:

> By frequent familiar conversations we make our students thoroughly acquainted with the chief impieties, blasphemies, absurdities, cheats and trickeries of the English heretics, as well as with their ridiculous writings, sayings and doings.

Specifically, such teaching aimed to fire mission by arousing 'a zealous and just indignation against the heretics' who had laid waste to England's traditional faith: so students were reminded of

> the utter desolation of all things sacred which there exists, our country once so famed for its religion and holy before God now void of all religion, our friends and kinsfolk, all our dear ones and countless souls besides perishing in schism and godlessness, every jail and dungeon filled to overflowing, not with thieves and villains but with Christ's priests and servants, nay with our friends and kinsmen.[9]

In some ways, of course, Douai *was* much like any other Counter-Reformation seminary. All seminaries had to equip their students with the essential pastoral skills of teaching and hearing confessions, and preparation in these areas at Douai wasn't much different from anywhere else in post-Tridentine Europe. The devotional regime at Douai – daily Mass, frequent confession and communion, devotion to the Virgin expressed in rosary sodalities, training in the use of the breviary and the celebration of the liturgy – was entirely conventional. For catechesis they used Trent's *Catechismus ad parochii*, as well as the more user-friendly catechisms of Peter Canisius, as most other seminaries did. The twice-weekly exposition of cases of conscience at Douai, an essential preparation for hearing confessions, was supplemented with material specially geared to the problems and dilemmas created by conditions back home, but was essentially based round the most popular of early Counter-Reformation textbooks of moral theology, the *Enchrydion* for confessors by Francis Xavier's maternal uncle Martín de Azpilcueta: seminarians all over early modern Europe took their formation from the same book.[10] Doctrinal instruction at Douai relied heavily on modern Jesuit scholastic interpreters of St Thomas, and once again this was routine for the period.

But Douai differed from other seminaries more than it resembled them. Trent itself had stipulated that candidates for the priesthood should be trained in 'grammar, singing, ecclesiastical computation, [...] Sacred Scripture, ecclesiastical books, the homilies of the saints, the manner of administering the sacraments [...] and the rites and ceremonies'. Only the emphasis on scripture in that list was in any way novel, and in actual practice through most of Europe the council's call for scripture study remained virtually a dead letter. Serious biblical training was conspicuous by its absence from most sixteenth- and seventeenth-century seminary syllabuses, which focused overwhelmingly on practical pastoral skills, to the neglect of dogmatic theology (as opposed to catechetics) and to the almost total exclusion of any serious engagement with scripture. Thomas Deutscher's studies of the curriculum at the seminary established by Cardinal Borromeo's disciple Mgr Carlo Bascapè in the Piedmontese diocese of Novara concluded that the course of studies there was conditioned by the need to equip priests quickly for parish life, giving them only what was deemed essential. Theological and scriptural studies were not deemed essential, especially since it was widely believed that country congregations 'would have been confused by subtle explanations of doctrine'. Similar practical and limited syllabuses were followed even in major centres such as Rome and Bologna. Few students even of the Jesuit Collegio Romano studied dogmatic theology, despite complaints by Cardinal Robert Bellarmine, who was concerned about the decline of theological expertise in Italy. And although the regulations for Borromeo's seminary in Milan followed Trent in prescribing scriptural study as part of the syllabus, in practice most students followed a similarly practical programme, only the very ablest being allowed to progress to work in scripture or dogmatic theology.[11]

By contrast, the account of the English college's syllabus that Allen set out in a letter to Vendeville late in 1578 laid overwhelming emphasis on expert knowledge of the Bible, constant practice in preaching and in disputation and a good grounding in dogmatic theology through the study of St Thomas.[12] It was, of course, the needs of the English mission that dictated that distinctive emphasis on Bible study, but we need to grasp just how very distinctive it was. Allen was intensely aware of the crucial importance of the vernacular Bible to the success of the Reformation, and was determined to eliminate the advantage this gave Protestants. Gregory Martin's Catholic translation of the Bible, and specifically the publication of his New Testament in 1582, was integral to this project. 'Our adversaries', Allen told Vendeville, 'have at their fingers' ends all those passages of scripture which seem to make for them, and by a certain deceptive adaptation and alteration of the sacred words produce the effect of appearing to say nothing but what comes from the Bible'. The remedy for this, Allen thought, was an authoritative Catholic translation of the Bible into English, a project for which, if papal permission could be procured, 'we already have men most fitted'. The man he had in mind was Gregory Martin, who had played a key role in the early stages of the establishment of the Venerabile Collegio Inglese in Rome in 1576, and who on his return to Douai from Rome had at once begun offering a course of lectures on the Hebrew Bible designed to enable his students to 'confound the arrogant ignorance of our heretics'.[13]

As that suggests, even before Martin's translation was begun, the course of studies at Douai was designed to ensure that Allen's men, like their Protestant opponents, would have the text of the Bible at their fingertips. Between three and five chapters of the Old or New Testaments in Latin were read aloud at each of the two main daily meals, followed while still at table by an exposition of part of what had been read, during which students were expected to have their Bibles open before them and pen and ink to hand. In three years the students heard the Old Testament read through in this way 12 times, the New Testament 16 times. Each was expected to do private preparatory work on the passages read communally, and there was a daily lecture on the New Testament, separate Hebrew and Greek classes, and regular disputations on the points of scripture controverted between Catholics and Protestants.[14]

These language classes were given by Gregory Martin, one of the ablest of the many young Catholic exiles from Elizabethan Oxford. The only surviving son of a family of minor Sussex gentry, Martin was an outstanding Greek and Hebrew scholar, who with his friend Edmund Campion had become a fellow of St John's in 1564. Early Elizabethan St John's was a notorious nest of papists: more than 30 of the early members of the college left Oxford for ordination at Douai or Rheims, and almost a third of Martin's and Campion's cohort of 20 founding members of the college eventually became Catholic priests. Bible study in early Elizabethan Oxford had a surprisingly strong Catholic dimension: Thomas Neale, regius professor of Hebrew from 1559, was a secret Catholic, and George Etheridge, regius professor of Greek, was deprived in 1559 for refusing the Oath of Supremacy but remained in Oxford tutoring private pupils in Greek throughout the 1560s and 1570s. But as pressure for conformity mounted in 1568, Martin resigned his fellowship and left Oxford, and found his way to William Allen's new college at Douai, in the Spanish Netherlands. Martin managed to persuade Campion, at the time Oxford's golden boy, to join him in exile in June 1571, but when Campion moved on to Rome, Martin stayed in Douai and from the mid-1570s taught scripture and biblical languages at the college.

And in October 1578 Martin set out on the mammoth project of translating the whole Bible single-handedly. He worked officially from the Latin Vulgate: this was inevitable, given the Council of Trent's privileging of the Vulgate above all other versions for doctrinal purposes, but in fact he made constant reference to the Hebrew and Greek. Martin turned out copy at the breakneck speed of two chapters a day. These chapters were then checked and corrected by Allen himself and by Allen's colleague and right-hand man, Richard Bristow. Between them these two also supplied most of the doctrinal and polemical notes to the published version. In addition to consulting the Hebrew and Greek texts alongside the Vulgate, Martin paid close attention to previous Tudor Bible versions, and despite his scorn for heretical mistranslation, he borrowed liberally from Tyndale and his successors. His New Testament was published in the year of his death, 1582, at the height of the national panic about popery triggered by the trial and execution of his friend Edmund Campion the previous year. His Old Testament had to wait till 1609 before the college had the money and the political breathing space to tackle the immense task of getting it to press.

Unsurprisingly, Martin's trawl through the English Protestant Bible translations was motivated not primarily by a search for the striking phrase to borrow – though borrow he did – but by a desire to document the wickedness of heretical translators in perverting the true meaning of holy scripture. He turned up hundreds of examples, which he published as a 300-page tract in the same year as his New Testament, in 1582, as *A discoverie of the manifold corruptions of the holy scriptures by the heretikes of our daie*. It's a relentlessly hostile case for the prosecution, designed to show that 'Heretikes (gentle Reader) be alvvaies like Heretikes, and hovvsoeuer they differ in opinions or names, yet in this point they agree, to abuse the Scriptures for their purpose by al meanes possibly.' So Protestant biblical translators and commentators systematically 'deny some whole bookes and parts of books […] call other some into question […] expound the rest at their pleasure [… and] fester and infect the whole body of the Bible with cankred translations'.

I've discussed the strengths and weaknesses of Martin's New Testament elsewhere, and I won't repeat that account in detail here. Notoriously, his translation was laughed at for its often impenetrable Latinisms: his version of the Psalms, and his rendering of the New Testament epistles especially were notoriously clumsy: 'Purge the old leaven, that you may be a new paste, as you are azymes. For our Pasche, Christ, is immolated' (1 Cor. 7); 'For our wrestling is not against flesh and blood, but […] against the rectors of the world of

this darkenes, against the spirituals of wickedness in the celestials'
(Eph. 6.12).

But by and large these problems arise only in the lyric and
argumentative parts of the translation. Martin's versions of
the Gospels, like his translation of the narrative books of the
Old Testament, are vigorous and idiomatic, and they can stand
comparison with any other Tudor Bible. Many of his distinctive
turns of phrase were vivid improvements on the renderings that
had preceded them: 'The footstool of thy feet' (Mt. 22.44); 'Why
what evil hath he done'(Mt. 27.23]; 'throng and press' (Lk. 8.45);
'his raiment white and glistering' (Lk. 9.29); 'set at nought' (Lk.
23.11); 'strive for mastery'(1 Cor. 9.25); 'to live is Christ and to
die is gain' (Phil. 1.21); 'questioned among themselves' (Mk 1.27);
'blaze abroad the matter' (Mk 1.45); 'mourn and weep'(Lk. 6.25);
'it came to pass' (Lk. 17.11); 'distress of nations' (Lk. 21.25); and
for ever and ever.

Martin was, of course, conscious of the oddity of many of his
Latinisms. But he considered that they were the price that had to
be paid for faithfulness to the (Vulgate) original: 'We presume not
in hard places to mollifie the speaches or phrases, but religiouslie
keepe them word for word, and point for point, for feare of missing
or restraining the sense of the holy Ghost to our phantasie.'[15] And
many of his Latinisms were in fact successful, subsequently being
adopted by the translators of the King James Bible, and from
there passing into the language – in the Epistle to the Romans
alone these include *separated, consent, impenitent, propitiation,
remission, concupiscence, revealed, emulation, conformed, instant* and
contribution.[16]

But it's the polemical notes and editorial material of the Rheims
Douai version that I want to consider here. No one could mistake
the ferocity of this material, and a modern reader is often perplexed
by its bitterness: this is not a new reaction. When he revised the
Rheims Douai Bible in the late 1740s, Richard Challoner removed
almost all the notes and commentary, as far too harsh for the polite
eighteenth century. As it happens, we have an unexpected window
into the source of the relentlessly polemical character of the Rheims

Douai Bible commentary in the teaching at Allen's seminary. The key figure here is not Gregory Martin but his slightly older and more famous colleague Thomas Stapleton. In his remarkable literary celebration of Counter-Reformation Rome, *Roma sancta*, written immediately after completion of his Bible translation, Martin described the course of studies at the English college in Douai, emphasizing the intensive instruction in biblical knowledge that was so distinctive a feature of the syllabus there. He was almost certainly summarizing Allen's account of the syllabus in his 1578 letter to Vendeville. But Martin added the information that at Douai the daily post-prandial discourses on the New Testament were given by 'one of the elder divines (a master in the facultie)'.[17] The 'elder divine' he was referring to was Stapleton, who had begun his teaching at Douai with a two-year stint as lecturer in scripture. As professor of scripture at Leuven in the 1590s he would publish two hugely influential sets of Gospel commentaries. The more substantial of these, the first volumes of which appeared in 1591, was his *Promptuarium morale super evangelica dominicala totius anni*, a pastoral commentary on all the Gospel readings for Sunday and feast days throughout the liturgical year, designed 'for the instruction of preachers, the reformation of sinners and the consolation of the devout'. It ran through an amazing 30 editions in as many years, and became a regular feature in clerical libraries all over early modern Europe.[18] The *Promptuarium morale* offered detailed verse-by-verse exposition of the Sunday Gospel passages, referring only rarely to current events but instead emphasizing the practical devotional, ascetical and moral application of the text, with cross-references to other places in scripture, the writings of the Fathers, saints lives, classical literature and scholastic theology, all designed to provide parish clergy with timeless material to instruct and edify Sunday congregations.

Stapleton's *Promptuarium catholicum ad instructionem concionatorum contra haereticos nostri temporis*, the first volume of which was published in Paris in 1589, was altogether more specialized in intent, though it proved almost equally popular. Much of the substance of both *Promptuaria* clearly recycled material from Stapleton's lectures at Douai and Leuven. But the *Promptuarium catholicum* must have drawn mainly on his Douai teaching, because publication of it began before he moved to the Leuven chair in scripture. And the *Promptuarium catholicum* didn't offer the generalized uplift of the *Promptuarium morale*. It was aimed specifically at preachers in regions such as England, Germany or the Low Countries, where Catholicism confronted the Protestant Reformation eyeball to eyeball. Accordingly, the *Promptuarium catholicum* was much more narrowly targeted and much more explicitly polemical, its Sunday offerings taking the form of short, sharp expositions, rarely more than a thousand words or so long, often taking just a single phrase or verse from the Gospel of the day, and designed to refute Protestant exegesis and to vindicate contested Catholic doctrines. And this, as we've seen, was precisely the agenda of the scriptural instruction on offer to seminarians at Douai College, 'wherin', as Gregory Martin explained, 'is urged [...] the true advantage of the Catholike and the pretensed argument of the Heretike, that studentes may learne out of the holy Scriptures how to prove and disprove, confirme the truth and infirme the Contrarie, and to spie both the advantages of the truth, and the treacheries [and] guiles of falsehood'.[19]

We can be fairly sure of the direct relationship between Stapleton's polemics in the *Promptuaria catholicum* and the scriptural instruction on offer in the college. As I've mentioned, Martin's translation came with copious marginal notes, introductions and commentary, the bulk of them the work of William Allen and Richard Bristow. But although the publication of the *Promptuaria* lay almost a decade in the future, these crucial Rheims Bible marginalia and commentaries show a close correspondence throughout to Stapleton's published polemical exegesis and, for the Gospels at any rate, are almost certainly directly indebted to it.

A single example will have to do in illustration of this dependence. The Rheims Bible's notes on the figure of John the Baptist in Mt. 3 cite the claim of St John Chrysostom and other Fathers that John was the model for the eremitic and religious life, the first monk, 'wherewith the protestants are so offended that they say

S. Chrysostom spoke rashly and untruely'. Despite the Gospel's description of John's desert dwelling, his rough clothing and austere diet, the note goes on, 'they are not ashamed to pervert all three with this strange commentarie, that it was a desert full of townes and villages, his garment was chamlet, his meate such as the country gave and the people there used [...] to make him thereby but a common man like to the rest.' These very specific accusations of Protestant misrepresentation of the Baptist have shorthand marginal page references to the Magdeburg Centuriators, to the obscure Rostock reformer David Kochhafe (Chythraus), a disciple of Philip Melanchthon from whom the otherwise baffling reference to John the Baptist wearing camlet was lifted, and to Martin Bucer. [20]

If we now turn from the Rheims New Testament note to Stapleton's homily for the second Sunday of Advent in the *Promptuarium catholicum*, a discussion of this same passage from Matthew which forms the Gospel for that day, we find precisely the same polemical points being made, in the same order, illustrated with extended quotations from the same Protestant authorities, but all at much greater length and framed within a blisteringly scornful commentary: *O delicatos homines et acutos, qui vt ex eremo loca pascuosà et amœna, sic ex veste aspera, vrbanam et elegantem norunt conficere : vel potiùs, ô homines impios, qui sic Scripturas sacras norunt peruertere* ('O pampered and over-clever men, who have contrived to turn the desert into a lush and charming spot, and from harsh vesture have woven elegant garments in the height of fashion : or, rather, you wicked men, who have learned thus to pervert the Holy Scriptures').[21]

It is of course possible that in compiling this homily for the *Promptuarium*, Stapleton had the terse Rheims New Testament note in front of him, that he went away and looked up the Protestant authors cited there, selected illustrative quotations from them and expanded the compressed point-scoring of the notes into full-scale homiletic vituperation. But it is far more likely that the truth is the other way round: that the brief Bible annotations represent a compressed version of Stapleton's lectures, which would in due course be absorbed wholesale into the *Promptuarium*. Stapleton

himself cannot have directly compiled the Bible note. He had
remained behind in Douai when the college relocated to Rheims,
and the annotations to the New Testament were composed after
the move to Rheims, as most of the translation itself was. But it is
overwhelmingly likely that the Rheims annotator was working from
detailed notes or the complete texts of Stapleton's Douai lectures
on the Gospels, and distilled them, and their learned citations from
European Protestant sources, into our marginal note.

If that's the case, the Rheims Douai New Testament takes on
a new significance. We've long been aware of the aggressively
polemical character of the editorial apparatus to Gregory Martin's
Bible; this was holy scripture conceived as a fighting manual
rather than an aid to devotion. The notes to Mt. 3 are entirely
characteristic of the rest of the marginalia, and the point to
emphasize here is that these notes and editorial commentary are
not only the work of the seminary staff, but they transport us to
the lecture room and the chapel of the first generation of Douai
seminarians, a community manifestly preoccupied by the calamity
of the overthrow of their Church at home by a heretical regime,
and who were being intensively coached to confront and to resist
that regime's Protestant apologists.

Allen understood perfectly well that he was creating a new kind
of priest, men

> well skilled in Latin and other learned tongues [...] brought upp
> to degree bothe in art and divinitye, such as should never have
> been refused, in any country chistianned, nether in this age nor
> of old time, to have been persons and pastors of men's souls
> [...] and some so well lerned that they might have passed with
> aestimation to any degree of divinitye in our universities [...]
> and none [...] unfytt but that they have much more convenient
> institution in all kind of pastorall doctrine than the common
> sort of curats had in old tyme.

But Allen wasn't just measuring his priests against the unlearned
parish clergy of pre-Reformation England. For although, as he told

the aged Carthusian prior Maurice Chancey, 'Mercury cannot be made of every log', and not all his men were 'of highest wit or learning', yet every one of them could stand comparison with the products of any of 'the seminaryes in Italy and other countryes [...] erected by commandement of the holy counsel of Trent for education and nurture of preests', and even with the elite products of 'the Jesuits trade'.[22]

We still await a scholarly history of Douai College, so it is difficult to say what, if any, were the long-term consequences of this remarkable if disconcerting early emphasis on expertise in controversial theology and scriptural study in the formation of priests for the mission. The training was designed to equip theological gladiators for public disputation, but from the start Allen's priests had few opportunities for public debate. Disguised, to the disgust of older Marian clergy, in 'colours, ruffes and rapiers', Allen's seminarians had to contend with 'miseryes in night journeys [...] perill of theves, of waters, of watches, of false brethren', and to endure 'close abode in chambers as in pryson or dongeoon without fyre or candell'. By the later 1580s and in the wake of the tragic end of Campion's mission, opportunities in England for safe disputation with Protestant opponents hardly existed. It's likely that the seminary curriculum reflected that change, and became more conventional.

And at this distance in time, however much we admire their heroism, we certainly can't simply appropriate or even retrospectively endorse the nature of their formation. From the perspective of the twenty-first century the confrontational stance in which these first English seminary priests were trained, their preoccupation with holy scripture conceived above all not as a shared Christian resource but as a magazine of proof texts condemning Protestantism, however understandable in the context of Reformation Europe, is bound to raise troubling questions. We are conscious now not merely of the historic tragedy of Christian disunity but also of the reality of good intentions and a concern for truth on both sides of the murderous religious divide that led sixteenth-century Christians to burn, strangle or disembowel each other. But for the priests trained at Douai, doctrinal disagreements were not intellectual or religious puzzles, or pardonable intellectual disagreements: the points in contention between Catholic and Protestant were armed with fire and blood. They were quite literally matters of life and death: Catholic and Protestant were in one another's eyes not merely mistaken but malign.

Yet whatever difficulty we may feel about an education in which theology was understood as a weapon of religious warfare, there can be no doubting the originality and distinction with which it was pursued at Douai and Rheims in that first Elizabethan generation. Never again would English seminaries match the urgent theological engagement and fierce eloquence of that first age, when English academics were still dominant presences in the universities of the Low Countries, and when, within Douai College itself, men of the calibre of Allen, Bristow, Martin and Stapleton were teaching. Not till the 1840s and another influx of Oxford converts could English Catholicism boast such a constellation of stars. And never again would English clergy stand at the very cutting edge of militant European Catholicism. The Rheims New Testament was a pioneering and in many respects risky project in a Church deeply suspicious of vernacular versions of the scripture, but for that very reason it would become the standard for other pioneering responses to the spread of Protestantism. When the Polish Jesuit Jakub Wujek confronted the Calvinist threat in Poland in the 1580s and '90s, it was to the example of Allen and his colleagues he turned, adopting the Rheims New Testament as the key precedent for the legitimacy of a Catholic vernacular Bible: his own Polish Bible, published in 1593, pillaged the Rheims version for its notes and editorial apparatus.[23] As Gerard Kilroy has demonstrated, in Edmund Campion's teaching and writing in Counter-Reformation Bohemia, the religious upheavals of Reformation Oxford cast a long shadow into the central European Counter-Reformation. But Campion's was not an isolated case. In the founding generation of Douai College, and in their great monuments, Stapleton's *Promptuaria* and Martin's Rheims Douai Bible, the exiles of Oxford spoke to Counter-Reformation Europe in a distinctively English accent.

5

The King James Bible

There are more than 350 different translations of the Bible into English, more than into any other language. And if we count English versions of the New Testament, or of individual books or clusters of books such as the Psalms or the Gospels, the number of different English Bible translations runs into the thousands. Yet, with all that abundance, all over the English-speaking world in 2011 there were events celebrating just one particular translation, the King James Bible, published 400 years earlier, in 1611. It wasn't the first complete English Bible: in fact, there had been five earlier versions in use in the churches of Tudor England, not to mention an illegal translation printed abroad at Rheims for English Roman Catholics. The King James Bible owes something to them all, and in fact it's not too much of an exaggeration to say that it wasn't so much a fresh translation as the distillation of 80 years of continuous Bible translation.

It was a conglomeration in other ways too, the collective work of no fewer than 47 mostly rather obscure clergymen and dons, divided up into six committees or companies – two apiece in Oxford, Cambridge and London.[1] Pantomime horses are prone to trot in two different directions, and it's hard to imagine anything beautiful or enduring being devised by so huge and baggy a pantomime horse as a committee of 47. The King James Bible is the great exception.

Amalgam it may be, but till relatively recently, when people talked or thought about the Bible in English, it was likely to be the King James Bible that they meant. And even now in the USA there is a powerful federation of more than a thousand evangelical churches who believe that this so-called Authorized Version is actually superior to the original Hebrew and Greek scriptures it translates: 'the perfect and infallible word of God [...] in the universal language of these last days, English'.[2]

And these American Baptists are not the only fundamentalists who think that the King James Bible is quite simply the most important book ever to have been published in the English language. That apostle of the New Atheism, Professor Richard Dawkins, gave his support to the King James Bible Trust, the body that organized many of the 2011 quatercentenary celebrations of its publication: you can even Google a YouTube clip of Richard Dawkins praising the King James Bible and reading a chapter from the Song of Songs.[3]

There is something comic about so ferocious a scourge of Christianity praising the Christian holy book, not least because Professor Dawkins has said how anxious he is that religious people aren't allowed, in his words, to 'hijack' this 'great cultural resource'. And he's not alone in thinking of it in those terms. For weeks in 2011 pundits who never darken the door of a church were queuing up on radio and television to tell us that the King James Bible is above all else a great work of literature, what the early twentieth-century scholar John Livingston Lowes famously called 'the noblest monument of English prose'.[4]

The King James Bible is indeed a magnificent translation of the scriptures, remarkable both for its fidelity to the original Hebrew and Greek and for the splendour and variety of its English: it is, without question, the best translation of the whole Bible into English, possibly even into any language. It has left an indelible mark in literature from Milton to Eliot, and in great cultural monuments such as Handel's Messiah, and its importance in the political history of the world was symbolized when Barack Obama began his presidency of the United States by swearing his oath of office on a battered copy of the King James Bible, printed in Oxford in 1855, the same copy that had been used at the inauguration of Abraham Lincoln.[5] But many sensitive Christians have expressed worries about the cult of the King James Bible as literature, and in any case profound social and linguistic shifts in Anglophone culture raise questions about whether or not it is ever likely to be once again the Bible of choice of most English-speaking Christians.

The King James's impact on our language is perhaps the most obvious measure of its importance, because English speech is saturated with vivid phrases straight from the King James Bible:

> to fall flat on your face, a man after my own heart, the land of the living, sour grapes, my brother's keeper, the fat of the land, far be it from me, image and likeness, an eye for an eye, nothing new under the sun, no peace for the wicked, the wages of sin, holier than thou, not a hair of your head, the skin of your teeth, the spirit is willing, from time to time, put words in my mouth, fell among thieves, from strength to strength, like a lamb to the slaughter, rise and shine, the writing on the wall, a fly in the ointment, a drop in a bucket, the salt of the earth, a law unto themselves, the wages of sin, all things to all men, the blind leading the blind, the patience of Job, the signs of the times, a thorn in the flesh, give up the ghost, the scales fell from his eyes, the burden and heat of the day, eat, drink and be merry, fight the good fight, be horribly afraid.[6]

So the language of the King James Bible is everywhere, which helps explain why someone like the novelist and philosopher Iris Murdoch, herself another famous atheist, could praise its 'unique religious eloquence' and even its 'linguistic perfection': it is a repository of 'treasured words', she wrote, which 'encourage, console, and save'.[7]

'Encourage, console, and save.' That sounds just the sort of thing that people who don't often read the Bible assume that it's supposed to do. But notice, there's not a hint there that it might actually matter whether or not the words that encourage, console or save are *true*. In this aesthetic frame of reference, what makes the words of the King James a treasure is their eloquence and beauty. There is in fact a complex and complicated relationship between beauty and truth, and it could be argued that often one implies the other. Nevertheless, this irreligious praise for the King James Bible is rather odd, and rather disturbing. Certainly, it would have disgusted the makers of the King James Bible, because what its translators wanted above all was a version of the Bible that said in English what God's own Hebrew and Greek said. Although they took pains to make sure that the translation sounded well, they probably hardly thought at all about whether or not their version might be *beautiful*, and they wouldn't have understood the notion that the Bible should be valued not for its saving truth but for its literary style.

The relationship between beauty and truth in religion is, of course, a very complicated issue, and I don't propose to enter into it here. But when King James commissioned his new version of the Bible, he certainly neither asked for nor expected to get a monument of English prose. He wanted a single Bible, to be the revered source of divine truth for all his people. His decision was driven by politics as much as piety, and I doubt if the literary aspect of the project entered his mind.[8] At any rate, for the first hundred years or so of his Bible's existence hardly anyone commented on or appears to have noticed its beauty. In fact, to begin with, nobody seemed all that keen on any aspect of what they called the 'New Version'. The great preachers of the day, even those who had themselves been involved in the translating, seemed to have preferred the older versions. It took King James's Bible 50 years or more to establish an exclusive claim to be *the* one and only English Bible. When it did, it was not because of its intrinsic merits, great as they were, but as one of the unexpected outcomes of a bloody civil war, and the disappearance and unavailability of rival versions. When they did get round to thinking about the Bible as prose, what they noticed was that it sounded like Hebrew prose, and often sounded rather strange as English. It was to take more than a century before anyone began to talk about the KJB as some kind of milestone for the language, and as a model for English style.

Bible translation in the English Reformation emerged almost fully formed with one man, working alone. He was William

Tyndale, a Gloucestershire priest who left England for Germany in the early 1520s, fell under the influence of Martin Luther and in 1526 published in Germany the first translation of the whole New Testament from Greek into English.[9] Tyndale was a fierce and prickly human being, but he was a great genius and his New Testament was a masterpiece, faithfully turning the Greek of the New Testament into marvellously vivid and salty English. But it was a provocative masterpiece. Tyndale hated the Catholic Church, and he deliberately translated some key words by English equivalents that flew in the face of traditional Catholic doctrine. *Presbyteros* became 'senior' or 'elder', not 'priest' or 'presbyter'; *agape* became 'love', not 'charity'; *ecclesia* became 'congregation', not 'church'. In using these terms Tyndale was deliberately flouting traditional Church teaching. But in 1526 Henry VIII was still a pious Catholic, so Tyndale's translation was banned and Tyndale himself outlawed. Nevertheless, his New Testament was so good that it proved definitive: it became the inevitable starting-point for every subsequent translation of the New Testament into English down to the twentieth century, even the Roman Catholic version produced at Rheims 50 years later. Almost 90 per cent of the King James New Testament is lifted unchanged or only slightly changed from Tyndale, and about 70 per cent of its Old Testament. It was, in fact, Tyndale who first coined many of the marvellous phrases I quoted earlier, as well as many more:

the burden and the heat of the day
in him we live and move and have our being
blessed are the peacemakers
the apple of his eye

And while he was about it, Tyndale invented many of the fundamental theological terms that were to shape religious thinking for centuries: the name Jehovah for God, and words such as 'Passover', 'scapegoat' and 'atonement'.

Having completed the New Testament, Tyndale moved on to the Old, and once again his version of the Pentateuch, the first five books of the Bible, was another masterpiece. He specialized in direct ordinary language. In Gen. 39, for example, later versions, including the King James Bible, would say 'The Lord was with Joseph, and he was a prosperous man'; but Tyndale translated that as 'The Lord was with Joseph, and he was a lucky fellow'. In Tyndale's Bible Joseph wore a gay coat, not a coat of many colours, Pharaoh's 'jolly captains' were drowned in the Red Sea and the serpent says to Eve, 'Tush, ye shall not die'. After the Pentateuch, Tyndale moved on to the historical books, but he didn't live to finish his work. Before he reached the prophets or the Psalms and wisdom literature he was arrested for heresy by the Catholic authorities in the Netherlands, executed by strangling, and his body burned, in 1536.

By now, however, Henry VIII had broken with the Pope over his desire for a divorce, and decided that an English Bible might be tolerable after all. So in the late 1530s three complete English Bibles were published in rapid succession, all stealing from Tyndale, culminating in 1539 in the so-called 'Great Bible', which every church in the land was required to buy. I don't have space here to discuss this explosion of Bible production, but the key figure behind it was the reformer Myles Coverdale. Coverdale knew no Hebrew and not much Greek, but he was a good Latinist and he'd lived and worked in Protestant Germany, so he built his Bible around the core of what Tyndale had left and supplied the rest himself by translating the other biblical books from modern Protestant Bibles in Latin and German. The Psalms in the Great Bible were Coverdale's work, beautiful but not very accurate. Ironically, they are the only part of these Henrician Bibles that has survived into modern times, because Coverdale's psalter is the version used in the 1662 Book of Common Prayer, and there it became the heart of the Anglican choral tradition.[10]

Protestant versions of the Bible were withdrawn, of course, under the Catholic Queen Mary, and her archbishop of Canterbury, Cardinal Pole, held a synod that authorized a new Catholic translation. But both Pole and the queen were dead before that project got started, and meanwhile many Protestant leaders fled abroad, taking refuge in Protestant cities such as Frankfurt, Basle and Calvin's

Geneva. And it was in Geneva that the greatest English Bible of the sixteenth century was created, by a group of exiled English scholars led by William Whittingham. Their New Testament, basically a tidied-up version of Tyndale's translation, appeared in 1557 and the complete Old and New Testaments three years later, in 1560, by which time the Catholic Queen Mary was dead, so this complete Geneva Bible, printed in Geneva, was dedicated to the Protestant Queen Elizabeth. The Geneva Bible was the first English Bible to be translated entirely from the original Hebrew and Greek, and in a way its appearance was more of a landmark than the King James Bible itself. In fact, it was such a good version that, as with Tyndale, a great deal of the King James version is recycled with minor changes or no change at all from the Geneva version. And the Geneva version had what the King James never provided: illustrations, maps, glossaries, introductions to each book, indexes and concordances to help the reader navigate round the text and extended marginal notes explaining all the difficult passages. It was also the first English Bible to number each verse. In fact, it was an ideal study Bible, printed in a handy small size on inexpensive paper so that ordinary people could afford to buy it and read it at home.[11]

However, Queen Elizabeth disapproved of the Geneva version. It had been produced and printed abroad, without royal permission. Some of its theological notes had a whiff of Presbyterianism about them, and one or two could be read as condoning rebellion against tyrannical rulers, a notion no Tudor monarch was prepared to put up with even for a second. The men who had produced the Geneva Bible were ardent Protestants, impatient to stamp out every surviving trace of popery in England. In her early years, Elizabeth was very conscious of being the Protestant queen of a still pervasively Catholic people. 'Softly, softly' was her motto in religious matters, and she distrusted anyone or anything that might rock the ship of state. A Protestant queen could hardly ban the Bible, even one produced in Geneva, but she and her tame archbishop of Canterbury, Matthew Parker, tried to freeze it out by pretending it didn't exist. Though the Geneva Bible ran through many editions, and became the Bible of preference for most Elizabethan readers, including Shakespeare, till almost half-way through Elizabeth's reign all copies had to be imported from Europe: not a single one was printed in England till after Archbishop Parker's death in 1575. Henry VIII's Great Bible was the only translation approved for use in churches for the first ten years of Elizabeth's reign, when it was replaced in 1568 by a revised version, the work of Parker and a small group of his episcopal colleagues and so, inevitably, known as the Bishops' Bible. [12]

The Bishops' Bible wasn't a patch on the Geneva Bible, and you can get some idea of the clunkiness of its style from the opening verses of Psalm 23:

> God is my shepherd, therefore I can lack nothing. He will cause me to repose myself in pasture full of grass, and he will lead me unto calm waters.

So Elizabethan Protestants had to choose between an official but rather uninspired version of the Bible, printed in large folio format for reading in church, and a much more accurate and memorable version, handily sized and equipped with forceful notes and commentaries advocating an ardent and committed Protestantism, a choice between a somewhat stodgy establishment Anglicanism and a fiercer, more strident, kind of Protestantism, nicknamed 'puritanism' by its enemies, which was sharply critical of the bishops and hostile to every remaining vestige of Catholicism in the worship and teaching of the official Church.

And it was out of that tension that the King James Bible was born. In 1603 Elizabeth died and was succeeded by her Scottish cousin James Stuart. James distrusted the puritans because he suspected that they were republicans, and he identified them with the presbytery of the Scottish Kirk, which had always made life difficult for him. He summed up his distrust in the slogan 'no bishop, no king'. The Geneva Bible was the official Bible of the Scottish Kirk, but that did not endear it to James, who thought he detected a treasonous distaste for the rule of kings in some of its notes on the Old Testament. [13]

So as James made his way south from Scotland in 1603, the puritans seized the opportunity to try to influence the new king by presenting him with a petition, allegedly signed by a thousand clergy, asking him to reform the things they disliked about the Church of England: saints' days, kneeling for communion, the wearing of the surplice, the use of the sign of the cross in baptism. James fobbed them off with the promise of a conference, which eventually took place at Hampton Court in January 1604, but there was no meeting of minds.[14] The handful of puritan delegates, led by Dr John Reynolds, the president of Corpus Christi College, Oxford, were swamped by a hostile posse of bishops and deans led by the ferocious Richard Bancroft, bishop of London, who in less than a year would be promoted to be archbishop of Canterbury, a man who had led a McCarthy-style witch-hunt against puritans under Elizabeth. For three days James and Bancroft stonewalled and ridiculed every puritan demand, and at one point the king even insultingly assured the distinguished puritan academics that if one of their university pupils had argued as badly as they did, 'so should the rodde have plyed upon the poor boys buttocks'.[15]

On the last day of this rather disastrous conference Reynolds asked whether the king might consider a new translation of the Bible, so that there might be 'one only translation [...] to be authentical and read in the church'. Reynolds was probably angling for the replacement of the despised Bishops' Bible by an improved edition of the Geneva Bible, complete with its notes. Predictably, Bishop Bancroft leapt in to rubbish the suggestion – if every quibble about the Bishops' Bible was heeded, 'there would be no end of translating'. But, to everyone's surprise, this was one puritan demand the king was ready to listen to.

James was always the shrewd politician, and he was conscious that the puritans were in danger of leaving the conference aggrieved and empty-handed. After all his refusals, a new Bible version was a concession he could afford to make without compromising the status quo: it would absorb puritan energies and establish James's credentials as a Protestant Solomon, a king who would provide his people with a new and improved version of the word of God, just as Henry VIII had once done.

So it was decided that the Bible should be divided up into six sections, each one to be translated by one of six committees, or companies as they were called: two based at Westminster, two in Cambridge, two in Oxford. The two Westminster companies were to be led by Lancelot Andrewes and William Barlow. Andrewes was the weighty figure here. Dean of Westminster Abbey, a ritualist high-churchman and a dedicated anti-puritan, he was also a profound scholar in Greek and the Semitic languages and one of the greatest preachers of that or any other age. His company, which met in the Jerusalem Chamber in the Deanery of Westminster Abbey, was responsible for the Old Testament from Genesis to the second book of Kings, and those books of the Bible would produce some of the King James Bible's mightiest prose. Barlow's Company translated the New Testament Epistles. The Cambridge companies were allocated the Old Testament from 1 Chron. to the Song of Solomon, and the Apocrypha. The Oxford companies were responsible for the prophets from Isaiah to Malachi, and the Gospels, Acts and book of Revelation.[16]

The companies were instructed that the Bishops' Bible was to be followed and as little altered 'as the Truth of the originall will permit'. To ensure this, they were issued with folio editions of the Bishops' Bible with very wide margins, into which the proposed alterations were to be entered. They were to stick to the familiar forms of Hebrew names, and when they were in doubt about the precise meaning of a Hebrew or Greek word, the translators were told to opt for the meaning most familiar from Church tradition: 'the old ecclesiastical terms' were to be kept. If Tyndale had had a grave, he would certainly have been turning in it.[17]

In the event, however, the translators went way beyond this narrow set of rules. They did indeed start with the Bishops' Bible as a working text, but they borrowed freely from all the existing translations, including even the Roman Catholic Rheims New Testament. But one aspect of their brief they did stick to religiously, with momentous consequences for the character of the King James Bible. Individual books were farmed out to men judged best qualified to translate them. Their translation then had to be scrutinized by the whole company, after which it was circulated to the other companies; difficult words or passages were to be sent, where necessary, for consultation to experts outside the companies, and the accumulated result of all this consultation and revision was finally approved by a committee of scrutiny made up of representatives of each of the companies.

That final process of scrutiny took nine months, and it was carried out in Stationers' Hall in London, the centre of the book trade in England. Crucially, this process highlighted the *sound* of the translation: one of the company responsible for the translation of the book being considered read it aloud slowly, while the members of the committee of scrutiny followed what they were hearing with Bibles in various languages in front of them, and as a contemporary witness, John Selden, put it, 'If they found any fault, they spoke up: if not, he read on'. That emphasis on testing the version by hearing it read aloud was quite new in translation into English, and it helps to account for the King James Bible's success as a version for reading in church.[18]

It is time now to have a brief look at what is distinctive about this very eclectic Bible translation and to try to see the King James translators at work. We start at the beginning, with one of the most dramatic confrontations in the story of creation and fall, the passage where God finds Adam and Eve hiding in the garden, and realizes that they have disobeyed his command and eaten the forbidden fruit. God asks Adam why he has done this and, spinelessly, Adam passes the buck: the woman gave me, and I did eat. So God turns to Eve, and says – well, first of all, here is Tyndale's version of what he says:

And the Lord God said unto the woman: wherefore didst thou so? And the woman answered, the serpent deceived me and I ate. (Gen. 3.13)

The Geneva Bible pruned this, and in the process improved the rhythm a little

And the Lord God said to the woman, Why hast thou done this? And the woman said, The serpent beguiled me, and I did eate.

That's definitely better: 'beguiled' is a more insinuating word than 'deceived', and 'and I did eate' has a more decisive closing rhythm than the balder 'and I ate'.

So the King James translators accepted most of the Geneva rendering, but they rephrased God's question to Eve, and in doing so they transformed the verse, making it unforgettably sinister and menacing:

> And the Lord God said unto the woman, What is this that thou hast done? And the woman said, the serpent beguiled me, and I did eate.

God's question is now spelled out in those seven terrifying monosyllables, every one like a hammer-blow, an effect increased by the translator's use of five hard consonantal sounds in a row, made with the tongue against the back of the upper teeth.

That sensitivity to the sound of words is on display over and over again in the King James Bible. Take another famous example, the passage in Job 38 where God challenges human questioning by describing the creation. In Geneva those verses go:

> Where wast thou when I laid the foundations of the earth? [...] when the stars of the morning praised me together, and all the children of God rejoiced. (Job 38.7)

Once again, the King James translators start by following Geneva, but they altered the final line to create an unforgettable piece of poetry:

> Where wast thou when I laid the foundations of the earth? [...] When the morning starres sang together, and all the sonnes of God shouted for joy.

Or, again, in Isa. 53.3 Geneva has 'a man ful of sorrowes and hath experience of infirmities', but King James has the phrase we all know, 'a man of sorrows, and acquainted with griefe'.

Now all these changes make the text sound better: to us they look like literary improvements, and they might incline you to think that what the King James version has to offer above all is style, or literary self-consciousness. And the King James version does seem deliberately stately: the translators often seem to nudge the earlier versions in the direction of greater formality. In the Genesis creation narrative they mostly follow Geneva closely, but where Geneva says 'and Darkness was upon the deep' the King James version has the more solemn 'And Darkness was upon the face of the deep' (Genesis 1.2). You find the same kind of deliberate stateliness in the King James's frequent use of phrases such as 'And it came to pass': that's an expansion not in the Hebrew, the kind of phrase that slows the text down and adds to its grandeur. It's definitely not common speech. Nobody ever actually spoke in the idiom of the King James Bible. Its translators don't give us any jolly captains or gay coats or lucky fellows; their serpent doesn't descend to slang with 'tush ye shall not die'. And precisely because the translators were deliberately drawing on the older versions, the language of the King James was archaic: it preserved a lot of usages that by 1611 were almost a century old.[19] This Bible was old-fashioned even when first published, and it would have had an antique ring to its first hearers and readers.

So not 'Our father, Who art in heaven', which would have been up to date in Shakespeare's England, but 'Our Father, *Which* art in heaven', which would have struck Shakespeare's contemporaries as quaint. The result was a stately rendering which announces itself as a sacred text by the very texture of its language, and which could sound magnificent when read aloud.

But not always. The translators were wrestling with obscure ancient texts, and they sometimes produced not magnificence but gobbledygook. What on earth, for example, does this mean?

O ye Corinthians, our mouth is open unto you, our heart is enlarged. Ye are not straitened in us, but ye are straitened in your own bowels. Now for a recompense in the same (I speak as unto my children) be ye also enlarged. (2 Cor. 6.11–13)

And that should alert us to a crucial feature of the King James Bible. Despite all the magnificence of its language, the translators were not out to produce literature: first and foremost, what they were after was fidelity to the Hebrew and Greek, as close a version as they could get to the Word of God set down in those ancient languages. When they changed earlier versions, it was not primarily in order to make them sound better but out of a concern to move the text closer to the originals. And that means that the language of the King James Bible is often anything but authentically English-sounding: it often abandons the natural word order of English, and replicates the sometimes odd-sounding word order of Hebrew. So in Isa. 1.7 the Geneva Bible has the natural-sounding 'Your land is waste, your cities are burned with fire: strangers devour your land in your presence'. The King James translators changed this to 'Your country is desolate, your cities are burned with fire: your land, strangers devour it in your presence', where the strange placing of 'your land' as a separate phrase reproduces the word sequence in Hebrew.

That determination to stick close to the originals meant that, when the King James translators didn't understand the Hebrew and Greek original, they settled for rendering the words as literally as they could, word for word, sense or nonsense: and impenetrable passages such as that verse from Corinthians are the result. So both the merits and the defects of the King James Bible come from a desire on the part of its translators not to write great literature but to pass on to readers as closely as possible what was in the original.

And certainly, to begin with, nobody thought it *was* great literature. One of the greatest Hebrew scholars of the day, Hugh Broughton, admittedly a chronically quarrelsome man who had been deliberately excluded from the committee of translators, published a vitriolic review of the new version, which he claimed had 'bred in me a sadness that will grieve me while I breathe'; the new edition, he wrote, 'crosseth me, I require it to be burned'.[20] Broughton's reaction was probably *parti pris*, but if anyone else thought this new Bible was a classic, nobody said so, and even the king's printer went on producing Geneva Bibles. The Church authorities tried to encourage sales of the King James Bible by forbidding the publication of new editions of the Geneva Bible, but the printers got round this by inserting bogus title pages dated 1599 into new editions of the Geneva. And the bishops themselves seemed dubious about the new Bible. Lancelot Andrewes, the great stylist who had headed the company responsible for some of the most magnificent books of the King James Old Testament, seems to have preferred to quote the Geneva Bible or the Latin Vulgate in his sermons, and as late as the 1630s so did Archbishop Laud himself.

But slowly the new translation made its way. The ban on English editions of the Geneva Bible gave the newer version a chance in the bookshops: the last English edition of Geneva was printed in 1616, and the last Geneva Bible printed anywhere before the twentieth century was in 1644. Even puritans began to switch to the so-called 'New Version', and by the time of the restoration of the Church and monarchy after the Cromwellian period in 1660, the King James Bible had begun to look venerable, a monument to the golden days of religion before the cataclysm of Civil War. The Church historian Thomas Fuller, writing in the 1650s, could look back on the King James translators, as 'worthy men [...] now gathered to their fathers and gone to God' whose 'industry, skilfulness, piety and discretion hath herein bound the church to them in a debt of special remembrance and thankfulness'.[21]

But not everyone agreed. Fuller's contemporary John Selden commented both on the King James Bible's accuracy and on its unnatural prose:

> If I translate a French book into English, I translate it into English phrase and not French phrase: but the bible into English words rather than English phrase: the Hebraisms are kept: as for example, 'he uncovered her shame' which is well enough so long as scholars have to do with it, but when it comes among the common people, Lord, what great mockery do they make of it.[22]

The English language was changing during the later seventeenth century, evolving much closer to modern English, so many sophisticated readers were inclined to be rather sniffy about what

one of them called 'the bald and barbarous language of the old
vulgar version'. That movement would culminate in 1769, when
an Oxford don, Benjamin Blayney, would be commissioned by
Oxford University Press to modernize the spelling and punctuation
and very occasionally the vocabulary of the King James version:
it is Blayney's tidied-up and polished version of the King James
Bible that people buy in a bookshop even today. It wasn't till almost
exactly a hundred years after the appearance of the King James Bible
that anyone said in so many words that it is a great classic of English
prose, and the first to say so was the Irishman Jonathan Swift. In a
pamphlet on the improvement of the language published in 1712
Swift claimed that the books of the Bible 'being perpetually read
in the churches have proved a kind of standard for the language,
especially to the common people'. The King James translators, he
thought, 'were masters of an English style much fitter for that work
than any we see in our present writings, which I take to be owing
to the simplicity that runs through the whole'.[23]

Swift's view of the beauty and influence of the King James Bible
was to become general: increasingly it was seen alongside the plays
of Shakespeare as one of the cornerstones of English literature and
English language, 'the first English classic'. Every educated man and
woman was immersed in the Bible, and even people with no time
for Christianity felt its power: the great scientific agnostic Professor
Thomas Henry Huxley, 'Darwin's bulldog' as he was nicknamed, a
Victorian Richard Dawkins, expressed the general view:

> For three centuries this book has been woven into all that is best
> and noblest in English history [...] it has become the national
> epic of Britain, and is as familiar to noble and simple, from John
> o Groats house to Land's End [...] it is written in the noblest and
> purest English, and abounds in exquisite beauties of mere literary
> form [...] By the study of what other book could children be so
> much humanised?[24]

But even as Huxley wrote the writing was on the wall for the
unchallenged dominance of the King James Bible that he

was describing. It was a masterpiece of translation, but it was sometimes obscure and often archaic. Above all, biblical scholarship had moved on since the sixteenth century: hundreds of newly discovered biblical manuscripts had made it obvious that the Hebrew and, especially, the Greek manuscripts from which the Jacobean translators had worked were very imperfect. Beauty alone was not enough for a book claiming to be the word of God. Truth mattered, so pressure grew for a fresh translation which would take these discoveries into account and so get closer to the Bible text as originally written down. The result was the Revised Version of the Bible published in 1881. That version never really caught on, but it was just the first of a wave of modern translations that in the twentieth century would replace the Authorized Version.

That shift in Protestant churches has been going on now for half a century, and it has produced many protests. By and large, those protests have emphasized the King James Bible as a national treasure, a great literary and cultural landmark without which future generations would be impoverished. But such protests have been more vociferous outside the churches than within: ten years ago I bought two identical King James Bibles in a second-hand bookshop in Cambridge, one of a batch of 20 or more with a memorial inscription inside that had been dumped by a local village church in favour of the Revised English Bible. And there have been some very surprising dissenting voices. One of them was that ardently conservative Anglican royalist the poet T. S. Eliot. Eliot loved the King James version, and he detested the New English Bible, which, he once said, 'astonishes in its combination of the vulgar, the trivial and the pedantic'. But he deeply distrusted praise of the King James Bible that tried to see it in isolation from its religious message as a cultural treasure:

Those who talk of the Bible as a 'monument of English prose' are merely admiring it as a monument over the grave of Christianity [...] the Bible has had a literary influence upon English literature not because it has been considered as literature, but because it has been considered as a report of the Word of God. And the fact that men of letters now discuss it as literature probably indicates the end of its literary influence.[25]

Eliot was arguing here against the attempt to turn the Authorized Version into a museum piece, but he also campaigned against attempts by clergy to displace the King James Bible from use in services, and his views were shared by his fellow poet and Anglican W. H. Auden. Like Eliot, Auden was revolted by the newer Bible versions, which he linked to clerical enthusiasm for fashionable new forms of worship. As he wrote to the pastor of St Mark's Church in New York,

> Our Church has had the singular good-fortune of having its Prayer-Book composed and its Bible translated at exactly the right time, i.e., late enough for the language to be intelligible to any English-speaking person in this century (any child of six can be told what 'the quick and the dead' means) and early enough, i.e., when people still had an instinctive feeling for the formal and the ceremonious which is essential in liturgical language.
>
> This feeling has been, alas, as we all know, almost totally lost. (To identify the ceremonious with 'the undemocratic' is sheer contemporary cant.) The poor Roman Catholics, obliged to start from scratch, have produced an English Mass which is a cacophonous monstrosity (the German version is quite good, but German has a certain natural sonority): But why should we imitate them?[26]

You might have expected that scourge of modern literary fashions and fads C. S. Lewis to share Eliot's and Auden's attachment to the King James Bible, but not a bit of it. For Lewis, the beauty and majesty that he recognized in the King James Bible were not necessarily an advantage. The New Testament in the original Greek, he argued, wasn't a work of literary art but was written in the Greek used by ordinary people, a utilitarian, commercial and administrative language. So:

> When we expect that the Gospel should have come before the World in all the beauty that we now feel in the Authorised Version we are as wide of the mark as the Jews were in expecting that the Messiah would come as a great earthly King. The real sanctity, the real beauty and sublimity of the New Testament (as of Christ's life) are of a different sort: miles deeper or further in.

In any case, Lewis thought,

> the Authorised Version has ceased to be a good (that is, a clear) translation. It is no longer modern English: the meanings of words have changed. The same antique glamour which has made it (in the superficial sense) so 'beautiful', so 'sacred', so 'comforting', and so 'inspiring', has also made it in many places unintelligible. The truth is that if we are to have translation at all we must have periodical re-translation. There is no such thing as translating a book into another language once for all, for a language is a changing thing. If your son is to have clothes it is no good buying him a suit once for all: he will grow out of it and have to be re-clothed.

And finally, though it may seem a sour paradox, we must sometimes get away from the Authorized Version, if for no other reason than simply because it is so beautiful and so solemn. Beauty exalts, but beauty also lulls. Early associations endear, but they also confuse. Through that beautiful solemnity the transporting or horrifying realities of which the book tells may come to us blunted and disarmed and we may only sigh with tranquil veneration when we ought to be burning with shame or struck dumb with terror. Does the word 'scourged' really come home to us like 'flogged'? Does 'mocked him' sting like 'jeered at him'? Lewis agreed with Eliot that the more people praised the King James Bible as a literary treasure, the less it would be read. It was, he argued,

> through and through, not merely a sacred book but a book so remorselessly and continuously sacred that it does not invite, it excludes or repels the merely aesthetic approach [...] It demands incessantly to be taken on its own terms: it will not continue to give literary delight very long except to those who go to it for something quite different. I predict that in future it will be read, as it has always been read, almost exclusively by Christians. For the Bible I foresee only two possibilities, either to return as a sacred book or to follow the classics, if not quite into oblivion yet into the ghost-life of the museum and the specialists' study.[27]

If Lewis was right, then the survival of the King James Bible is not in the hands of the chattering classes who may admire its prose but ignore its teaching. It is in the hands of the Protestant churches. And by and large, the Protestant churches have been abandoning it. They have done so for some good and some bad reasons. The good reasons are easily stated, and Lewis stated some of them in the extracts quoted above. The churches are anxious to communicate the message of Christianity, and in a culture where people are less and less familiar with the Bible in any version, and where the voices we hear on the media speak a demotic English with a restricted vocabulary, the archaic grandeur of the language of the King James Bible seems ever more exotic and more alien. In the age of the email, the text message and an eleven-minute programme attention span, our culture doesn't do profundity; people are less able and less willing to grapple with difficult or complicated speech. So clergy increasingly turn to new translations to make the Gospel message simpler and clearer.

The problem with that of course is that the message of the Bible, translated or not, is not always simple or clear. Some truth is deep and difficult, slow to unfold itself in our experience, so that to put it into words of one syllable may be to betray it. Language that has no obscurities has no depth, and the language of many modern Bible translations is often flat, uninspiring, two-dimensional. If we never encounter anything more demanding we become emotionally and morally impoverished. Above everything else, the King James Bible was born out of a determined attentiveness to language and all its nuances. Its translators were the contemporaries of Shakespeare; they spoke an English blossoming into its greatest age of creativity, and they brought to their work a devout attentiveness to every nuance of the original Hebrew and Greek, and of the words in which they sought to render that Hebrew and Greek. The King James Bible should be read in churches not because it is venerable, not because it is beautiful, not even because it is authorized, but because, despite its age, its difficulties, its reliance on bad manuscripts and outdated scholarship it is still, more often than not, the most accurate as well as the most eloquent English rendering of the word of God.

6

Richard Baxter, Reminiscent

The seventeenth century was the first great age of confessional literature, the century in which the spiritual diary, the intimate memoir and the gossipy reminiscence all achieved the status of art. So it's also the first century in which we get real insight into the inner lives of men and women who were both like and unlike ourselves. There had, of course, been autobiographical writing in English in earlier times, and in late sixteenth-century France one of the greatest of all autobiographers, Michel de Montaigne, perfected the art of the self-revealing utterance in the novel form of the essay.[1] But in England it's only really with the age of the Stuart monarchy, and under the influence of earnest Protestant religion, that autobiographical writing becomes widely practised.

Historians and literary critics use the blanket term 'life-writing' for all kinds of personal writing – diaries, memoirs, biographies and autobiographies, confessional letters or speeches – and everyone reading this is likely to have encountered well-known examples of seventeenth-century life-writing, such as the diaries of John Evelyn and especially of Samuel Pepys.[2] Pepys's diary, in particular, offers perhaps our most vivid and entertaining window into the everyday life of Stuart England – not least, of course, its sex life. And even the more formal historical works of the time, such as Thomas Fuller's *Worthies of England* or the Earl of Clarendon's *History of the Great Rebellion* or Isaac Walton's *Lives* have a continuing appeal because their authors relied on personal recollection as much as documentary sources in compiling them.[3] They have stayed vivid because their pages are filled with pen portraits of their authors' contemporaries but also, above all, because they reveal something of themselves.

In all this life-writing the specifically religious autobiography has an important but perhaps less popular place. John Bunyan's autobiography *Grace Abounding to the Chief of Sinners* and George Fox's *Journal* are just the two best-known examples of a kind of writing that was produced by the shelf-full in early modern England.[4]

But these religious autobiographies have a specialist appeal. For the texture and taste of ordinary life in seventeenth-century England we usually have to look to the secular diarists and reminiscencers, to all too fallible and sinful men such as Pepys or that equally genial recorder of his times, John Aubrey, whose *Brief Lives* is saturated with entertaining and often scurrilous personal recollections, almost as immediate and vivid as Pepys's *Diary*.[5]

In the galaxy of readable and racy Stuart biographers, autobiographers and reminiscencers Richard Baxter is liable to be overlooked.[6] Historians of religion, of course, rate him as a major figure who self-consciously set about providing for future historians detailed testimony of events in which he played a major role. But his posthumously published autobiography and historical memoir *Reliquiae Baxterianae* has never commanded the same kind of popular readership as Pepys, Evelyn or Aubrey.[7] It's a baggy monster, assembled five years after Baxter's death from the mountain of his personal papers and atrociously edited by his friend and disciple Matthew Sylvester. It's a betwixt-and-between book. The autobiographical core of the *Reliquiae* is perched uneasily somewhere between the out-and-out puritan conversion narrative and the secular autobiography. It has a good deal in common with Bunyan or George Fox, since it traces the progress of a devout soul towards religious assurance. Like them, Baxter wrote to 'own and honour' the hand of God in leading him to faith, and his book is, among other things, a record of God's dealing with his soul. But, unlike either Bunyan or Fox, Baxter describes no moment of personal conversion, and he deliberately distanced himself from the relation of 'soul-experiments' and what he considered the over-intimacy of much puritan confessional writing. As he declared:

> for any more particular account of heart-occurrences and God's operations on me, I think it somewhat unsavoury to recite them: seeing God's dealings are much the same with all his servants in the main, and the Points wherein he varieth are usually so small, that I think not such fit to be repeated.[8]

This was not the whole truth, though he repeatedly expressed similar reservations about the dangers of self-absorbed spiritual reminiscence in many of his works – not least in his astonishing and at times disturbingly credulous tract *The Certainty of the World of Spirits*, from beginning to end a horribly entertaining collection of pious gossip about ghosts, witches, answers to prayer and things that go bump in the night, much of it allegedly drawing directly on personal reminiscence.[9] But Baxter, in theory at least, held back from sustained confessional self-revelation precisely because he knew his own religious experience did *not* fit the standard puritan pattern: in fact, he doubted whether there was a single pattern that fitted every soul. As he says elsewhere in the *Reliquiae*, 'I understood at last that God breaketh not all men's hearts alike'.[10] He certainly disliked and distrusted religious fanaticism and resisted forcing his own gradual progression towards mature religious conviction into a ready-made puritan mould, or the expectation that every good Christian must experience a Damascene moment of conversion.

He was to versify this distrust of over emotional self-scrutiny in the autobiographical poetic fragments he published in 1681, after the death of his wife, Margaret.

> Long was I sadly questioning thy Grace,
> Because thy Spirits steps I could not trace.
> [...] I fear'd the change which rais'd my soul no higher
> Would not suffice to save me from Hell fire.

I wonder'd, things so great as Heav'n and Hell,
Did on my heart with no more feeling dwell!
That words which such amazing things import,
Did not sink deeper, and my soul transport!

[...] But as thy Wisdom gives in fittest measure;
Not all at once: It's meet we wait thy leisure.
I thought that things unseen should *pierce* and *melt*,
With as great Passion as things *seen* and *felt*.
But now I find it is their proper part,
To be *most valu'd*, to be *next the Heart;*
To be the *highest Interest* of the *soul;*
There to *command*, and all *things else controul.* [...]
[...]
New-lighted Candles, darkened by the snuff,
Are ready to go out with every puff:
[...] Thus GRACE like NATURE entereth in a *seed;*
Which with man's labour, heav'nly dews must feed:
Whose *Virtue* and *first Motions* no eye sees;
But after comes to ripeness by degrees.[11]

That was the wisdom of a man in his sixties: the young Baxter had, of course, longed for the sort of conversion experience that the classic textbooks on self-examination had led him to expect, and he feared that he lacked the holy spirit because he had grown gradually into his Christian convictions, without any dramatic conversion from sin and unbelief. By the time he compiled the autobiographical material that Sylvester gathered into the *Reliquiae*, however, he'd come to terms with the undramatic character of his own remarkable religious journey:

But I afterward perceived that *Education* is God's ordinary way for the Conveyance of his Grace, and ought no more to be set in opposition to the Spirit, than the preaching of the Word; and that it was the great Mercy of God to begin with me so soon, and to prevent such sins as else might have been my shame and sorrow while I lived; and that Repentance is good, but Prevention and Innocence is better.[12]

Nevertheless, Geoffrey Nuttall observed more than 60 years ago that, despite this self-conscious religious reticence, an unstoppable autobiographical urge pervades Baxter's writing. He

> could never write for long without inserting some autobiographical reminiscence, some reference to his own experiences. The argument of his most serious works is relieved by such an illustration as 'When I was young, I was wont to go up the Wrekin-Hill with great pleasure (being near my dwelling) and to look down on the country below me'; or 'I cannot forget that in my youth [...] sometimes the morrice-dancers would come into the church in all their linen and scarfs, and antic-dresses, with morrice-bells jingling at their legs'; or 'the case, as I remember, when I was a boy, our school was in, when we had barred out our master'; or 'the raining of that grain about ten years ago in England [...] I tasted it, and kept some of it long, which fell on the leads of the church, and of the minister's house in Bridgnorth'; or 'I never awaked since I had the use of memory, but I found myself coming out of a dream'.[13]

But Baxter's memoir was meant to be far more than a set of reminiscences or a spiritual autobiography. He had been involved in great events, as a chaplain in the Parliamentarian army in the 1640s, as a leader of the attempt to reconstruct a Protestant national Church along semi-voluntarist lines in the 1650s and as one of the chief negotiators in the attempt to find a religious settlement in the Restoration that could include both the triumphant episcopal party and the now defeated puritans.[14]

The *Reliquiae* was begun just as it became clear that Baxter's life's work was in ruins and the Church of England irreparably divided. So his huge, sprawling narrative was written as a monument to his part in trying to prevent all that, and it's a self-conscious history of his own times as well as a religious autobiography. Among other things, it was designed to justify Baxter against criticisms that his own cantankerous personality had helped ensure the defeat of the puritan cause in the negotiations at the Restoration and to place the blame for the shattering of England's religious unity firmly at the door of his Anglican opponents. He wanted to set the record straight, as he wrote, 'lest the fable pass for truth when I am dead'.[15]

The *Reliquiae* is not an elegant or even a very coherent work. Nearly two-thirds of its 800 folio pages are devoted to the catastrophic years 1660–62, and the narrative of Baxter's life and of the historical events in which he was caught up is clogged and at times buried under hundreds of pages of contemporary documentation and tangled argument. In the early eighteenth century much of the material on Baxter's nonconformist contemporaries and colleagues was edited into a separate work by Edmund Calamy as the *Nonconformists' Memorial*,[16] and in 1925 the more strictly autobiographical narrative, together with Baxter's coverage of some of the major events of the Civil War, Cromwellian period and Restoration was filleted out of the *Reliquiae* and published by the Revd J. Lloyd Thomas as *The Autobiography of Richard Baxter*.[17] Lloyd Thomas's selection made Baxter's fascinating portrait of his own life and times easily available to ordinary readers for the first time, but in the process of abbreviation some of the most vivid detail was lost. Sylvester's tome, for all its faults, remains indispensable, and it's good to know that Neil Keeble's and John Coffey's annotated five-volume Oxford edition of the *Reliquiae* is at last complete.

I've emphasized the differences between the *Reliquiae* and conventional puritan spiritual autobiography, and these spring partly from Baxter's cooler temperament and from his central involvement in the great events of the time, as a chaplain in the Cromwellian army, as the leader of the Association Movement in the 1650s and as chief puritan negotiator at the Savoy conference at the Restoration. Baxter began writing the *Reliquiae* in 1664, fresh from the failure of the puritan cause at the Savoy and while he himself was experiencing persecution and harassment under the draconian legislation against nonconformity enacted by the Cavalier Parliament. So he had far more in mind than describing his own spiritual journey. He wanted to explain the religious vision that underlay his kind of moderate puritanism, and he wanted to convince people of the progress towards religious reform and moral renewal that had been achieved in the 1650s, not least by giving a full picture of the success of his ministry in Kidderminster. In the fervid and paranoid royalism of the 1660s he needed to excuse himself from any compromising association with Cromwell, to explain that, though he was a puritan, he had always rejected the killing of Charles I. Hence his unrelentingly hostile portrayal of Oliver Cromwell, whom he presents as a hypocrite and a manipulative usurper. And, finally, he wanted to lay the blame for the ejection of almost 2,000 puritan clergy from the parochial ministry firmly at the door of the intolerant high-church clergy and their lay supporters who had triumphed with the return of Charles II.

So Baxter's book has major historical importance as an eyewitness source for the writing of history. But his narrative often also has the vividness of reportage whose imaginative appeal reaches far beyond the professional historian. His writing is full of surprising and memorable side-glances at the great and terrible events of his time. I'm thinking here of moments like his account of his preaching a sermon at Alcester on Sunday, 23 October 1642, when his voice was drowned and the congregation drawn outside by the noise of cannon fire from the Battle of Edgehill. The next morning he went to view the battlefield for himself, and, as he tells us, he

> found the Earl of *Essex* with the remaining part of his Army keeping the Ground, and the King's Army facing them upon the Hill a mile off; and about a Thousand dead Bodies in the Field between them [...] and neither of the Armies moving toward each other.[18]

That glimpse of the battlefield choked with corpses, and the silent armies facing each other across the carnage, has all the vivid immediacy of a war correspondent's photograph.

But of course Baxter rarely merely reports, rarely merely reminisces. He was, notoriously, an incorrigible polemicist, and personal memory was repeatedly pressed into service to add impetus to polemical brickbats. In his 1658 treatise *Confirmation and Restoration* Baxter buttressed an argument for the superiority of his proposals for fencing the communion table by ministerial scrutiny of every would-be communicant with a recollection of his own teenage experience of the scandalously slack discipline in what he called 'the Bishop's days':

When I was a Schoole boy, about 15 years of age, the Bishop coming into the Country, many went in to him to be Confirmed: we that were boies, runne out to see the Bishop among the rest, not knowing any thing of the meaning of the business: when we came thither, we met about thirty or fourty in all, of our own stature and temper, that had come for to be Bishopt, as then it was called: The Bishop examined us not at all in one Article of the Faith; but in a Church-yard, in haste, we were set in a rank, and he past hastily over us, laying his hands on our head, and saying a few words, which neither I nor any that I spoke with, understood; so hastily were they uttered, and a very short prayer recited, and there was an end. But whether we were Christians or Infidels, or knew so much as that there was a God, the Bishop little knew, nor enquired. And yet he was one of the best Bishops esteemed in *England*.[19]

Such barbed reminiscences abound in Baxter's polemics, but beyond controversy he was, above all, a moralizing preacher. For him history was a theatre in which was displayed the workings of providence, and the God of providence. Though he was suspicious of religious fanaticism and discouraged those who wanted to see the hand of God in every trivial happening, he believed history was driven by God's mercies and judgements, and the moral behind most of the stories he tells is never far to seek. That's true even when making the moral explicit might be considered treasonous, as in his account of the unexpected and ominous thunder on Charles II's coronation day:

> On *April* 23. was his Majesty's Coronation Day; the Day being very serene and fair, till suddenly in the Afternoon, as they were returning from *Westminster-hall,* there was very terrible Thunders, when none expected it. Which made me remember his Father's Coronation, on which, being a Boy at School, and having leave to play for the Solemnity, an Earthquake (about two a Clock in the Afternoon) did affright the Boys, and all the Neighbourhood. I intend no Commentary on these, but only to relate the Matter of Fact.[20]

He is not always so restrained: his book is full of reports of providential events with an unmissable moral, such as the story of the orphaned baby after the Civil War massacre at Bolton

> found lying by her Father and Mother, who were slain in the Streets: an Old Woman took up the Child, and carried it home, and put it to her Breast for warmth, (having not had a Child her self of about 30 Years) the Child drew Milk, and so much, that the Woman nursed it up with her Breast Milk a good while: The Committee desired some Women to try her, and they found it true, and that she had a considerable proportion of Milk for the Child: If any one doubt of this, they may yet be resolved by Mrs. *Hunt,* Wife to Mr. *Rowland Hunt of Harrow on the Hill,* who living then in *Manchester,* was one of them that by the Committee was desired to trie the Woman, and who hath oft told it me, and is a credible, godly, discreet Gentlewoman, and Wife to a Man of most exemplary Holiness, and of the primitive Sincerity without Self-seeking, Hypocrisie and Guile.[21]

Amusingly, having told that story and named the witnesses (should anyone doubt it), Baxter was immediately reminded of a similar incident, this one set in Ireland in 1641; and as a good reminiscencer he felt obliged to tell us that as well. The delight for a modern reader in this second story, which is also about a baby in desperate need of milk, comes from the name of the main protagonist of the tale, who is wonderfully appropriately called Mrs Teat.

> This putteth me in mind of that worthy Servant of Christ, Dr. *Teat,* who being put to fly suddenly with his Wife and Children from the Fury of the *Irish* Rebels, in the Night without Provision; wandred in the Snow out of all ways upon the Mountains till Mrs. *Teat,* having no suck for the Child in her Arms, and he being ready to die with Hunger, she went to the Brow of a Rock to lay him down, and leave him that she might not see him die, and there in the Snow out of all ways where no Footsteps appeared, she found a Suck-bottle full of new, sweet Milk, which preserved the Child's Life.[22]

That story and its stream-of-consciousness link – 'this putteth me in mind' – to the account of the old woman whose breasts yielded miraculous milk, is worthy of John Aubrey, the most magpie-minded of seventeenth-century gossips. But the resemblance goes only so far. Baxter can gossip, but the gossip almost always has a point to it, which is never far below the surface. We can get a sense of the distance between Baxter and his merely secular contemporaries by looking at two rather similar reminiscences, both concerned with the transience of earthly memory: one from Aubrey and one from Baxter.

The story from Aubrey is one of his most famous. It occurs in his pen portrait of Lady Venetia Stanley, the celebrated early Stuart beauty who had married Sir Kenelm Digby and who died young in mysterious circumstances. Having played up Dame Venetia's beauty and her youthful reputation for risqué sexual adventure, Aubrey adds:

> About 1676 or 5, as I was walking through Newgate Street, I saw Dame Venetia's Bust from off her tombe standing at a stall at the Golden Crosse, a Brasier's shop. I perfectly remembered it, but the fire had gott off the Guilding: but taking notice of it to one that was with me, I could never see it afterwards exposed on the street: they melted it down. How these curiousities would be quite forgot, did not such idle fellowes as I am put them downe.[23]

That's a wonderful vignette: in a few apparently throwaway lines Aubrey vividly conjures up for us the continuing legacy of the great fire of London, an unforgettable glimpse, ten years on from the disaster, of a fire-damaged monument from the burned-out church, waiting to be melted down for scrap on a barrow in the street. The vignette poignantly catches a favourite theme in the art of the time: the fleeting nature of earthly fame, the fragility of beauty, the inexorability of time. And in a final throwaway sentence Aubrey explains and justifies his own literary dilettantism, his obsessive collection of useless information: the preservation of these curiosities justifies the activities of 'idle fellows like himself'.

No one could ever have described Baxter as an idle fellow, and when *he* recounts stories of this kind it is almost always to score a point, or to drive home a moral. As it happens, he does have a reminiscence very like Aubrey's, though it comes not from the *Reliquiae* but at the end of his moving tribute to his dead wife, *A Breviate of the Life of Mrs Margaret Baxter*. Like Aubrey's story, Baxter's centres on the memory of a much-loved woman, and, by a remarkable coincidence, this story too features another funeral monument in Newgate Street, this one in Christchurch there, one of the many churches destroyed by the Great Fire of London. His wife, Margaret, Baxter tells us,

> was buried on June 17 1681 in Christ Church, Newgate, in the ruines in her own mother's grave. The grave was the highest, near the old altar or Table in the chancel, on which this her daughter had caused a very fair, large Marble stone to be laid, anno 1661, about 20 years ago, on which I caused to be written her titles, some Latin verses, and these English ones:
>
> > Thus must thy flesh to silent dust descend
> > Thy mirth and worldly pleasures thus will end:
> > Then happy holy souls, but wo to those
> > Who Heaven forgot, and earthly pleasures chose:
> > Here now this preaching grave without delay
> > Believe, repent, and work while it is day.

And then Baxter adds:

> But Christ's-Church on earth is liable to those changes of which
> the Jerusalem above is in no danger. In the doleful flames of
> London 1666, the fall of the Church broke this great Marble all to
> pieces, and it proved no lasting monument. And I hope this Paper
> Monument, erected by one that is following, even at the door, in
> some passion indeed of grief, but in sincerity of truth, will be more
> publicly useful and durable than that Marble-stone was.[24]

The memoir of Margaret Baxter belonged to a particular kind of
edifying memorial literature, and Baxter's somewhat heavy-handed
moralizing over his wife's and mother-in-law's graves was intended
to inspire an appropriate mood of piety. Even the gravestone in the
story is called a preacher. Both stories are touching, but most of us
would prefer Aubrey's, as gentler and subtler in its method and lack
of didacticism.

But the *Reliquiae* has its own artistry, and in the best and most
personal parts of it Baxter's method is usually both subtler and
more oblique than in that story from the *Breviate*. He is capable
of a consummate skill in mobilizing his memories. The stories he
chooses to tell are, of course, designed to contribute to the critique of
episcopal Anglicanism and to justify his life of nonconformity, which
together are the main objectives of his book: neither the apologist nor
the preacher is ever quite off duty. But time and again the underlying
objectives of justification and of edification are established with a
literary instinct that outshines anything in Aubrey.

Take, for example, the very well-known account of the hostility
of the 'Vulgar Rabble' to the Baxter family in his home village of
Eaton Constantine, a hostility aroused by his father's moderate
puritanism. To gauge the brilliance of the passage it needs to be
considered more or less unabridged. Baxter is here recalling the
Sunday afternoons of his teenage years:

> In the Village where I lived the Reader read the Common-Prayer
> briefly, and the rest of the Day even till dark Night almost,

except Eating time, was spent in Dancing under a May-Pole and a great Tree, not far from my Father's Door; where all the Town did meet together: And though one of my Father's own Tenants was the Piper, he could not restrain him, not break the Sport: So that we could not read the Scripture in our Family without the great disturbance of the Taber and Pipe and Noise in the Street! Many times my Mind was inclined to be among them, and sometimes I broke loose from Conscience, and joyned with them; and the more I did it the more I was enclined to it. But when I heard them call my Father *Puritan,* it did much to cure me and alienate me from them: for I consider'd that my Father's Exercise of Reading the Scripture, was better than theirs, and would surely be better thought on by all men at the last; and I considered what it was for that he and others were thus derided. When I heard them speak scornfully of *others* as Puritans whom I never knew, I was at first apt to believe all the Lies and Slanders wherewith they loaded them: But when I heard my own Father so reproached, and perceived the Drunkards were the forwardest in the reproach, I perceived that it was mere Malice: For my Father never scrupled Common-Prayer or Ceremonies, nor spake against Bishops [...] But only for reading Scripture when the rest were Dancing on the Lord's Day, and for praying [...] in his House, and for reproving Drunkards and Swearers, and for talking sometimes a few words of Scripture and the Life to come, he was reviled commonly by the Name of *Puritan, Precisian* and *Hypocrite:* and so were the Godly Conformable Ministers that lived any where in the Country near us, not only by our Neighbours, but by the common talk of the Vulgar Rabble of all about us. By this Experience I was fully convinc'd that Godly People were the best, and those that despised them and lived in Sin and Pleasure, were a malignant unhappy sort of People: and this kept me out of their Company, except now and then when the Love of Sports and Play enticed me.[25]

This is an artful piece of writing, which delivers a subtle social narrative under the guise of a piece of picture-painting. It's a study in light and shade, in which inner light and darkness reverse the physical light and darkness in the story. The careless villagers, dancing round the maypole on the village green 'where all the town did meet together', are in the summer sunshine. By contrast, separated from 'all the town' is the isolated puritan family, who gather round the Bible in the shadowy indoors on those golden sunny Sunday afternoons. The portrait of Baxter's father is a little study in frustrated earnestness, trying and failing to silence the sport, even though he is the pipe-and-tabor man's landlord. Baxter himself, a wistful uncertain teenager, is conflicted, clearly embarrassed and worried by his father's unpopularity, longing to be outside dancing himself. Yet in the course of the narrative he comes to see that his father, portrayed here as earnestly ineffective, is nevertheless a better man than the drunks who mock him. The picture is a classic puritan separation of the world into sheep and goats: the little godly remnant indoors reading the Bible, the profane ungodly mob outside, dancing themselves to hell in sin and pleasure. Baxter's language underlines this polarity. When he calls the mockers 'a malignant unhappy people', he's not just being rude. 'Malignant' and 'unhappy' were technical theological terms for the reprobate, those predestined to be damned. But the stark separation of the good and the bad, which might have made the passage sound merely priggish, is softened and subverted by the disarming honesty of Baxter's confession of his own rather wobbly religious convictions. The passage enacts both Baxter's growing awareness of the opposition between the ungodly and the godly and his half-reluctant identification with his father. But it simultaneously enacts his boyish back-sliding, the betwixt-and-between state of a teenager with conflicted loyalties, not yet sure of who he is. So although he shuns the ungodly, he does so 'except now and then, when the love of sports and play enticed me'.

There is something of the skill of the novelist in Baxter's teasing out of his own conflicted psychology here, though the novel as a form had hardly been invented. And, of course, the anecdote also demonstrates the truth of his central religious conviction, that one grows into godliness not by a blinding flash of conviction, a Damascus road conversion, but by a painful, slow process of education and maturing.

He can be equally deft in his handling of more intimate themes of human relationships such as marriage or friendship. This is perhaps an unexpected side of Baxter, whose notoriously abrasiveness tetchiness might make him seem an unlikely celebrant of intimate friendship: indeed, in the chapter on friendship and sociability in his study of seventeenth-century attitudes *The Ends of Life*, Keith Thomas presents Baxter as a hostile critic of close, exclusive male friendship. Thomas quarries Baxter's *Christian Directory* (1673) for warnings against the dangers of 'intimate special friendship', and denunciation of the excessive love of another human being as 'a sin of deeper malignity than is commonly observed'. But the *Christian Directory* belongs to a specific kind of proscriptive genre, in which almost by definition the moral bar is set too high. A very different and more humane picture emerges if we set all that alongside Baxter's far more sympathetic life-writing.

One of the most moving passages in the *Reliquiae* is the account he gives of the part played in his own religious development by the anonymous friend who was his closest companion while they were both being tutored in the house of the Revd Richard Wickstead in Ludlow. This adolescent friendship was Baxter's first close encounter with ardent puritanism outside the closed circle of his own immediate family, and it left a deep impression on him. But the friend who was instrumental in consolidating Baxter's puritanism was himself to fall away from godliness, and Baxter's account of that fall is a brilliant study of tragedy in miniature. Once again, to grasp the quality of Baxter's artistry, we need the whole story. Here he is describing his two years in Ludlow:

> though the Town was full of Temptations [...] it pleased God not only to keep me from them, but also to give me one intimate Companion, who was the greatest help to my Seriousness in Religion, that ever I had before, and was a daily Watchman over my Soul! We walk'd together, we read together, we prayed together, and when we could we lay together: And having been

brought out of great Distress to Prosperity, and his Affections being fervent, though his Knowledge not great, he would be always stirring me up to Zeal and Diligence, and even in the Night would rise up to Prayer and Thanksgiving to God, and wonder that I could sleep so, that the thoughts of God's Mercy did not make me also to do as he did! He was unwearied in reading all serious Practical Books of Divinity; especially *Perkins, Bolton,* Dr. *Preston, Elton,* Dr. *Taylor, Whately, Harris,* &c. He was the first that ever I heard pray *Ex tempore* (out of the Pulpit) and that taught me so to pray: And his Charity and Liberality was equal to his Zeal; so that God made him a great means of my good, who had more knowledge than he, but a colder heart.

Yet before we had been Two years acquainted, he fell once and a second time by the power of Temptation into a degree of Drunkenness, which so terrified him upon the review (especially after the second time) that he was near to Despair; and went to good Ministers with sad Confessions: And when I had left the House and his Company, he fell into it again and again so oft, that at last his Conscience could have no Relief or Ease but in changing his Judgment, and disowning the Teachers and Doctrines which had restrained him. And he did it on this manner: One of his Superiours, on whom he had dependance, was a man of great Sobriety and Temperance, and of much Devotion in his way; but very zealous against the Nonconformists, ordinarily talking most bitterly against them, and reading almost only such Books as encouraged him in this way: By converse with this Man, my Friend was first drawn to abate his Charity to Nonconformists; and then to think and speak reproachfully of them; and next that to dislike all those that came near them [...] And the last I heard of him was, that he was grown a Fudler, and Railer at strict men. But whether God recovered him, or what became of him I cannot tell.[26]

Once again, in this passage we are in the hands of a master storyteller, who gets his effects from a carefully worked out set of contrasts. Baxter, as yet cold-hearted and cerebral, falls under the spell of his more spiritually adventurous friend, and is stirred or perhaps shamed into greater ardour by his impetuous zeal. Yet the portrait of that friend has just a hint of fanaticism about it, in the midnight prayer sessions and the reproaches to Baxter for his lack of fervour. The intensity of their boyish friendship is captured with a wonderful economy of words – 'We walk'd together, we read together, we prayed together, and when we could we lay together' – and the picture of its fading and the parting of the ways is a masterly novella in brief. His friend's ardour is revealed as part of an unstable and addictive personality, as he succumbs to drunkenness: he gradually retreats into rationalizing his fall from virtue as the abandonment of an unreasonably over-strict Puritanism, till he becomes a pathetic figure, 'a fudler and railer at strict men'. But in a master-stroke, Baxter refuses to prejudge the end of the story: this little drama of the death of a friendship that once meant everything to the two involved is left open-ended, though we fear the worst, and although the sentence drives home the pathos of lost affections: 'But whether God recovered him, or what became of him I cannot tell.' And, of course, it's part of the artistry of the story that the incident consolidates Baxter's overarching spiritual argument in the *Reliquiae*, that slow and gradual is best. Once again we see Baxter's own unspectacular journey towards godliness, his education into puritanism, proving to have more staying power than the spiritual fireworks of more radical puritans.

I hope I have done enough to demonstrate the power and artistry of Baxter's autobiographical writing, the skill with which he deploys carefully crafted incidents in a larger argument about the nature of puritanism, the subtlety with which he depicts and justifies his own slow and undemonstrative religious evolution. I want to end now with an example of Baxter simply as chronicler of his times. We think of him, I suppose, mainly as he was in Kidderminster in the 1650s, at the height of his success as a religious leader, in a pioneering ministry that became the trigger and the model for similar religious experiments all over Cromwellian England. But for the second half of his long life he was a Londoner, like Pepys and Evelyn, and like them he witnessed the two great calamities

Pilgrims draw holy oil from taps built into the shrine of St William of York, one of 95 scenes illustrating the holy bishop's life, miracles and *cultus* in the early fifteenth-century window of the north choir aisle of York Minster. The miraculous oil began to flow three years after the much-publicized translation of Becket's relics to a new shrine in 1220, perhaps an example of market rivalry.

Lepers at the shrine of St William, a reminder that many pilgrims came in hope or desperation, seeking cures for diseases medieval medicine could not help.

Scenes from the life of St Etheldreda: part of a sequence illustrating the saint's life and miracles stripped from her shrine during the Reformation, the panel is attributed to Robert Pygott, who created a new shrine canopy for Ely Cathedral in 1455. The panel was discovered serving as a cupboard door in a house in Ely in the eighteenth century.

The fourteenth century Lady Chapel at Ely was once decorated with a cycle of 93 carved and painted scenes from the life and miracles of the Virgin Mary, the most complete sculptural cycle of its kind. Mary's cult was a particular target of the protestant reformers, and Bishop Thomas Goodrich had the heads of every one of the carved figures pulverized.

The grave slab of John Brimley, choirmaster at Durham Cathedral from 1535 until his death in 1576. During the Northern Rebellion, he trained the boys to sing for the restored Catholic liturgy, but retained his post after the suppression of the uprising.

THE
NEVV TESTAMENT
OF IESVS CHRIST, TRANS-
LATED FAITHFVLLY INTO ENGLISH,

out of the authentical Latin, according to the beſt corrected copies of the ſame, diligently conferred vvith
the Greeke and other editions in diuers languages: Vvith
ARGVMENTS of bookes and chapters, ANNOTA-
TIONS, and other neceſſarie helpes, for the better vnderſtanding of the text, and ſpecially for the diſcouerie of the
CORRVPTIONS of diuers late tranſlations, and for
cleering the CONTROVERSIES in religion, of theſe daies:

IN THE ENGLISH COLLEGE OF RHEMES.

Pſal. 118.

*Da mihi intellectum, & ſcrutabor legem tuam, & cuſtodiam
illam in toto corde meo.*

That is,

Giue me vnderſtanding, and I vvil ſearche thy lavv, and
vvil keepe it vvith my vvhole hart.

S. Aug. tract. 2. in Epiſt. Ioan.

*Omnia quæ leguntur in Scripturis ſanctis, ad inſtructionem & ſalutem noſtram intentè oportet
audire: maximè tamen memoriæ commendanda ſunt, quæ aduerſus Hæreticos valent plu-
rimùm: quorum inſidiæ, infirmiores quoſque & negligentiores circumuenire non ceſſant.*

That is,

Al things that are readde in holy Scriptures, vve muſt heare vvith great attention, to our
inſtruction and ſaluation: but thoſe things ſpecially muſt be commended to me-
morie, vvhich make moſt againſt Heretikes: vvhoſe deceites ceaſe not to cir-
cumuent and beguile al the vveaker ſort and the more negligent perſons.

• PRINTED AT RHEMES
by Iohn Fogny.

1582.

CVM PRIVILEGIO.

Title page of the Rheims/Douai New Testament, Gregory Martin's Catholic translation of
1582, whose fiercely polemical marginal notes drew on the lecture notes and commentaries
of Dr Thomas Stapleton.

Sieben Köpffe Martini Luthers
Vom Hochwirdigen Sacrament des Altars / Durch
Doctor Jo. Cocleus.

Doctor
Martinus
Luther
Ecclesiast
Schwirmer
Visitirer
Barrabas

Martinus Luther
Siebenkopff.

Dr Thomas Stapleton (1535–1598), the English Catholic theologian and controversialist, whose biblical commentaries became a staple reference work of the European Counter-Reformation.

'Seven-Headed Luther', the frontispiece to a 1529 pamphlet attacking Luther by Dr Johann Cochlaeus: the heads, from left to right, identify the reformer as heretical 'doctor' (theologian), apostate monk, turbaned ally of Christendom's Turkish enemies, false preacher pandering to the mob, crazed fanatic, schismatical founder of breakaway churches, and the club-carrying brigand Barabbas, released when Christ was crucified. The seven heads identify Luther as the seven-headed dragon in the Book of Revelation.

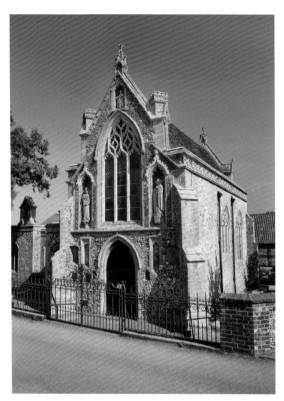

The medieval 'Slipper Chapel' in the hamlet of Houghton St Giles, acquired by philanthropist Charlotte Boyd before her conversion to Catholicism, replaced a Victorian chapel in King's Lynn as the official Roman Catholic shrine of Our Lady of Walsingham in 1934.

The exotic Anglican 'Holy House' at Walsingham was built on the outskirts of the village in 1931 by the Anglo-Papalist Vicar of Walsingham, Alfred Hope Patten, on land he mistakenly believed to be the site of the medieval shrine.

The annual summer procession with the image from the Anglican shrine, targeted here by banner-waving protestant protesters, who view the processions and shrine as idolatrous betrayals of the Reformation.

The changing demographic of Roman Catholicism in England has made Walsingham a favoured pilgrimage venue for thousands of Syro-Malabar Catholics originating from Kerala, Southern India.

Holbein's Frick Collection portrait of Thomas More, 'one of the most noble presences in the whole of British portraiture'.

Holbein's bleak Frick Collection portrait of Thomas Cromwell helped shape the traditional view of its sitter as a ruthless bureaucrat.

Mark Rylance's physical appearance as Cromwell in the TV adaptation of *Wolf Hall* seems closer to Holbein's More than to his Cromwell.

The casting of Leo McKern as the thuggish Cromwell in the film version of *A Man For All Seasons* was clearly indebted to the Holbein portrait.

that befell restoration London in the mid-1660s, the plague and the fire. Baxter has a great deal to say about both, famously evoking the heroism and fidelity of the nonconformist clergy who ministered to the sick and dying while the clergy of the established Church fled to safety during the plague. He gives us an unforgettable glimpse of the graveyard at Acton, where he was living during the plague, the ground there ploughed up like farmland from the hasty burial of the dead. But it's with his extended description of the Fire of London that I want to end. In its power and vividness it rivals the more famous and extended account in Pepys's diary. And who but Baxter could have brought home to us the terror and tragedy of the fire by dwelling on the catastrophic loss of books and papers that holocaust involved? His description of the burned pages, found drifting from the skies further and further from the fire, is a wonderful imaginative stroke. So I give the last word to Richard Baxter, reminiscent.

On *Septemb.* 2. after midnight, *London* was set on fire; and on *Sept.* 3. the *Exchange* was burnt; and in Three Days almost all the City within the Walls, and much without them. The season had been exceeding dry before, and the Wind in the *East,* where the Fire began. The people having none to conduct them aright, could do nothing to resist it, but stand and see their House burn without Remedy; the Engines being presently out of Order, and useless. The streets were crowded with People and Carts, to carry away what Goods they could get out: And they that were most active, and befriended (by their Wealth) got Carts, and saved much; and the rest lost almost all. The Loss in Houses and Goods is scarcely to be valued: And among the rest, the Loss of Books was an exceeding great Detriment to the Interest of Piety and Learning: Almost all the Booksellers in St. *Paul's* Church-Yard brought their Books into Vaults under St. *Paul's* Church, where it was thought almost impossible that Fire should come. But the Church it self being on fire, the exceeding weight of the Stones falling down, did break into the Vault, and let in the Fire, and they could not come near to save the books. The Library also of *Sion-Colledge* was burnt, and most of the Libraries of Ministers, Conformable and Nonconformable, in the City; with the Libraries of many Nonconformists of the Countrey, which had been lately brought up to the City. I saw the half burnt Leaves of Books near my Dwelling at *Acton* six miles from *London;* but others found them near *Windsor,* almost twenty miles distant. [...] Thus was the best, and one of the fairest Cities in the world turn'd into Ashes and Ruines in Three Days space, with many score Churches, and the Wealth and Necessaries of the Inhabitants.

It was a sight that might have given any Man a lively sense of the Vanity of this World, and all the Wealth and Glory of it, and of the future conflagration of all the World. To see the Flames mount up towards Heaven, and proceed so furiously without restraint: To see the streets filled with people astonished, that had scarce sense left them to lament their own calamity. To see the fields filled with heaps of Goods, and sumptuous Buildings, curious Rooms, costly Furniture and Houshold-Stuff: Yea, Warehouses and furnished Shops and Libraries, *&c.* all on a flame, and none durst come near to receive any thing. To see the King and Nobles ride about the streets, beholding all these Desolations, and none could afford the least Relief. To see the Air, as far as could be beheld, so filled with the smoak, that the Sun shined through it, with a colour like Blood; yea even when it was setting in the *West,* it so appeared to them that dwelt on the *West* side of the City. But the dolefullest sight of all was afterwards, to see what a ruinous confused place the City was, by Chimneys and Steeples only standing in the midst of Cellars and heaps of Rubbish; so that it was hard to know where the streets had been, and dangerous, of a long time to pass through the Ruines, because of Vaults, and fire in them. No man that seeth not such a thing, can have a right apprehension of the dreadfulness of it.[27]

PART TWO

Writing the Reformation

7

Luther through Catholic Eyes

For half a millennium the posting of Luther's 95 Theses on the door of the castle church in Wittenberg on Halloween 1517 has been seen as one of the few precisely datable turning points in world history. Luther was the catalyst for the ideological explosion that shattered Western Christendom. Without him there would have been no Reformation, so to discuss the theme of Reformation involves discussing him.

And Roman Catholics shared the celebrations of the Reformation quincentenary in ways that would have been unimaginable even 30 years earlier. Luther detested the papacy: 'I believe the pope is the masked and incarnate devil', he declared, 'because he is the Antichrist. As Christ is God incarnate, so the Antichrist is the devil incarnate. [...] The kingdom of the pope really signifies the terrible wrath of God, namely, the abomination of desolation standing in the holy place.'[1] But in October 2016 Pope Francis travelled to Lund in Sweden to join in the Lutheran celebrations of Reformation Day. During his visit he and the president of the Lutheran World Federation signed a joint declaration, expressing gratitude both for 'the spiritual and theological gifts received through the Reformation' and for 50 years of fruitful ecumenical engagement. The document acknowledged the wounds inflicted on the unity of the church by both traditions, and committed both sides to renewed striving towards full communion.[2] In the same year the Evangelical Lutheran

Church of America (ELCA) endorsed the *Declaration on the Way*, a document listing a series of 32 consensus statements between Catholics and Lutherans, including the most important of these, the Joint Declaration on Justification, of 1999. The *Declaration* identified key doctrinal issues, including justification by faith, the priesthood of all believers and the presence of Christ in the Eucharist, which the ELCA considered to be no longer 'church-dividing'.³ And all of this had been preceded back in 2013 by the jointly agreed guidelines for a common celebration of the Luther quincentenary, 'From Conflict to Communion', sponsored by the Pontifical Council for Promoting Christian Unity, which offered an agreed outline of Reformation history, listed the milestones and significant documents in Lutheran Catholic dialogue and laid down guidelines for future engagement.⁴

This edifying unanimity of Catholic and Lutheran ecumenists was satirized early in 2017 on an Australian Anglican website, which published what purported to be a leak by a disgruntled Curial insider, horrified that Pope Francis was planning to mark Reformation Day 2017 by canonizing Martin Luther. Last-minute details were still being finalized, according to the report, but there was to be a Vatican City stamp with Luther's portrait, a sure sign of sanctity, and the various recent doctrinal agreements between Roman Catholics and Lutherans were being drawn on to clarify exactly how the intercession of St Martin would be called upon, for example, 'to aid the suffering souls in Purgatory'. The report elicited a great deal of indignant spluttering from outraged conservatives in both camps, but the game was given away by the date of the alleged leak, and the Latin title of the proposed *motu proprio* embodying all this, whose opening words were to be '*Stultus Aprilis*'.⁵

Whether bogus or authentic, all these symbolic gestures were key to the Halloween anniversary of the posting of the 95 Theses. So it's ironic that the story of Luther nailing the theses to the castle church door is almost certainly a myth: to quote the title of a famous and still controversial Catholic book, 'the theses were not posted'. So this momentous anniversary commemorated a non-event: I'll have more to say about the careful historical deconstruction of that myth by

Fr Erwin Iserloh in 1966, and its religious significance, later in this essay, whose theme is not Luther himself but what Catholics over the last century or so have come to think about him. For it is really only over the last 100 years that Catholics have attended to the father of the Reformation with anything approaching open-mindedness.

The tone of the Catholic default mode of rabid denunciation of Luther was set by Leo X in the Bull of Excommunication, *Exsurge Domine*, of 1520: in that document Luther features as a ravening and destructive beast – *exterminate nititur [Ecclesiam] aper de silva, et singularis ferus depasci eam* ('The wild boar from the forest seeks to destroy [the Church] and every wild beast feeds upon it').[6] As late as the mid-1870s Gerard Manley Hopkins could paraphrase the rhetoric of *Exsurge Domine* by alluding to Luther in *The Wreck of the Deutschland* as the 'beast of the waste wood'.

Violent abuse was the staple of Catholic language about Luther for centuries, and the decisive figure in the shaping of sixteenth-century Catholic polemic against Luther was Johann Cochlaeus, himself one of Luther's earliest theological opponents, whose 1529 tract 'Seven-Headed Luther', with its brilliantly effective frontispiece portraying Luther as the dragon of Revelation, traced the reformer's degeneration from monk to crazy visionary to murdering robber Barabbas. In 1549 Cochlaeus published a major biographical study of Luther which raked together everything bad that could be said about him, a well of falsehood and misunderstanding into which most subsequent Catholic polemicists would dip their buckets, in quest of mud to sling.[7]

Serious Catholic study of Luther's life and writings was a late Victorian and Edwardian phenomenon, but in its early stages it too was a product of this rancid polemical tradition. Catholic Luther scholarship got off the ground in 1904 with the publication of the first volume of Heinrich Denifle's pioneering *Luther and Lutherdom from Original Sources*.[8]

Denifle, a Dominican who became sub-prefect of the Vatican Library, was a world authority on medieval scholasticism. The abiding value of his multi-volume and ultimately unfinished book on Luther, in reality a collection of essays on various aspects of

Luther's life and works, was its massively learned contextualization of Luther's early thought against the late medieval theological background. Denifle was a meticulous scholar, but he was also a gladiator for ultramontane Catholicism, unrelentingly hostile to Luther, whose decline from a talented and conservative reformer into a heretical moral pervert he attributed to egotism, drunkenness and undisciplined sensuality.

Denifle searched the reformer's published and unpublished works for evidence of heresy, ignorance and moral turpitude: as the American Luther scholar Preserved Smith remarked, Denifle's great work was 'a day of judgment in which Luther is called to account for every idle word, and he said many'. Denifle even drew on Victorian criminological theories to suggest that the reformer's face was of the 'criminal type'.[9] In Gordon Rupp's words,

> the climax of the work is the cry 'Luther, there is nothing of God in you!' The trouble is that, by the time Denifle has done with him, there is nothing of man in Luther either. His caricature, liar, blackguard, clown, sot, lecher, knave is a monster fit only for the records of criminal pathology.[10]

The massive if malign scholarship of Denifle's work would force Protestant defenders of Luther to raise their game and strive for new levels of accuracy and realism: even hostile Protestant reviewers recognized that Denifle's book marked a milestone in Luther scholarship, which had given the *coup de grâce* to a long tradition of Protestant hagiography.

And hard on Denifle's work, another Catholic scholar-priest brought outstanding scholarship to bear on Luther's failings. In 1911 Hartmann Grisar, a German Jesuit papal historian based in Rome, published the first part of a multi-volume psychological biography of Luther. Grisar was both formidably learned and formidably honest: when his unflinching 'warts and all' history of Rome and the papacy in the Middle Ages was published, it was said that novenas were offered all over Rome for Fr Grisar's conversion to Catholicism. If Grisar was harsh on the medieval

LUTHER THROUGH CATHOLIC EYES

popes, he was a good deal kinder to Dr Luther than Denifle. Grisar devoted chapters to disproving ancient Catholic calumnies about the reformer, and he rejected Denifle's allegations of Luther's sexual turpitude. Instead, Grisar substituted a picture of a troubled neurotic, morbidly pessimistic about human nature in general and his own sinfulness in particular. Grisar's Luther is coarse, quarrelsome, obstinate, dogmatic, lacking in humility – failings that help explain his ultimate apostasy – and Grisar deployed a good deal of psychological analysis to proving that the reformer's theology had its origins in a pathologically disordered personality. Grisar did include a long chapter on what he called 'Luther's better features', which paid tribute to the reformer's intellectual abilities, his kindness to friends and pupils, his courage, his love of simplicity. But it was immediately followed by an even longer chapter headed 'Luther's mode of controversy a counterpart of his soul', exploring Luther's anger, his rabid hostility to the Jews, the psychopathology of his abusive language and his conviction of his own greatness and superiority to criticism.[11]

Both Denifle and Grisar were men of the nineteenth century, products of the church of Pius IX for whom Protestantism was simply a great apostasy and Luther a guilty heresiarch. But in the aftermath of the Modernist crisis in the years before the Second World War a profound shift took place in German Catholic theology, as theologians sought to escape the rigidities of ultramontane ecclesiology and explored the patristic and early medieval periods as resources for a renewed Catholicism. This shift, represented in theology by figures like Romano Guardini and Erich Przywara, had momentous consequences for Catholic attitudes to the Reformation and the major reformers – Luther, of course, among them. The key historians in this shift were Hubert Jedin, biographer of Cardinal Seripando and historian of the Council of Trent, and Joseph Lortz, the first volume of whose *History of the Reformation in Germany* appeared in 1939, an event that represented a watershed in Catholic attitudes to Luther.[12]

Lortz is a complex figure: his work played a major role in the evolution of Catholic ecumenism in Germany, and he was an

influence on Vatican II's ecumenical decree *Unitas redintegratio*.
But he was also, in contrast to Jedin, Przywara and Guardini, an
advocate of accommodation between the Church and National
Socialism, and he didn't resign his membership of the Nazi Party
till 1938. His significance for our story lies in the fact that more
or less single-handedly he brought about a revolution in Catholic
thinking about Luther and the Reformation, with profound and
continuing implications not only for the ecumenical movement
but also for Catholic theology.

Volume 1 of Lortz's *Die Reformation in Deutschland* (1939)
contained a profoundly negative assessment of the state of the
late medieval Church and an extended discussion of Luther's
development and career as a reformer up to 1525. The two aspects
of the volume were to prove almost equally influential. Lortz
portrayed the Catholic Church in Germany and beyond on the
eve of the Reformation as dominated by a corrupt hierarchy,
promoting a mechanical and materialistic popular piety remote
from the Gospels, and adrift from the patristic and high medieval
theological synthesis created by giants such as Aquinas. Among the
chief villains of Lortz's story were Occam and Occamism, the latter
a system that Lortz thought had distanced God as an arbitrary and
angry judge, unknowable by human reason, and which had also
taught that believers could fulfil the commands of God as revealed
in scripture, thereby propagating a practical Pelagianism which
Lortz condemned as '*wurzelhaft unkatolisch*' ('uncatholic to its very
roots'). The Reformation therefore was a tragic necessity, 'caused by
the disintegration of the fundamental principles and basic forms
on which the Middle Ages were built'. Because of its flawed origins
and equally flawed agents, the Protestant Reformation would evolve
into 'a denial of the visible church, rooted and grounded in the
objective teaching authority and in the sacramental priesthood',
which it replaced with a subjective appeal to the individual
conscience. In that sense, the Reformation was itself not a remedy
for but a manifestation of the breakdown of the medieval Catholic
synthesis: but however badly directed, Luther's Reformation
originated not as wanton rebellion against holy Church but as an

indignant and fundamentally religious response to a radical crisis within late medieval Catholicism.

Lortz's Luther was a deeply though anxiously religious man, brought to despair by fear of the Occamist God whom he imagined was the God preached by the Church, a man struggling to find a truly Catholic solution to his profound sense of sin. Lortz believed that Luther's rediscovery of that solution in the healing righteousness of God, appropriated by faith alone, was a personal breakthrough into a true perception, but Luther had not in fact discovered a new doctrine: it had been taught, Lortz insisted, 'by all the exegetes of the Middle Ages'. What was both genuinely new, and profoundly mistaken in its extremism, was Luther's overwhelming sense of the utter helplessness of the human will in this process, a pessimism rooted in his own psychopathology. Combined with a radical subjectivism which reduced the objective reality of salvation within the doctrinal and sacramental system of the Church to a purely personal experience, that pessimism led Luther beyond the genuine Catholic truths he had rediscovered and into heresy. Lortz summed all this up in a lapidary formulation: 'Luther overcame in himself a Catholicism that was not Catholic'.

You may have spotted in Lortz's emphasis on 'objective teaching authority and in the sacramental priesthood' the essentially ultramontane character of his theology in 1939. For all his receptivity to positive aspects of Luther's life and work, the propositional Catholicism distilled into the pages of Heinrich Denzinger remains the yardstick against which Luther's theological revolution was being measured.[13] But Lortz would go on developing his portrait of Luther into the age of Vatican II, and the Council's more scriptural, expansive and less propositional theological style did move Lortz towards an even more positive view of Luther. He remained certain that Luther was the victim of a 'strained and tormented conscience', a ' Doctor Hyperbolicus' who thought and wrote 'explosively and eruptively', too readily swayed by emotion and whose teaching was accordingly often distorted by his reaction to particular situations or opponents. Nevertheless, by the mid-1960s Lortz was insisting that 'Luther is in fact more Catholic than I realized', and that 'this

great believer, who led a constant and rich life of prayer, belongs
[...] among the great pastors'.

It's worth pausing at this point to register the precise extent to
which Lortz sought to rehabilitate Luther as a theologian with
something vital to say to the *Catholica*, and the limits of that
rehabilitation. Lortz conceded that the Reformation was a tragic
historical necessity, because the late medieval Church, institutionally
corrupt and theologically and spiritually decadent, had lost hold on
fundamental truths of the faith such as justification by faith, and
was in thrall to a nominalist misunderstanding of God as arbitrary
and unknowable. Luther, he believed, was a genuinely religious
and intensely earnest Christian, a theological genius driven by
conscience to see through the materialism and practical Pelagianism
that was poisoning and enfeebling Catholic piety, and a man of
'astounding vitality [...] captivated by the spirit of scripture' who
had rediscovered for himself and proclaimed the sovereignty of
grace. But deep flaws in Luther's own personality – his 'strained
and tormented conscience', his subjectivity and egocentrism, his
tendency to fly to extremes in order to best his opponents, his
violent and combative language – had all combined to propel him
into error. Lortz pointed in particular to the disastrous influence
on Luther of a passage from the writings of the fifteenth-century
conciliarist Cardinal Nicolò de Tudeschi, known as Panormitanus
('the man from Palermo'), who had argued that 'in matters
concerning the faith, even the statement of a private individual
might be preferred to that of a pope if the former is guided by
better reasons from the Old and New Testaments than the latter'.
Luther, Lortz insisted, had seized on this principle, abandoning
the constraints of obedience to Church and *magisterium* that had
kept Panormitanus within the bounds of orthodoxy, and had set
his own brilliant but subjective interpretations of 'my Gospel, my
bible' over against the universal testimony of the Church.

Lortz's growing sense that underneath the egotism and heretical
overstatement there was a Catholic Luther to be rediscovered owed
something to the fact that by the mid-1960s many theologians had
come to believe that there was fundamental agreement between

Catholics and Protestants on the contested issue of justification, for Luther the *articulum stantis aut cadentis ecclesiæ*. 'Today', Lortz wrote in 1964 ' the doctrine of Justification is hardly anywhere considered to divide Protestants and Catholics.' This breathtaking claim had been made possible by a generation of scholarship by Jedin and others on the debates leading up to the Tridentine decree and anathemas on justification, and on related matters such as the relationship between scripture and tradition, and a new interest in the ideas and importance of the generation of Catholic theologians in the circle of Cardinals Contarini and Pole who had been favourable to some of Luther's views.

Crucial triggers for this shift were two books published in the mid-1950s: Louis Bouyer's *The Spirit and Forms of Protestantism*, which argued for the Catholic orthodoxy of Luther's rediscovery of justification by grace alone; and the young Hans Kung's *Justification: The Doctrine of Karl Barth and a Catholic Reflection*, in which Kung claimed to have demonstrated the fundamental compatibility between Catholic teaching on justification, rightly understood, and that of the greatest living protestant theologian, Karl Barth. Kung's claim, in particular, was vigorously contested from both sides of the Reformation divide, but Barth himself endorsed it, as did both Karl Rahner and Hans Urs von Balthasar, and it was to prove hugely important in ecumenical discussion.

Kung himself notably did not engage Luther directly, and Barth was not, of course, a Lutheran. Nevertheless, the 1999 joint declaration on justification by the Lutheran World Federation and the Catholic Church would have been unimaginable without Kung's distinctive exposition of Catholic teaching on justification, and from the early 1960s widespread interest in Kung's contentions promoted Catholic receptivity to Luther. And the large-scale recasting of Catholic theology and ecclesiology in the wake of the Council seemed to point in the same direction. As Lortz wrote in 1964, 'The Second Vatican Council has taught us to see or to sense that the deplorable onesidedness of many Catholic formulations can be legitimately complemented so that the Catholic element expands [...] to include a previously ignored [...] biblical fullness'.[14]

The ambivalent feelings this new Catholic receptivity aroused on the other side of the Reformation divide were highlighted by the furore over the claim by one of Lortz's brightest students, Fr Erwin Iserloh, that Luther had never in fact posted the 95 Theses on the door of the castle church in Wittenberg. First floated by Iserloh in a lecture in 1961, the claim was developed in a short book, *The Theses Were Not Posted: Luther between Reform and Reformation*, published in 1966, the year of Iserloh's premature death.[15] There ensued a flood of rebuttal, recrimination and outrage. Iserloh was, of course, by no means the first scholar to cast doubt on the heroic myth of a dauntless young Luther defying the world by nailing his colours more or less literally to the door of the castle church. What made his book controversial was the ecumenical spin he gave his claim. Both Protestant and Catholic tradition had interpreted the posting of the theses as a deliberate act of defiance, the first blast of the trumpet of Protestant Reformation against the papal tyranny. But according to Iserloh, Luther had intended no defiance: he had punctiliously first sent the theses privately to his bishop, the accepted procedure for initiating a theological debate, and had intended only such a debate within the normal conventions of university theology. As my old supervisor Gordon Rupp commented, if Luther did not make what Iserloh repeatedly calls 'a scene', then 'we have Luther as an obedient rebel indeed', one whose theological protest a good deal of modern Catholic theology could support, so that the Catholic authorities themselves, by their inaction on the one hand, and by their repudiation of Luther on the other, must bear a large responsibility for the outbreak of the Western schism.

But however commendable Iserloh's intentions, not all Protestants were delighted. The fact that his book had appeared on the eve of the 450th anniversary of the posting of the theses did not go unnoticed, and this Catholic portrait of a 'reformer without a hammer' was seen as an attempt to tame Luther and defuse his protest. As Gordon Rupp grumbled rather sourly,

> It can alas be no accident that as the 450th anniversary looms, it should be Catholic historians who have called in question the historicity of this event [...] At first sight, Lortz and his pupils

mark the end of an old, bad polemic tradition. In a manner which would seem strange, say, to Catholics in Ireland, they dwell on Luther's great virtues—and are frank to the point of daring about the faults of the medieval church—the practical abuses, the theoretic errors of individual theologians, above all that 'Unklarheit' of culpable vagueness of fifteenth-century theological definition. Yet under the surface they still exploit Luther rather than sit down under him, and support the old thesis that what is true in Luther is Catholic, so that the over-all effect is pre-Vatican II.[16]

The remarkable flowering of positive Catholic Luther scholarship in these years ranged from essentially historical studies, such as John Todd's notably good 1964 Luther biography,[17] to major theological reassessments such as Otto Pesch's 1972 comparative analysis of Aquinas and Luther on justification, which suggested that Thomas's sapiential theology was complemented, not contradicted, by Luther's more existential engagement with scripture. And despite Rupp's barb about the pre-conciliar assumptions underlying the work of Iserloh and the Lortz school more generally, a major part of the energy from all this came from the post-conciliar theological ferment, and an optimistic drive towards Church unity. So, for example, the most notable North American Catholic Luther scholar, Jared Wicks SJ, was and is a distinguished ecumenical theologian, heavily involved in national and international Lutheran–Catholic dialogues.

But by no means all Catholic attention to Luther had such friendly intent. Even in the newly ecumenical 1960s and '70s there were dissenting voices warning against what they insisted was the fundamentally uncatholic nature of Luther's poisonous legacy. This sourer note was struck by Remigius Bäumer, who revived some of Denifle's moral charges against Luther, and by Theobald Beer, who argued that many of Luther's key ideas had pagan roots in Gnosticism and Neoplatonism. But perhaps the most insistent and influential of these voices was that of the controversial Indologist Paul Hacker, a layman and himself a convert from evangelical

Protestantism.[18] In 1966 Hacker published a polemic against Luther whose drift was evident in its title, *Das Ich im Glauben*, soon translated as *The Ego in Faith: Martin Luther and the Origin of Anthropocentric Religion*.[19]

Hacker's fundamental accusation against Luther was that he had preached what Hacker called 'a reflexive faith', which 'bends back upon its own subject in its very act'. According to Hacker, Luther located the certitude of salvation in the believer's own self, and 'the consoling conviction of being in God's favour'. Hacker illustrated what he considered the introverted subjectivity of Luther's teaching by contrasting the overwhelming predominance of first-person singular pronouns and corresponding possessive adjectives in Luther's exposition of the Apostles' Creed with the entire absence of such pronouns and adjectives in the text of the creed itself. In Luther, Hacker maintained, 'The doctrine of God the Father means first and above all that God has created *me* and everything that belongs to *me*. The salvation wrought by Christ means that the Saviour has redeemed *me*. The third article means that the Spirit has called *me*.' Hacker pointed to passages such as Rom. 8:31–9, which since Luther's time had been interpreted as expressing this individual certitude, but where in fact Paul repeatedly and pointedly speaks of salvation as a communal reality: 'If God is for US, who is against US?' The consciousness of salvation in apostolic times was not individualistic, as in Luther, Hacker insists, but universal, 'comprised within the consciousness of being the people of God'. In this Apostolic preaching the individual's salvation was 'inconceivable outside the primary comprehensive relationship of the Lord to his Mystical Body'. Luther had thus 'twisted the texts' of the New Testament to produce an account of faith in which 'the ego bends back upon itself', an understanding 'alien to Scripture and to all Christian spirituality and teaching before his time'. Authentic Christian tradition offers none of the false and self-reflexive certitude that Luther and Lutheranism regard as 'the essence of Christianity'. And even beyond Christianity, the effects of the destructive novelty of Luther's teaching lived on even in a secular world in the subjectivism of some forms of German idealism and existentialism. [20]

LUTHER THROUGH CATHOLIC EYES

The early 1980s saw elaborate Luther celebrations for the 450th anniversary of the Augsburg Confession in 1980 and the fifth centenary of Luther's birth in 1983. These anniversaries prompted an accompanying stock-taking of the generation of modern Luther studies, much of it by Roman Catholics, that had flowed since the 1960s. And among those taking stock was the recently appointed prefect of the Congregation of the Doctrine of the Faith, Cardinal Joseph Ratzinger. In the autumn of 1984 *Communio* printed an extended interview with Ratzinger, in which he reflected on two generations of Catholic Lutheran scholarship and their significance for practical ecumenism.[21] While appreciative of its achievements, Ratzinger discerned in the Lortz tradition a dangerous tendency to trivialize the Reformation divide:

> Though Lortz did not minimize the deep rift which really began to take shape in the controversies of the Reformation, it seemed simple enough, following his work and by simplifying his statements, to develop the thesis that the separation of the churches was, really, the result of a misunderstanding and that it could have been prevented had the church been more vigilant.

But this, Ratzinger thought, was to patronize the people of the past, 'a form of rationalistic arrogance which cannot do any justice to the impassioned struggle of those men as well as the importance of the realities in question'. Emphasizing the work of scholars such as Hacker and Beer who had rejected the eirenicism of the Lortz school, Ratzinger pointed to Luther's deep and considered repudiation of much that was fundamental to Catholicism: 'there exist not only Catholic anathemas against Luther's teachings but also Luther's own definitive rejections of Catholic articles of faith which culminate in Luther's verdict that we will remain eternally separate.' Unity could not be achieved by 'interpretative tricks' minimizing real differences; ecumenism involved 'insights which will overcome the past', not the remodelling of the past to explain away fundamental disagreements. In a distinction that was in essence derived from early Lortz and perhaps even Grisar, Ratzinger discerned two Luthers: an earnest and Christ-centred devotional genius on the one hand and a radical theologian whose personality and intellectual radicalism led him into heresy on the other. 'With his catechism, his songs and his liturgical directives Luther created a tradition of ecclesiastical life in the light of which we can both refer to him as the "father" of such an ecclesiastical life and interpret his work with evangelical churchliness in mind': this was Luther as the founder of the tradition that gave birth to Bach, and which Catholics could learn from and share with gratitude. But 'on the other hand, Luther also created a theological and polemical opus of revolutionary radicality', and to approach this Luther 'on the basis of his revolutionary break with tradition' is to 'arrive at quite a different overall view'.

Ratzinger saw examples of these radical and decisive departures from Catholic truth in Luther's exclusion of charity from the act of faith, in his fundamental lack of any theology of a visible universal Church as distinct from the Church as the local congregation and in his effective dissolution of any effective ecclesial *magisterium*.

> The history of reformed Christianity very clearly illustrates the limitations of exegetic unity: Luther had largely abandoned the line separating the teachings of the church from theology. Doctrine which runs counter to exegetic evidence is not a doctrine to him. That is why, throughout his life, his doctorate in theology represented to him a decisive authority in his opposition to the teachings of Rome. The evidence of the interpreter supplants the power of the *magisterium*. The learned academic (Doctor) now embodies the *magisterium*, nobody else.

But the unity derived from scholarly consensus 'is essentially revisable at any time', whereas 'Faith is a constant'.

This distinction led Ratzinger to pour scorn on the eight-point proposals for practical unity put forward in 1982 by Karl Rahner and Heinrich Fries. With Lutheran/Catholic unity in mind they had suggested acceptance of the scriptures and the creeds as a sufficient basis for Church unity, together with an agreement that none of the uniting Churches would overtly repudiate any doctrinal formulary accepted as binding by another uniting Church. This, Ratzinger suggested, was ecumenism by political trickery, a mere papering over the cracks, imposed from above, and doomed to failure: 'the unifying effect of theological pluralism is [...] only temporary and sectional. There is inherent in pluralism the inability ultimately to become a basis for unity.'

Ratzinger's sombre text was a warning against unrealistic expectations that a more positive scholarly assessment of Luther would translate directly into ecclesial convergence. It was also perhaps a prognostication of what Rahner dubbed the 'ecumenical winter' which, despite real advances such as the 1999 Joint Declaration on Justification, would deepen perceptibly throughout the pontificate of John Paul II. Certainly the extraordinary expansion of Catholic scholarship on Luther that was so remarkable a feature of the 1960s and 1970s slowed down in the 1990s and the early second millennium. More recent Catholic studies of Luther, including those triggered by the quincentenary, have been notably reticent and on the whole less sanguine about any likely ecclesial impact. Some of this no doubt can be attributed to the draining away of the post-conciliar ecumenical euphoria and the marked change of theological ethos in the pontificates of Papa Wojtyla and Papa Ratzinger. But it also reflects important changes that had taken place in the writing of Reformation history more generally.

Ratzinger had declared in his 1984 interview that 'there cannot be any Luther scholarship which does not at the same time involve research into his theology. One cannot simply approach Luther with the distant eye of the historian.' That perception owed something to the fact that in Germany Reformation history was almost exclusively studied and taught within theology faculties, and most European Catholic Church historians were priests, in whose training and interests theology loomed large. From the 1990s onwards that was changing, and Reformation history was increasingly studied and taught by scholars without overt religious commitments, as much or more interested in the social and political dimensions of the Reformation as in the theological. Increasingly, the success or failure of the German Reformation was assessed not on whether or not 'true' religion triumphed over false but in terms of the success of the reformers and their successors in suppressing traditional Catholic beliefs and replacing them with different doctrines, practices and sensibilities. The result was a reduction of ideological investment in Luther's story, one way or another.

A key figure here was the brilliant left-leaning Irish-Australian historian Bob Scribner, firmly lapsed for most of his career, though he returned to the Church during his final illness. Both as a former Vatican II enthusiast and as a secular-minded social historian, he was unimpressed by the Lutheran pieties that had dominated German Protestant scholarship about Luther, and which had influenced even Lortz and his school. Scribner rejected the religious value judgements that had sanctified Luther's revolt even in the eyes of Catholics like Lortz. For Scribner all religion was religion, none of it worse or better, none any more or any less authentic than any other kind. In this perspective, the narrative framework in which Luther featured as a purifier of corrupt religion disappeared, relativized by the anthropological techniques Scribner brought to bear on the religious life of late medieval and Reformation Germany. He demonstrated, for example, that Luther's startling popularity with his German contemporaries largely depended on the extent to which the 'cult' of the reformer borrowed from rather than simply repudiated the Catholic cult of the saints.[22] Scribner's work initially faced real hostility from the German academic establishment, but he established himself as a formidable voice offering fruitful new approaches, and he was hugely influential with a new and more secular-minded generation of Reformation historians.

There's a broader point here about the confessional underpinnings of Reformation historiography. It was a fundamental presupposition of the whole Lortzian school that Luther's Reformation, whatever its shortcomings from a Catholic perspective, was in some sense necessary and even legitimate, because of the woeful state of the late medieval Catholic Church. Lortz and his followers conceded the theological and religious decadence of fifteenth-century Catholicism, and the feebleness of the defence of traditional religion mounted by Luther's opponents. So Catholic historians did not question that, at least till Trent, Luther had all the best theological tunes, and the new religious style made such progress because it had more to offer than the debased and debilitated Catholicism it challenged.

Now, till the late 1980s, much the same assumptions had conditioned writing about the English Reformation also. But a generation of revisionist historians – some, though by no means all, Catholic – contested that basic assumption, arguing for the vigour and secure social embedding of religion in late medieval England. As that contention gained traction, the English Reformation, and the religious stature of the sixteenth-century English reformers, came to look different.[23] Even now, the historiography of the German Reformation has yet to undergo a similar large-scale revision.[24]

Some recent Catholic treatments of Luther have reworked some of the basic contentions of Lortz and his followers: one example is the question-begging subtitle of Peter Stanford's recent popular biography of Luther, characterized as 'Catholic Dissident'.[25] But different and more Ratzingerian notes are sounded in a much more scholarly recent study of Luther, my friend and colleague Richard Rex's *The Making of Martin Luther*.

Rex is best known as a historian of the English Reformation, but his doctoral work was on the theology of John Fisher, and Fisher's writings against Luther were among the most influential early Catholic responses. Rex's book is a pacy and vivid exploration of Luther's theological evolution to 1530, by which time all his distinctive positions were in place. Rex recognizes Luther's genius as a polemicist, religious activist and expositor of scripture: his book is in no sense a hatchet job. But he is equally clear that many of Luther's distinctive teachings represented a decisive break with a millennium of Catholic teaching, and not merely with late medieval misunderstandings of that teaching. 'Luther's problems', he writes,

were medieval problems, but his solutions were new solutions. The big novelties in his thought were the invisible church, the ineradicable persistence of sin in this life, and the certainty of grace (through justification by faith alone). Each of these central ideas directly contradicted the presuppositions of a thousand years of

Christian writing and preaching – and, ironically, contradicted
Luther's favorite ancient Christian writer, Augustine of Hippo.[26]

And, according to Rex, the man in the pew pre-empted modern
historians in recognizing that the religion of Luther was not that
of their forefathers: 'Ordinary people, as witnessed by everyday
speech and usage, had a clear idea of what was going on. What they
saw in Luther's movement […] was novelty […] as much a novelty
in sixteenth-century Germany as Islam in seventh-century Arabia
or Mormonism in nineteenth-century America.'[27]

Echoing Lortz, Rex argues that Luther's deployment of 'the
Panormitanus Principle' was 'profoundly corrosive because it was
profoundly individualistic'.[28] Along with 'the personal certitude
of divine favor which grew out of the doctrine of justification
by faith', that principle would lead ultimately to the triumph of
subjective private judgement as the only judge of truth within the
Reformation. And there is an echo of Bäumer in Rex's contention
that 'the deployment of peace of conscience as a practical yardstick
of doctrinal truth amounted to an assertion of the self, shrouded
beneath a professed subjection to scripture […] the egotism of his
rhetoric drowned out the intrinsic individualism of his logic'.[29]

Rex's take on Luther can be commended as both an entertaining
and a challenging read for anyone with an interest in the subject.
He writes as a historian, not a theologian, but he engages vigorously
with Luther's key ideas. And he is clearly much closer to Ratzinger
than to Lortz on the question of the compatibility of Catholicism
with Luther's key doctrines. His Luther is, in the end, a heretic,
not a Catholic dissident. This most recent product of a century of
Catholic Luther scholarship is far more measured, more objective
and more receptive to Luther than the character assassinations
of Denifle and Grisar with which I began. But they would have
recognized some of Rex's key points, and his book certainly points
us in a very different direction from the work of Lortz and those
who took their lead from him. Pope emeritus Benedict will probably
have enjoyed it.

James Anthony Froude and the Reign of Queen Mary

Great historical writing, perhaps all historical writing, holds a mirror up to two different worlds: the age it sets out to describe and the age in which it is written. The historian aims to understand and explain the past. But the questions historians bring to the past often reflect the anxieties and preoccupations of the present. Of no great historical work is this more true than James Anthony Froude's monumental 12-volume study of *The History of England from the Fall of Wolsey to the Defeat of the Spanish Armada*, published between 1858 and 1870.[1]

Froude's intellectual career was stormy even by the contentious standards of Victorian England. Born in 1818, he was the fourth son of a stern West Country parsonage. His father was an old-fashioned high and dry churchman, archdeacon of Totnes from 1820 till his death in 1859; his mother had died two years after James Anthony's birth. The future historian was raised in a male-dominated household of rigid discipline and little overt affection, disapproved of at home and bullied at school. He was overshadowed by his brilliant, ebullient and egotistical eldest brother Hurrell, whose idea of toughening his timid and sickly sibling was to lower him head-first into a Devon stream and stir the mud with his hair.[2] Before his premature death from tuberculosis

in 1836, Hurrell was to become one of the founding fathers of the
Tractarian Movement, the Oxford-based clerical ginger group that
sought to recover and promote the Catholic aspects of the Anglican
tradition. The publication of Hurrell Froude's inflammatory and
opinionated literary *Remains* by his friend and admirer John Henry
Newman in 1838 was both a turning point in the history of the
movement and a staging post on Newman's own journey into the
Roman Catholic Church.

James Anthony arrived in Oxford just months before his brother's
death, and fell at once under the spell of Newman's magnetic
personality. His first historical work was a life of the Saxon St Neot,
contributed to a hagiographical series on the English saints edited
by the older man. Froude was never to lose his personal reverence
for Newman, 'one of the ablest of living men'.[3] But he soon found
himself repelled by Newman's religion, with its emphasis on the
importance of dogma and the continuity of Catholic tradition.
Unsettled by a *Zeitgeist* in which traditional religious certainties
seemed increasingly contradicted by advances in science and
biblical criticism, Froude abandoned what he saw as the hot-house
churchiness of Tractarianism. After much agonizing, he took refuge
in a self-consciously low-church Protestantism, fiercely patriotic,
deeply anticlerical, dismissive of doctrine and ceremonial. Froude
emphasized instead religion as moral goodness informed by faith in a
providentialist God, known in the course of history by the individual
conscience.[4] For him, the triumph of the Reformation did not lie in
the replacement of a Catholic creed by a Protestant one, for Froude
himself had reservations about all creeds. What Henry VIII and his
daughter Elizabeth had achieved instead was the shattering of clerical
power and the liberation of the lay conscience from ecclesiastical
control and nonsensical mumbo-jumbo. In the Tractarian nostalgia
for the Catholic past, and even more in the contemporary revival
in England of the Roman Catholic Church, Froude saw a mindless
retreat into superstition and intellectual oppression.

Victorian England was militantly Protestant. Yet disparagement
of the Reformation was common among early Victorian writers.
The great Whig historian Thomas Babington Macaulay valued

the sixteenth-century break with the papacy as a step away from obscurantism on the road to modernity, but he saw the Reformation itself as an ignoble episode, initiated by tyranny and driven by the basest of motives:

> Elsewhere, worldliness was the tool of zeal. Here, zeal was the tool of worldliness. A King, whose character may best be described by saying that he was despotism itself personified, unprincipled ministers, a rapacious aristocracy, a servile Parliament, such were the instruments by which England was delivered from the yoke of Rome.[5]

For quite different reasons the Tractarians also distanced themselves from the first reformers, because they had repudiated the Catholic inheritance that the Oxford Movement now sought to reinstate. In one of the most notorious sentences in Hurrell Froude's *Remains*, James Anthony's brother declared the English Reformation to be 'a limb badly set – it must be broken again to be righted'. Newman too had cast a bleak eye on the founding fathers of Anglicanism: 'Cranmer will not stand examination', he had written in 1838, 'the English Church will yet be ashamed of conduct like his.'[6]

These jaundiced views of the Reformation and its leaders had been given formidable scholarly underpinning by the work of a learned Catholic historian, the priest John Lingard. His soberly understated 12-volume *History of England*, completed in 1830, had marshalled new material from hitherto unexploited European archives into a deeply unflattering picture of the origin and progress of Henry VIII's break with Rome.[7] Despite his suspect status as a Catholic priest, Lingard's scholarship was widely respected, and though he seldom mentioned him by name, Froude often had this influential Catholic historian firmly in his sights.

Froude's great *History* was therefore deliberately conceived as a defence of the English Reformation. It was, however, financial necessity that drove Froude to the writing of that history. In 1849 he published a lurid semi-autobiographical novel, *The Nemesis of Faith,* whose clerical hero is plagued by religious doubts, flirts with adultery and suicide, becomes a Roman Catholic and enters a monastery, but who ultimately dies in despair. The scandal that erupted around this sensational novel changed the course of Froude's life. His horrified father disowned him, and he was forced to resign his fellowship at Exeter College, Oxford. To hold his fellowship in the first place, he had been obliged to accept ordination as a deacon in the Church of England, despite his religious doubts. This unwanted clerical status now legally prevented Froude from earning a living in any of the other professions. Married, and with a growing family, he settled in idyllic if impoverished seclusion at Plas Gwynant, near Snowdon in north Wales, in 1850. He commenced work as a jobbing journalist, writing reviews and essays for many periodicals. Froude also conceived the idea of a biography of Elizabeth I, and began reading the available printed sources. As he became more absorbed, the scope of the project widened, to take in the whole of the English Reformation, understood as 'a revolt against idolatry and superstition [...] of the laity against the clergy, and of the English nation against the papal supremacy'.[8]

Froude was fortunate in his timing. Till the early nineteenth century the history of England had been written largely from printed sources: manuscript archives were mostly uncatalogued, difficult to locate and to gain access to once located. Lingard had recognized the importance of going to the archives if old stereotypes were to be overthrown, and had made pioneering use of manuscript material in the Vatican and other European depositories. But the bulk of the state papers for sixteenth-century England were not yet accessible to historians, and the great Victorian publication series of state papers not yet conceived.

By the time Froude came to write, however, that situation was changing. The Public Record Office (PRO) had been established in Chancery Lane in London in 1838, the first step towards centralizing and opening to researchers the National Archives, till then scattered in more than 50 different locations. The Deputy Keeper of the Public Records, Sir Francis Palgrave, had begun transcribing and calendaring the records for the reign of Henry VIII, and made these transcriptions available to Froude. They provided him with both the framework for the early volumes of his history and a sense of the sheer quantity of the treasure as yet unexplored. He moved to London to be near the sources and became a dedicated archival historian, searching out sixteenth-century papers not just at the PRO but also in great family collections such as the Cecil Papers at Hatfield.[9] For the Elizabethan volumes of his history, he would spend gruelling months in the heat, dust and uncatalogued chaos of the Spanish archives at Simancas.[10]

Froude's reliance on manuscript sources was his proudest boast as a historian. Nine-tenths of his source materials, he insisted, were manuscripts that no one else had used. Ironically, that very claim became a favourite target of gleefully hostile reviewers. Froude worked rapidly on manuscript materials in five languages, under constant pressure of time, in atrocious conditions, too dark, too cold, too hot, often without the benefit of calendars or finding lists and with no research assistants. Never a careful proofreader, and with no formal training in palaeography, he sometimes had to guess as much as read the meaning of the crabbed and blotted texts he was deciphering, and he did not always guess right. In taking notes, sometimes he transcribed verbatim, sometimes he paraphrased. When reproducing his sources in print, he did not always distinguish between transcriptions and summaries. He could be sloppy and careless, and hostile readers pounced on the slips. But considering the pioneering nature of the work and the circumstances in which it was executed, he made amazingly few major errors. More than a century on, no less an authority than the late Sir Geoffrey Elton endorsed the essential soundness of Froude's use of the English state papers. And when the official calendars of the state papers relating to England in the Spanish archives were being prepared at the end of the nineteenth century, the editors found Froude's notes and transcripts a constant and reliable guide.[11]

Froude always maintained that he had come to the writing of history with the usual inherited preconceptions and prejudices, but had had them blown away by exposure to the sources themselves.[12] In fact, his immense 12-volume narrative was profoundly shaped by his own tormented religious journey, and by a distinctive and rather pessimistic world view which he brought to the sources, rather than derived from them. Having shaken free of the influence of Newman, Froude had fallen under the spell of the Scottish writer and thinker Thomas Carlyle. The fascination would last a lifetime, and Froude was to become Carlyle's literary executor and, more controversially, his embarrassingly frank biographer.

Carlyle's greatest work was a history of the French Revolution, and his perception of human history was volcanic, not evolutionary. The world was indeed a moral arena in which the purposes of God worked themselves out, but always unpredictably, never gradually. The vital forces of present and future erupted shatteringly through the carapace of moribund social structures and outworn creeds. Carlyle despised optimistic Whiggish theories of the inevitability of progress through constitutional development, and he identified modern democracy with the rule of little people. Instead, he believed that the spirit of the age and the great forces of change manifested themselves, for good and ill, not in the rank and file but in the world-transforming figure of the hero – titanic individuals such as Socrates, Julius Caesar, Jesus, Shakespeare, Cromwell, Frederick the Great, Napoleon.[13]

Though he would not have subscribed formally to all these ideas, they had a profound influence on Froude's understanding of the sixteenth century. He shared Carlyle's distrust of the masses, accepted contemporary racial theories which emphasized the innate superiority of some human beings to others (for example, of the English over the Irish and of the white over the black races). He regarded the advent of Protestantism and the repudiation of papal authority as an immense blessing, a necessary step in the emergence of the modern world and of English values, and a prelude to future imperial greatness. Yet he understood perfectly well that the majority of the English people in the sixteenth century would have preferred to remain Catholic, and that the Reformation was in fact imposed on the nation by Henry VIII and his daughter Elizabeth:

> I regarded the Reformation as the grandest achievement in English history, yet it was equally obvious that it could never

have been brought about constitutionally according to modern methods. The Reformation had been the work of two powerful sovereigns [...] backed by the strongest and bravest of their subjects. To the last up to the defeat of the Armada, manhood suffrage in England would at any moment have brought back the Pope.[14]

It was the power of a personal monarchy – above all of Henry VIII, therefore – that had enabled and indeed enforced the transition to a new age. Though Froude recognized that there were monstrous aspects of Henry's life and actions, his instinct was to find a 'rational' justification for them, and he considered that for his great service to his people Henry could be forgiven much. To his Victorian contemporaries one of the most controversial aspects of Froude's history was this willingness to justify even the most autocratic and cruel actions of Henry, provided they had advanced the cause of reformation. He defended even the law imposing boiling alive as a punishment for poisoners, and insisted that many of Henry's victims, including his executed wives, were justly punished for real crimes. Henry's Treason Act had introduced capital punishment for those unable to acknowledge the Royal Supremacy, and was loathed by both Catholic and Whig historians as a prime example of tyrannical government attempting mind control. Froude would have none of it:

> There are times [...] when the safety of the State depends upon unity of purpose [...] At such times the *salus populi* overrides all other considerations: and the maxims and laws of calmer periods for awhile consent to be suspended [...] I assume that the Reformation was in itself right [...] If this be allowed, those laws will not be found to deserve the reproach of tyranny. We shall see in them but the natural resource of a vigorous Government placed in circumstances of extreme peril.

It was indeed a matter of regret that 'in this grand struggle for freedom, success could only be won by the aid of measures which bordered on oppression', but when all was said and done, the

Catholics themselves were natural persecutors, and so had deserved the worst that was done to them: 'here also the even hand of justice was but commending the chalice to the lips of those who had made others drink it to the dregs.'[15]

In this spirit Froude defended the executions of More and Fisher and the excruciating death by disembowelling of leading Carthusian monks for refusing the Oath of Supremacy in 1535. He admitted their courage and personal nobility, but saw that very nobility as an anachronism, an obstacle to the necessary advance of reformation. 'We cannot blame the Government' driven to 'so hard a necessity', since 'the future of the world could not be sacrificed to preserve the exotic graces of medieval saints'.[16] This was a defence that might, of course, be used to legitimate the most arbitrary actions of any authoritarian regime, as many of Froude's contemporaries were quick to point out. In the margin of these very passages, the Victorian medievalist Professor E. A. Freeman, one of Froude's most relentless reviewers, scribbled indignantly 'Bah!', 'Beast!', and 'May I live to embowel James Anthony Froude'.[17]

The necessary triumph of the Reformation provided Froude's sprawling narrative with an overarching general theme. But the work itself, though written with the easy grace and eloquence of a gifted journalist, was in structural terms a loose and baggy monster. It was vast in scale, leisurely in pace, sometimes racing forward in vaulting narrative, sometimes pausing for pages at a time to unravel a single incident, often incorporating vast blocks of undigested original documentation, from private letters to entire Acts of Parliament. Froude had originally intended to take the narrative to the death of Elizabeth, but decided late in the 1860s on the defeat of the Armada as a more dramatic end-point. The message as well as the form of the book evolved as Froude's own opinions shifted in response to his materials. His treatment of the reigns of Henry, Edward and Mary was originally intended essentially as an extended prelude to his much fuller treatment of the reign of Elizabeth, which did indeed eventually occupy six of the twelve volumes of the completed work. Elizabeth, rather than Henry, was therefore the intended hero(ine) of Froude's narrative. But as he read his way deeper into the sources, his respect for the Virgin Queen dwindled. Though she remained for him a providential instrument in preserving English protestant liberties, he came to believe, 'with reluctance', that 'the wisdom of Elizabeth was the wisdom of her ministers, and that her chief merit [...] lay in allowing her policy to be guided by Lord Burghley'.[18]

Froude's treatment of the reign of Mary I, published in 1860, was the culmination of the six volumes that make up the first half of the *History* as a whole. It forms a genuinely pivotal point in the unfolding of Froude's narrative, together with the reign of Edward forming a trough between the twin peaks of achievement represented by Henry and Elizabeth. For Froude, Henry was a man perfectly matched to the historic moment. At the point at which the English people needed to unleash their potential by striking against the 'enormous tyranny' of clerical oppression, and to cast off the foreign interference of the popes, Henry had led their bid for freedom. Even his personal inconsistencies, the radicalism of his break with Rome and the (richly deserved) destruction of the monasteries, the conservatism of his belief in the Mass, matched the mood of his people:

> As the nation moved, the King moved, leading it, but not outrunning it; checking those who went too fast, dragging forward those who lagged behind.[19]

It was Henry who had masterminded the English Reformation and given it its distinctively national character, and it was Henry who had established Parliament as 'the first power in the State under the Crown'.[20] And correspondingly, Elizabeth had re-established and stabilized Henry's Reformation and had defended England from being gobbled up by a politicized European Catholicism, from papistical disloyalty within and papistical invasion from abroad. The defeat of the Armada was therefore the last act in a drama that had opened with the divorce of Henry from Catherine of Aragon.

But with the death of Henry, Froude believed, the Reformation had taken a wrong turn. A national reformation implied 'the transfer of power [...] from the ignoble to the noble, from the incapable to the capable, from the ignorant to the wise'. Under Edward, however, ambition, greed and selfishness had triumphed, and the rule of those around the child king had poisoned English public life. Liberated from the Egyptian bondage of the papacy, the people had been led not to the promised land but into a barren wilderness where even the manna had been stolen by the Duke of Northumberland and his cronies:

> To the Universities the Reformation had brought with it desolation. To the people of England it had brought with it misery and want. The once open hand was closed; the once open heart was hardened; the ancient loyalty of man to man was exchanged for the scuffling of selfishness; the change of faith had brought with it no increase of freedom, and less of charity. The prisons were crowded as before with sufferers for opinion, and the creed of a thousand years was made a crime by a doctrine of yesterday.[21]

In these circumstances the accession of Mary seemed a deliverance

> In the tyranny under which the nation was groaning, the moderate men of all creeds looked to the accession of Mary as to the rolling away of some bad black nightmare.[22]

In fact, however, Froude believed, what was to ensue was a winnowing, a nightmare ten times worse than the reign of Edward. But it was a salutary nightmare, which Providence would use to demonstrate beyond all doubt the blessings of Protestantism and the incompatibility of Catholicism with English liberties. If indeed the Edwardine Reformation had proved to be, in Hurrell Froude's words, 'a limb badly set', then Mary's reign had broken it again with a vengeance, so that it might be set right again under Elizabeth. For Froude, therefore, Mary's reign was a tragic drama in which the queen, misguided by bigotry, hysteria and evil counsel, would squander a nation's goodwill and doom her inherited Catholicism for ever to the margins of English history. The nation had cast off clerical oppression under Henry, but the people were otherwise religiously conservative. Nobody cared for the pope, or wanted the re-establishment of the religious orders, or 'the odious domination of the clergy'. But most people, Froude thought, did want the Mass, the ancient ceremonies and a celibate clergy. Mary's fatal decision to try to turn the clock back behind Henry's reforms, therefore, to introduce the tyranny of heresy tribunals and the slavery of papal obedience once more, snatched defeat from the jaws of victory and doomed her regime to ignominious failure.

> Could Mary have been contented to pursue her victory no further, she would have preserved the hearts of her subjects; and the reaction, left to complete its own tendencies, would in a few years, perhaps, have accomplished in some measure her larger desires. But few sovereigns have understood less the effects of time and forbearance. She was deceived by the rapidity of her first success; she flattered herself that difficult though it might be, she could build up again the ruined hierarchy, could compel the holders of church property to open their hands, and could reunite the country to Rome.[23]

The ensuing slide into catastrophe and monstrous injustice – the folly of the Spanish marriage, the crime of religious persecution, the humiliation of the loss of Calais – followed inexorably. For Froude, Mary's failure derived in part from her own inflexible temperament. He was by no means entirely unsympathetic to her: her courageous fidelity to her religion under Edward 'determined, downright and unaffected, cutting through official insincerities and fearless of consequences', commended her to him. Froude dwelt on the paradox that it was Mary, 'the defender of a dying superstition', rather than Edward's Protestant Council, 'the patrons of liberty and right', who had then held the moral high ground.[24]

But Mary as queen was a different matter. Here her frailty as a woman and her religious bigotry united to form a literally lethal combination. The 'unhappy Queen, unloved, unlovable, yet with her parched heart thirsting for affection', pined with 'hysterical

longing' for a husband who would care for her, and found instead
only the icy indifference of Philip II. Her love for him became a
torture to her, and a calamity for her people.

> With a broken spirit and bewildered understanding, she turned
> to heaven for comfort, and instead of heaven, she saw only the
> false roof of her creed painted to imitate and shut out the sky.[25]

Froude dwelt on Mary's desolation after Philip's departure and
her first false pregnancy: 'with stomach swollen and features
shrunk and haggard, she would sit upon the floor'. And he made
a direct connection between that bitter disappointment and the
increasingly ferocious campaign against heresy. The queen, he
thought, attributed her childlessness to supernatural causes, a
divine punishment.

> And what could that crime be? The accursed thing was still in
> the realm. She had been raised up [...] for the extermination of
> God's enemies, and she had smitten but a few.[26]

But if Froude saw in Mary's 'hysterical' temperament one of the
major causes of the cruelties and failures of her reign, he laid at least
equal blame on her clerical advisers Bishops Gardiner and Bonner,
'straining at the leash' to revenge themselves on their Protestant
enemies, and above all, the Queen's cousin Cardinal Reginald Pole.
Pole is one of the recurring villains of the first six volumes of the
History. Educated in Italy at Henry's expense and groomed for high
office in the Church, Pole had bitten the hand that fed him by
turning against the king after the executions of More and Fisher.
His treatise against the Royal Supremacy, *De unitate*, sent to the
king in 1536, embodied for Froude the ultimate treason, for in it
Pole denounced his own monarch, exalted the papacy and called
on the emperor Charles V to invade England, depose Henry and
halt the Reformation. Pole's elevation to the cardinalate in 1536,
and his attempts to organize an imperial or French 'crusade' against
Henry, confirmed him in Froude's mind as a betrayer of his country.

Till Froude's *History*, Pole had in fact enjoyed a surprisingly good press from English writers, which perhaps owed something to his European stature, his Plantagenet blood and his personal virtues. But for Froude the cardinal represented fanaticism untempered by common sense. He seems to have seen in him something of the same clerical single-mindedness that had repelled him in the Tractarian movement.

> His character was irreproachable; in all the virtues of the Catholic Church he walked, without spot or stain; and the system to which he had surrendered himself had left him of the common selfishness of mankind his enormous vanity alone. But that system had extinguished also in him the human instincts, the genial emotions by which theological theories stand especially in need to be corrected.

It seems likely that recollections of Froude's own brother Hurrell were not far beneath the surface when he placed Pole in

> a class of persons at all times numerous, in whom enthusiasm takes the place of understanding; who are men of an 'idea'; and unable to accept human things as they are, are passionate loyalists, passionate churchmen, passionate revolutionists, as the accidents of their age may determine.[27]

Fanatical zeal, untempered by common sense or common humanity, was for Froude the clue to the calamities of Mary's reign. He repeatedly contrasted this hysterical lack of realism with the 'judicious latitudinarianism to which the lay statesmen of the better sort were inclining'.[28] It was these pragmatic realists (above all William Cecil, Lord Burghley) who saw that England's salvation lay in a return to the wholesome rationalities of the Reformation, an outcome dependent on the accession of Mary's Protestant half-sister. Elizabeth 'was the person to whom the affections of the liberal party in England most definitely tended', not least because, though she firmly rejected Catholic superstition, she was 'opposed as decidedly to factious and dogmatic Protestantism'.[29] Accordingly, the preservation of Elizabeth from the hatred of the Queen and the wreckage and self-destruction of Mary's doomed regime formed an important sub-theme in Froude's narrative.

Froude's portrayal of what he saw as the increasingly self-deluded character of Mary's reign focused on the queen's false pregnancies. He positively gloated over the heightened emotion and un-English excess with which both Cardinal Pole and Queen Mary deluded themselves that their regime had a future. Froude makes much of the first encounter between cardinal and queen, when Pole, amid much un-English weeping and kissing, blasphemously greeted Mary with the words of Gabriel to the Virgin Mary, 'Hail Mary Full of Grace, the Lord is with thee, blessed art thou amongst women, and blessed is the fruit of thy womb'. For Froude the fundamental emptiness of Marian Catholicism was reflected in the fact that, though there were to be no fruits of Mary's womb, the queen persuaded herself and others that the baby had leaped within her at Pole's words.[30]

For Froude, not only the queen but the Marian regime in general was characterized by these doomed and insubstantial emotional excesses. They 'indulged their fancy in large expectations'; Catholic enthusiasm 'flowed over in processions, in sermons, masses and te Deums'. The regime was full of show, but ultimately as empty within as the heartless King Philip's cynical pretence of religion:

> Whatever Philip of Spain was entering upon, whether it was a marriage or a massacre, a state intrigue or a midnight murder, his opening step was ever to seek a blessing from the holy wafer.[31]

And if unreality was one of the defining marks of the Marian regime, murderous cruelty was the other. Froude detested dogmatic Protestantism almost as much as he did Catholicism, and many of the victims of the Marian burnings were very dogmatic indeed. He nevertheless devoted a sixth of his narrative of the reign to the burnings, using material from John Foxe's *Actes and Monuments* to good effect to tug at his readers' heart strings. In the process he offered a psychologically perceptive and persuasive rehabilitation of Cranmer, who had been disparaged by both Macaulay and Newman. Froude devoted so much space to the burnings because he believed that they above all else had opened the nation's eyes to the true horrors of a Catholic regime, thereby ensuring that an otherwise conservative people would return to Protestantism under Elizabeth. The 'cruelty of the Catholic party' converted the general population to the Reformation cause 'with a rapidity like that produced by the gift of tongues on the day of Pentecost'. It was a decisive step on the emergence of English identity. The 'horrible sight' of the burnings 'worked upon the beholders as it has worked since, and will work for ever, while the English nation survives': the martyrs alone 'broke the spell of orthodoxy, and made the establishment of the Reformation possible'.[32]

To begin with, Froude's history had a rough ride from his academic contemporaries, and most of the early reviewers fastened gleefully on the work's weaknesses and errors. But public reaction was very different, and the *History* rapidly became a best-seller. The vividness and pace of the narrative, the author's contagious excitement at his many real discoveries in the archives, the brilliance of his character-drawing and the sheer scale and grandeur of Froude's theme, the emergence of the Protestant nation in defiance of the might of Catholic Europe, caught the mood of mid-Victorian England. Tennyson was inspired by Froude's treatment of Mary's reign to write his now neglected verse drama *Queen Mary*, which Froude understandably thought the greatest of the poet laureate's works. Gladstone, at the time embroiled in his own fierce polemic against the Pope and Papal Infallibility, declared that the play, and by implication Froude's narrative which underlay it, had 'struck a stroke for the nation'.[33] Academic recognition of Froude's achievement as a historian would come belatedly, just two years before his death, in the form of his election as regius professor of modern history at Oxford in 1892.

No one would now rely uncritically on Froude's 12 volumes for an understanding of the history of sixteenth-century England. His prejudices are too blatant, his tendency to read sixteenth-century evidence through nineteenth-century spectacles too anachronistic. But many of his fundamental emphases – above all, his insistence on the central role of Henry VIII in shaping the future course of English nationhood – did in fact endure, being taken up and refined by more sober (and tamer) twentieth-century academic historians. They included the most influential Tudor historian of the first half of the twentieth century, A. F. Pollard. From the 1950s onwards Pollard's influence gave way to that of the Cambridge historian Professor G. R. Elton. Elton departed drastically from Froude's reading of the sixteenth century by transferring Henry's central role in Tudor politics and religion to his minister, Thomas Cromwell. But more recent treatments of the period have returned to Froude in reinstating the king as the chief mover and shaker, even if few historians have gone as far as Froude in putting a positive spin on Henry's every action.[34]

Less happily, Froude's treatment of Mary as a hysterical personality has also survived, and has coloured accounts of the queen down to the present day.[35] And in the treatment of religion in the period, Froude's influence has been even more persistent. A. G. Dickens, whose textbook on the English Reformation dominated English school and university teaching from the 1960s to the 1990s, did not depart essentially from the interpretation laid down by the great Victorian. Only recently has Froude's negative and confessionally driven assessment of the Marian regime come under critical scrutiny.[36]

Froude has to be read in bulk to appreciate the vigour and pace of his narrative writing, his mastery of evocative description, his brilliantly dramatic character sketches. The main themes of Froude's handling of Mary's reign are predictable enough: the illusory optimism of the Catholic restoration itself, the cruelty of the persecution of Protestants, and the nature of Cardinal Pole's influence over the queen. Most of them are touched on in Froude's long opening chapter of the volume on Mary's reign, his account of the Privy Council plot to exclude her from the succession and enthrone Jane Grey in her place, her seizure of power and the downfall of the Duke of Northumberland, with its merciless analysis of Northumberland's desperate last days and scaffold recantation. His aphoristic summary of the career of a bold bad man who just missed greatness shows Froude at his most characteristic:

> In his better years Northumberland had been a faithful subject and a fearless soldier, and, with a master's hand over him, he might have lived with integrity and died with honour. Opportunity tempted his ambition – ambition betrayed him into crime – and, given over to his lower nature, he climbed to the highest round of the political ladder, to fall and perish like a craven.[37]

And any notion that Froude aspired to be a scientific historian of studied neutrality would be banished by a perusal of the concluding pages of his treatment of Mary's reign, which are a sustained and deliberate exercise in inspirational rhetoric, reminding the reader that, although Froude repudiated his Anglican ordination and considered himself a layman, he never quite exorcized the ghost of the fervent revivalist preacher he might have become.

9

A. G. Dickens and the Medieval Church

You might be forgiven for thinking that a discussion of A. G. Dickens as a historian of the late medieval Church need detain the reader no more than a very few minutes. Dickens, in his day the leading historian of the English Reformation, was a pupil of K. B. McFarlane, one of twentieth-century Oxford's most brilliant medievalists, and the godfather of wonderful work by pupils such as Colin Richmond. McFarlane pointed Dickens not in the direction of the Middle Ages, however, but to post-Reformation Yorkshire Catholicism. So most of what Dickens had to say about the medieval Church is to be found in preliminaries and asides, and at an angle to his main concerns. Nevertheless, one of his first major publications was an edition of the chronicle of Butley Priory, a house of Augustinian canons near Woodbridge in Suffolk, and towards the end of his life Dickens reissued it, saying that the original edition had been the most enjoyable academic project of his entire career. And although he devoted relatively little printed space to it, Dickens's view of late medieval English Christianity was in fact a crucial component of his account of the Reformation, so it certainly merits a closer look.[1]

Dickens came to maturity as an historian in something of a golden age for English medieval studies. The generation or so before the appearance of his edition of the Butley chronicle saw the publication of a series of major editions of synodical and episcopal statutes, registers and monastic and secular visitation returns by outstanding scholars such as Hamilton Thompson, W. A. Pantin, Christopher Cheney and Eileen Power. Monasticism was especially well served. In Cambridge, David Knowles had published his defining masterpiece, *The Monastic Order in England*, in 1940, and the first volume of his great survey of late medieval English monasticism, *The Religious Orders in England,* appeared in 1948. In Oxford a generation of medievalists, formed in the shadow of Sir Maurice Powicke, flourished. Nigel Ker had begun cataloguing the monastic, cathedral and college libraries of medieval England, and McFarlane was at work on his biography of Wyclif, the first of a series of studies, all of which were a good deal more sceptical about the coherence and influence of Lollardy than anything Dickens would ever write on the subject. W. A. Pantin, most of whose earlier work had focused on monastic history, gave his important series of Birkbeck lectures at Cambridge in 1948 on *The English Church in the Fourteenth Century*, and the published version offered what is still in many ways the fullest and most judicious account of the English Church in the age of Wyclif.[2]

The materials from which an informed and sympathetic appraisal of late medieval Christianity might emerge were already, therefore, being assembled. But throughout the years of Dickens's education discussion of the late medieval Church, monastic and secular, was coloured by frankly sectarian polemic, in the form of the unequal gladiatorial struggle between Cardinal Aidan Gasquet and Dr George Gordon Coulton.[3] This is not the place to recount the detail of what had become by the mid-1930s, when Dickens began independent historical work, an excruciating and unrelenting exercise in bear-baiting by the terrier-like Coulton. Gasquet was a generously talented man, whose first book, *Henry VIII and the English Monasteries* (1888), contained a good deal of fresh and worthwhile research and offered a spirited challenge to traditional Protestant historiography of the Reformation. It caused a considerable stir, became a best-seller and was welcomed not only by Catholic but also by Anglo-Catholic historians, as doing much to rescue a crucial aspect of late medieval religion from the calumny of centuries. Gasquet was to follow it with a series of almost equally successful books with titles such as *The Old English Bible and Other Essays*, *The Eve of the Reformation* and

Parish Life in Medieval England, all of them containing a good deal
of valuable information, and all offering a highly idealized picture
of Catholic England from which every shadow and blemish had
been airbrushed out or explained away. His last book of real value
was the collaborative study, with Edmund Bishop, *Edward VI and
the Book of Common Prayer*, published in 1890. Thereafter his work
was increasingly based on hasty and half-remembered reading, and
it was riddled with gross mistakes which, however often or politely
pointed out to him, he failed, and sometimes refused, to correct.
As David Knowles remarked, towards the end of his life, 'Gasquet's
capacity for inaccuracy amounted almost to genius': in a serious
historical essay offered to one of the greatest and most meticulous
historians of the day, his friend and collaborator Edmund Bishop,
he could write blithely and repeatedly about Gibbon's '*Rise and
Fall of the Roman Empire*'. As Coulton declared contemptuously,
'inaccuracy grew on him like a crust'.[3]

Coulton was, by contrast, a man of considerable intellectual
distinction, and was judged by Dom David Knowles to be one of the
most learned medievalists of a learned age, and a man of unflinching
integrity. He was, however, also a fanatic, with a deep loathing and
fear of Roman Catholicism in general, and of monks in particular. He
was convinced, and often said, that monastic life was fundamentally
unnatural, and even in the modern world only the vigilance of
Protestant civilization, and a watchful police force, restrained its
worst abuses. Given half a chance, Stanbrook and Ampleforth would
be sinks of iniquity, as he believed most monasteries of the Middle
Ages had been. And Coulton's understanding of the historian's craft
was curiously and characteristically Victorian in the Gradgrind
manner. He thought it was the job of the historian to establish facts
in order to confute errors, and in the writings of Cardinal Gasquet
he saw error incarnate. For 40 years he pursued him, writing letters
to newspapers and journals, challenging him to debate, publishing
pamphlets, denouncing his duplicity, listing his errors and ramming
home the moral that lies, superficiality and unprofessionalism were
the constant marks of Catholicism. Coulton hated Catholicism,
but he despised Anglo-Catholicism, which he saw as a self-deluding

ecclesiastical fad, maintained by woolly thinking and an ignorance of the realities of the Middle Ages. His own most popular book, *Ten Medieval Studies*, one of Cambridge University Press's more profitable ventures, was a set of polemical historical essays from reviews such as the *Hibbert Journal*, explicitly designed to 'defend the moderate Anglican position against the misrepresentations of writers who disparage modern civilisation in comparison with a purely imaginary and unhistorical idea of medieval life'. The essay titles –'The monastic legend', 'Romanism and morals', 'The failure of the friars'– speak for themselves.[4]

In 1906 Coulton produced a fascinating fictional equivalent to these scholarly labours, the novel *Friar's Lantern*, in which a decent but deluded Anglo-Catholic curate, Herbert 'Rasher' Rashleigh, and a sly and duplicitous Catholic priest, Fr Duvet, are magically transported back to England in the 1320s, to learn the hard way how brutal, ghastly and unhygienic the Middle Ages were. The novel dwells a good deal on the ubiquity in Merry England of snot and sewage; it portrays the fourteenth-century episcopate as greasily cruel and corrupt; and it gives a gleeful account of the killing of Lord Halifax (thinly disguised as Lord Halfwayhouse) by a popish mob. Rashleigh himself, the Anglo-Catholic scales at last removed from his eyes by his terrifying encounter with the moral and intellectual squalor of medieval Christianity, survives by disguising himself as a Franciscan friar, but is eventually driven to confess his newly rediscovered Protestantism and is burned at the stake. He promptly reawakens in his own time, to labour henceforth as a decent and devoted muscular Protestant. His erstwhile friend Fr Duvet is equally disillusioned but, being a popish priest, will not admit it. Nevertheless, he eventually quietly abandons his parish and his religion and sneaks away, as popish priests do, to marry a plump little widow and set up as a stockbroker in the city.[5]

For all his prejudices, Coulton had an unrivalled knowledge of medieval complaint literature and episcopal and monastic visitation records (from which he distilled his bleak picture of the realities of monastic and parochial life in the Middle Ages), and there is no question that he wiped the floor with Gasquet. But, although he was almost always right, and Gasquet almost always wrong, there is a deadening and unrelenting feel to his ceaseless marshalling of ugly facts to discredit the legend of the Ages of Faith, and a modern reader of their works cannot avoid the sense that Gasquet, for all his criminal carelessness and breathtaking disregard for evidence, had a surer sense of what medieval religion had actually been about than did his formidable opponent. Coulton's Whiggishness, and his total lack of sympathy for the materials of which he was superficially the master, rendered him tone deaf to anything but dissonance and decay: his picture of medieval Christianity, painted entirely in shadow, ultimately fails to convince.

When Dickens began to write, therefore, the history of the late medieval English Church had long been a sectarian battleground, and as a historian he would scrupulously seek to avoid sounding like Coulton. As we shall see, his treatment of institutions such as monasticism was far more judicious and even-handed than the relentless case for the prosecution that underlies everything that Coulton wrote on the subject. But Dickens himself could not help being touched by Coultonian presuppositions. He too came from impeccably Protestant stock. Dickens's paternal grandfather, chief inspector of the Alexandra Dock in Hull, was an old-style Tory Anglican churchwarden. His maternal grandfather, by contrast, was a Liberal in politics and a Primitive Methodist local preacher, given, in Dickens's own words, to 'emotional testifyings' and 'denouncing strong drink from the eminence of a wagonette'. Dickens remembered as a child walking Sunday by Sunday hand-in-hand to chapel with the old man, the latter 'resplendent in silk hat, morning coat, gold Albert and whiskers', and he recalled with affection a household where 'strict sabbatarianism, teetotalism and fundamentalism' went alongside 'the utmost tenderness to a child', and where, every Sunday morning, a packet of sweets from his grandparents helped to brighten 'the endless deserts of sermonising'.[6]

He was therefore, by both lines of descent, a Protestant to his fingertips, and his inherited religious outlook was to colour all his work on the Middle Ages. Despite meticulous courtesy and a conscious desire to be fair in all that he wrote, for him 'Catholic' would always carry a whiff of the exotic, would always in his hands be a term of at least mild disapprobation, and 'Protestant', by contrast, an accolade. This emerges with startling and comical clarity in one of his most charming books, his *Portrait* of the East Riding of Yorkshire (*charming*, by the way, is a thoroughly Dickensian word, although in his hands it usually means engagingly untrue – thus Catholic legends of the saints were 'charming'). Dickens closed this genial and unbuttoned guidebook to the East Riding with a pen-picture of the town of Beverley. Discussing the minster there, he developed a revealing comparison with Chartres Cathedral. Chartres, he thought, in its exuberant elaboration represented 'the Catholic Church, organised on every side by logic and law, yet within this compass luxuriously human, infinitely anthropomorphic', 'seething' with the figures of men and women, not merely the 'bible in stone' but 'a petrification of all Christian and pagan history'. 'Early English Beverley seems by contrast proto-Protestant; it suggests the crags of the mountain-top or, more properly, the bare glade in early spring, where the individual soul stands in loneliness face-to-face with its own sense of God.' 'I call it half protestant', he wrote,

> the symbol of *ecclesia anglicana* [...] yet might one not rather regard the spirit which informed its builders as a survival of the Celtic strain in English Christianity? Despite the Roman philosophies and forms of administration, did not this more truly native strain continue to grow underground and then, in the thirteenth century, when English literature also broke its long silence, did it not escape from the closer forms of continental tutelage to create these grave, sweet harmonies?[7]

This is, of course, the purest tosh, and one can only hope that he had his tongue in his cheek as he wrote it, although he was prone to get carried away by the temptation to fine writing. But it is revealing tosh all the same, every word of which is worth weighing as a key to his thinking about medieval Christianity, and not least his manifest conviction that all that is best and dearest in English religion, even in the Middle Ages, must somehow have remained free of the influence of 'Roman philosophies and forms of administration', and must either look forward to the Protestantism that was to come or backwards to an unsullied Celtic strain of Christianity, reflecting the purity of the bare crags and vales, and the lonely soul in communion with its maker.

And more overtly Coultonesque sentiments, too, would inform his writing about the Middle Ages. It was a constant emphasis of Coulton's work that romanticism about the Middle Ages was deeply anachronistic. Catholics and Anglo-Catholics viewed medieval institutions from the benign perspective of four centuries of Protestant civilization, centuries during which respect for law, decency and hygiene had become second nature to us. He conceded the civilizing and religious value of much in medieval Christianity, but the rhetorical thrust of most of his work emphasized its corruptions and its infinite inferiority to Protestant civilization. Because the average clergyman now was honest and chaste and decent, we erroneously assumed that the same must have been true in the Middle Ages. But it ain't necessarily so: had not the cathedrals been built 'partly out of the fines of unchaste priests, partly by a traffic in indulgences which one of the greatest medieval chancellors of Oxford described as more immoral still'? Ignorant of the social realities of the Middle Ages, romantic Victorians read with awe the small handful of profound 'mystical writings in which the great men of the Middle Ages tried to escape from the sordid realities of life around them by dreaming of a new heaven and a new earth'.[8] Dickens too, would sound this note, citing Coulton in the process: in the first edition of *The English Reformation* he was to warn against the 'pre-Raphaelite spectacles of our grandfathers', and insist that 'a more exact knowledge of the social background of medieval art and architecture has struck some heavy blows at Puginesque sentiment'. We should not take the church buildings of the so-called Ages of Faith as evidence of widespread zeal or devotion, for, were not these 'attractive creations', he asked,

> often commissioned by wealthy magnates anxious to buy their way into heaven, or by superstitious worldlings who subscribed to building funds by buying indulgences? Do not the works themselves show that superstition and legend constantly stood at the elbows of designers and carvers? [...] Such questions

have been asked by scholars in their zeal to deflate that absurd Victorian romanticism which threw the age of the reformation into a false perspective.[9]

If he shared some of Coulton's presuppositions, however, Dickens's practice as a historian of medieval religion differed radically from that of the older man. The essential difference lay in Dickens's awareness that, for a real understanding of late medieval religion, we had to move beyond institutional sources such as chronicles and visitation records to mine more local and personal materials – most momentously, in his case, wills and their preambles but also ecclesiastical court books, personal correspondence and commonplace books, and specifically the abundant manuscript holdings of the great northern depositories. Dickens's Reformation writing, therefore, would consistently be set against the background not merely of external institutions such as monasteries and chantries, or the writings of major figures like More or Erasmus. He had a good knowledge of fourteenth-century mystical writers such as Richard Rolle and Walter Hilton. But he also brought to the study of the Reformation a new late medieval perspective afforded by his own detailed research on the unpublished writings of Yorkshire clerics from Thomas Ashby, an Augustinian canon of Bridlington, to Robert Parkyn, the mid-Tudor vicar of Adwick le Street near Doncaster, work undertaken originally at the suggestion of Sir Maurice Powicke in the 1930s.

All of this material would be very effectively and powerfully reprocessed in the opening chapter of *The English Reformation* into his picture of the archaisms and inadequacies of late medieval Christianity, what he called 'the popular and conventional religions' (notice the revealing plural there). For some of this material Dickens had a real respect: in a lecture on the Decorated Gothic of his parish church at Cottingham he reflected on Victorian prejudice against the decadence of late medieval Gothic styles in favour of the more chaste early English, and had this to say:

the fourteenth century [...] saw not merely Flamboyant and Perpendicular [architecture], but Chaucer, Boccaccio, Petrarch, the rise of vernacular literatures, the origins of the Classical renaissance, and some of the greatest mystics in Christian history [...] altogether, if fourteenth century religion, art or literature were decadent, then Midsummer must be decadent as compared with Spring! When dogmatic theories bring us to such a point, it seems time to jettison the dogmas and start thinking again.[10]

Dickens's admiration and sympathy for certain aspects of late medieval religion is manifestly sincere and well informed – he spoke of the writings of Walter Hilton, for example, as the work of 'an obvious spiritual aristocrat – lucid, sane, exquisitely discriminating'. He wrote eloquently and movingly about the reformed Franciscans and the Carthusians, fountains of living water in 'the desert of late monasticism'. Recalling bitter Protestant denunciations of midnight pilgrimages in quest of holiness and blessing to the ruins of the Yorkshire Carthusian priory of Mount Grace by 'diverse sundry and superstitious and popishly affected persons', he commented that 'For once the folk-memory did not greatly err'. But that 'for once' is revealing, and despite these genuine sensitivities, images of decadence and decay are never far away whenever he writes about the religion of the fifteenth and early sixteenth centuries.[11]

For all his protestations about the need to think again, Dickens's discoveries in the devotional commonplace books of late medieval Yorkshire clergymen were presented less as integrated elements in a coherent religious symbol system than as exhibits in a freak show. Like Erasmus, one of his intellectual heroes, he looked at the framework of medieval religion and saw no coherence or design, only a monstrous heap of littleness. The first chapter of the first edition of *The English Reformation* begins with the words 'There was once a certain knight', and goes on to tell at length an elaborate and improbable medieval miracle story of the rescue of a knight from a demon by the Virgin Mary, culled from the commonplace book of Thomas Ashby. The chapter continues by itemizing the rest of the contents of Ashby's book: prayer texts to Mary and St John of Bridlington, a commentary on the Hail Mary, miracle stories, an account of the value of the opening words of

St John's Gospel in Latin as a charm, an exposition of Psalm 50, a treatise on the privileges and rites of various festivals, a scholastic disputation about whether the resurrected will be naked or clothed on Judgement Day, an English rhyme teaching transubstantiation and so on. Dickens comments wonderingly that this material was written 'not round the year 1200 but by a man who mentions Pope Julius II as still alive'. At Bridlington, therefore, 'a twelfth-century world lingered on while Machiavelli was writing *The Prince*, while the sophisticated talkers at Urbino were giving Castiglione the materials for his *Book of the Courtier*'. This world of fable, relic, miracle and indulgence, he thought, allowed 'the personality and teaching of Jesus to recede from the focus of the picture', and it could be demonstrated with 'mathematical precision' that its connection with the Christianity of the gospel 'is rather tenuous'. Medieval people were alienated by such stuff, not least by the unscriptural horrors of purgatory, which cut them off from the mercy and love of Christ: 'faced with quite terrifying views of punishment in the life to come [...] it was small wonder that they felt more comfortable with the saints than with God.'[12]

As these passages suggest, Dickens operated with a sharply polarized understanding of the difference between the medieval and humanist world views, the world of Machiavelli, Castiglione and Erasmus, on the one hand, and the wonder-world of the Golden Legend, indulgences and what he more than once called the 'crazed enthusiasm for pilgrimage', on the other. This distinction was very clear and stark in his mind: humanism looked forward, to a rational religious world in which belief was firmly based on solid biblical evidence, not on unwritten verities and ecclesiastical tradition; it stood in marked contrast to the world of 'scholastic religion', petering out in 'disharmony, irrelevance and discredit'.[13]

The obfuscating effect of this stark distinction in Dickens's own pioneering attempts to assess the religion of non-elite Catholics during the Reformation emerges most clearly in his handling of what he once called 'an old friend of forty years', the Yorkshire priest Robert Parkyn. Dickens had first encountered Parkyn in 1932, when Sir Maurice Powicke pointed him to some of Parkyn's manuscripts in the Bodleian

Library. Curate of Adwick le Street from the early 1540s until his death in 1569, Parkyn was a fascinating example of an educated but non-graduate parish priest of conservative religious convictions. Although he never attended a university, his brother John was a fellow of Trinity College, Cambridge, and through him Parkyn had access to a world of learning not commonly available to parish clergy. Parkyn was a copious, although unpublished, writer. Dickens edited Parkyn's ferocious narrative of the Reformation, written in Mary's reign, as well as some of his 'charming' devotional writings.

Dickens understood perfectly well that Parkyn was an important and emblematic figure, but his evident intellectual difficulty in categorizing or accounting for Parkyn's religion throws a great deal of light on the critical standards he brought to the study of the late Middle Ages. From the historiographical perspective of the early twenty-first century, Parkyn looks like a fairly typical intelligent mid-Tudor churchman. Much in his religion, it is true, was old-fashioned. His parish included the ruins of Hampole Priory and he was keenly interested in spiritual direction and the life of prayer: unsurprisingly, his commonplace books include copies of three of the major works of Richard Rolle of Hampole. But he was emphatically not a backwoodsman: he was, for example, intensely interested in the Bible, and he compiled his own 20,000-word concordance to the Vulgate, made a chapter-by-chapter analysis of the epistles of St Paul and wrote a 10,000-line versified life of Christ incorporating material from many of the standard late medieval Bible commentaries, designed to be read aloud to his parishioners. And he was alert to the struggle for the soul of the nation being enacted all around him: he composed savage verses on Henry VIII's 'utter destrucion of holly Churche', and copied into his book a series of Thomas More's Tower prayers and a meditation by John Fisher. He was also in touch with contemporary spiritual and polemic developments: his devotional compilations drew on the writings of the London Dominican William Peryn, the first English writer to absorb and adapt the techniques of Loyola's *Spiritual Exercises*; and some time in the mid-1560s he copied out large sections of Thomas Stapleton's translation of a Spanish Counter-Reformation treatise against indiscriminate Bible-reading and the fissiparous nature of Protestantism.

Parkyn's religious and intellectual interests, with their characteristic blending of traditional spiritual and doctrinal interests with contemporary concerns and emphases, align him with many mid-Tudor intellectuals, and to describe them, as Dickens did, as 'reactionary' or 'backward-looking', is to beg a multitude of questions. Like John Fisher himself, or the Cambridge-educated monks of Syon, many Tudor ecclesiastics availed themselves of humanist writings and techniques, while seeing no contradiction or inconsistency in the presence on their shelves, alongside these new writings, of devotional and theological classics from earlier periods. We have to beware of the mistake of the makers of the *Poirot* television series, where all the houses, furniture, clothes and décor are pure 1930s, as if people endlessly purged their houses and their minds of any contents that were not of the latest fashion.

But Dickens published his most extended treatment of Parkyn under the title 'The last medieval Englishman', and his treatment of traditionalist elements in Parkyn's writings is revealingly moralistic and censorious. Parkyn's versified life of Christ, for example, composed between 1548 and 1554, includes some apocryphal material, devotional comment and theological elaboration borrowed from patristic and medieval sources, although in its prologue Parkyn declared his intention of sticking to authentic scripture, and he normally distinguishes non-biblical material with some explicit marker. However, Dickens took the presence of this extra-biblical material to represent an incorrigible medievalism, and commented severely, 'despite these good intentions he nevertheless devotes many stanzas to the pretty legends' and '*most reprehensibly of all* [...] he invents long discussions between the apostles as they await Pentecost'. Dickens was specially shocked that Parkyn's poem gave the Virgin Mary a central role among the apostles at Pentecost, deliberately making her 'the dominating figure of the nascent Church', and he shook his head sorrowfully that, as late as 1550, 'a virtuous, sincere and by no means uneducated parish priest could so manipulate these passages', evidence of 'an obstinate

denial of the principle which had its origin in humanism – that
belief must be based upon a close scrutiny of original sources,
rather than upon the unsupported authority of medieval doctors
or upon writers of pious fiction': all this was a demonstration of the
intellectual slackness of much late medieval religion.[14]

One needs to remember that Dickens is talking here about a
poem, albeit not a very good one. Would he have applied the same
stark criteria, one wonders, to the long and equally unscriptural
conversations invented by Milton for God, Adam and Eve, Lucifer,
Michael and the apostles in *Paradise Lost* and *Paradise Regained*? And
it is surely astonishing that a man so sensitive to painting as Dickens
should see no connection between Parkyn's allegedly incorrigible
medieval obscurantism in placing Mary at the centre of the apostles
in the upper room at Pentecost and the powerful images of precisely
the same scene painted, for example, by Botticelli in the flood tide
of the Florentine Renaissance. These are pictures in which Mary,
her billowing robe making her look pregnant, has her eyes thrown
upwards and hands raised in trance like a sibyl while the apostles
cower around her under the rain of the Holy Fire – providing an
unforgettable image of Holy Mother Church, caught up in the
spirit, pregnant with the future that Pentecost inaugurates.

In many ways Dickens admired the conservative spirituality of
Robert Parkyn, but he thought it sapped by the weaknesses of all
late medieval ascetical piety, which he tended to lump together
under the blanket term *devotio moderna*. It was too demanding and
esoteric for the common man, and it offered no 'fighting creed' that
could stand up against the cold winds of reform. Parkyn's world
thus seemed to him irremediably backward-looking and powerless
to counteract or to absorb the Reformation, above all because of its
lack of intellectual rigour. He blamed this lack on the 'dead hand of
University scholasticism', on the deficiency of reforming zeal among
what he called civil service bishops, and on the general 'stodginess'
of clerical leadership: by 1500, he thought, it was too late to mend.

I doubt if Dickens in fact *knew* very much about the content
of university scholasticism around 1500. At the point at which he
was writing nobody did, and his judgement on the stodginess and

inadequacy of the early Tudor episcopate has not been borne out by subsequent studies.[15] And the quality of episcopal leadership was not the only specific aspect of late medieval religious life on which Dickens's views have come to seem dated: already when Dickens was writing *The English Reformation*, proto-revisionist work such as that of Peter Heath on the early Tudor clergy was available to him. But much of what makes modern historians of the late medieval Church uneasy with some of Dickens's views is a matter not so much of fact as of emphasis. His judgement on late medieval monasticism was not notably more negative than that of Dom David Knowles, but the conclusions he drew from the evidence were significantly different. They both, for example, chose Prior William More of Worcester as an emblematic picture of the worldliness of late medieval Benedictinism. But where Dickens saw in More's genteel and decent worldliness a token that late medieval monks had forfeited all right to the respect of the laity, Knowles saw in it rather the characteristic Erastianism and spiritual philistinism not of medieval but of Tudor England, and the main reason for the failure of the monks to rise to the challenge of the Reformation. In all respects, he wrote, Prior More 'was the child of his age. When the moment came, he and all his community duly subscribed to the Oath of Succession and to the series of declarations repudiating the pope. He followed, in fact, both for good and for evil, the way of the world.'[16]

It is instructive also to compare their apparently very similar treatments of Butley Priory. Knowles, like Dickens before him, used the chronicle of Butley to portray a monastery whose fundamental values had been invaded and subverted by gentry and aristocratic patronage. Once again, Dickens took this to mean that medieval monasticism had forfeited the respect of the laity. Knowles, however, saw in it the 'characteristic Tudor exploitation of a religious house without any evidence of gratitude or patronage of its best interests', an indication of something amiss in lay society as much as in the monasteries. Despite his own stern assessment of the slackness of monastic life on the eve of the Reformation, he would not, I think, have endorsed Dickens's judgement that the respectable worldliness of the canons of Butley proved that

'English monasticism was too old, too enfeebled, too forgotten to die violently amid dramatic passions'.[17]

For all Dickens's attempts at fair-mindedness, then, and despite his concession that late medieval religion contained both 'inspiring and mitigating features', his sense of the bankruptcy and failure of the late medieval Church was all-pervasive. He was aware of the problematic nature of the evidence for the persistence of Lollardy, and took aboard McFarlane's and Thompson's scepticism about its intellectual coherence, but he believed nonetheless that it was growing in the late fifteenth century, essentially as a manifestation of anticlericalism, and the intellectual restiveness of laymen and women, weary of the replacement of central beliefs by marginalia such as purgatory and saint worship, starved by a reactionary episcopate of proper biblical nourishment. Like Coulton, if less stridently, change and decay in all around he saw, and that perception sometimes led him into inconsistency. Dickens thought, for example, that the doctrine of purgatory was a terrifying, if unscriptural, central plank of late medieval devotion: relief from its fears was one of the reasons why Tudor men and women listened to the reformers. But in an early study of the municipal dissolution of charities in York in 1536 he considered that chantries in general by 1530 'commanded little veneration', and in *The English Reformation* he deduced from this fact the possibility that even before the Reformation 'a marked decline of interest, a more sceptical and secular attitude, was beginning to manifest itself'.[18]

The Reformation, therefore, merely completed a work already begun in the late Middle Ages. His essay on the York chantries opens boldly: 'When the ministers of Edward VI finally dissolved the chantries and similar foundations they were striking at a complex of institutions already in process of decay and liquidation.' This notion that the decline of chantry foundation on the eve of the Reformation implied the collapse of late medieval lay confidence in the value of intercession for the dead and the doctrine of purgatory has not been supported by subsequent work in the area. Barry Dobson, considering the same York material, concluded that the cessation of chantry foundation was a consequence of the economic difficulties of the city, and reflected no diminution of interest in intercession for the dead. On the contrary, on the eve of the Reformation, 'the endowment of prayers for the dead [...] continued to be the aspiration of every York merchant who could possibly afford it'.[19]

To sum up, Dickens's treatment of the late medieval Church was novel and groundbreaking in its attentiveness to hitherto neglected or undervalued sources such as clerical commonplace books. He understood, as few historians before him had done, that the liturgy was a key element in the religion of the late Middle Ages, and that much in the liturgy was noble and Christian. But he never pursued that insight, and he divorced the piety that he found in the clerical manuscripts he studied from the liturgical piety that lies at the centre of every priest's experience. It does not seem to have occurred to him that the daily celebration of Mass and office might have put Christ, rather than 'flying demons and saintly thaumaturges', somewhere near the centre of these men's religion. He was appreciative of the more refined features of late medieval ascetical and mystical piety but thought it too arcane for the common man, and not robust enough to withstand the bracing airs of biblical Protestantism. At the root of all this was his own Protestant conviction that what the Reformation taught was healthy and true, and that what Catholicism taught was unwholesome and false. In the devastatingly revealing opening sentence of the 1989 edition of *The English Reformation*, he declared that 'In England as elsewhere, the Protestant Reformation sought first and foremost to establish a gospel-Christianity, to maintain the authority of the New Testament evidence over mere Church tradition and human inventions'.[20]

That fundamental perception coloured his approach to every aspect of late medieval religion: with perfect sincerity, considerable originality and a good deal of technical finesse he weighed the late medieval Church and invariably found it wanting. In short, Dickens thought that late medieval Christianity was ailing and played out, and that as a result it had died on its feet. To some of us, on the other hand, it looks rather as if it had those feet shot out from under it.

Walsingham:
Reformation and Reconstruction

Let us begin with an ending, with the haunting Tudor lament for the destruction of the shrine of Our Lady of Walsingham:

> In the wrackes of Walsingham
> Whom should I chuse,
> But the Queene of Walsingham
> To be guide to my muse?
> Then, thou Prince of Walsingham,
> Graunt me to frame
> Bitter plaintes to rewe thy wronge,
> Bitter wo for thy name.
> Bitter was it oh to see
> The seely sheepe
> Murdered by the ravening wolves
> While the sheephardes did sleep.
> Bitter was it, O, to view
> The sacred vine
> (Whilst the gardeners played all close)
> rooted up by the swine.
> Bitter, bitter, O, to behold
> The grass to grow

Where the walls of Walsingham
So stately did show.
Such were the worth of Walsingham
While she did stand;
Such are the wrackes as now do show
Of that so holy land.
Levell, levell with the ground
The towres doe lye,
Which with their golden glittering tops
Pearsed once to the skye.
Where were gates no gates are now, –
The ways unknown
Where the press of peers did pass
While her fame far was blown.
Oules do scrike where the sweetest himnes
Lately weer songe;
Toads and serpents hold their dennes
Wher the Palmers did thronge.
Weep, weep, O Walsingham,
Whose days are nights,
Blessings turned to blasphemies,
Holy deeds to despites.
Sin is where our Lady sat;
Heaven turned is to hell.
Satan sits where our Lord did sway;
Walsingham, O, farewell.[1]

This poem is often attributed to St Philip Howard, which would
mean it was written late in the reign of Elizabeth I by a man
who never saw the shrine in its heyday, but it seems to express
a sharper outrage at a more recent destruction, and it's been
plausibly suggested that it may in fact be the work of an eyewitness
writing earlier, perhaps in the 1540s.[2] The shrine it laments, and
which Henry VIII's commissioners destroyed in 1538, had been
established early in the twelfth century by a wealthy woman,
Richeldis de Favrache, the widow of a local Norman landowner,

Geoffrey de Favrache, mentioned but not named in the pipe rolls for 1131, from which we learn that she was about to remarry and that she had an infant son. This son must be Geoffrey junior, the founder of Walsingham Priory, established in 1153 to administer his mother's chapel, which had by then evidently become a shrine of at least local celebrity.[3]

So much can be documented from a handful of surviving contemporary records. Everything else that is usually said about the origins of the shrine, and especially its alleged foundation in 1061, is derived from a single and, sadly, extremely unreliable late fifteenth-century source, a very bad 140-line poem in rhyme royal, originally displayed for the benefit of pilgrims on a panel in the Holy House, and printed for the shrine authorities in 1496 by the London publisher Richard Pynson; it survives in a single copy in the Pepys Library of Magdalene College, Cambridge. Rediscovered and republished in the nineteenth century, this ballad is the source for the elaborate story of Richeldis's visions of Our Lady, for the account of the miraculous relocation of the Holy House from the site on which Richeldis's workmen had first tried to erect it and, crucially, for the foundation date of 1061.[4]

But no medieval document before the Pynson pamphlet offers any date for the foundation of the shrine, or of any vision of Our Lady at Walsingham, and we can only speculate what Richeldis had in mind in building her chapel. That said, there is no reason to doubt that she did indeed build a chapel to the supposed measurements of the Holy House at Nazareth. At least since the sixth century, pilgrims to the Holy Land had measured the Holy Places using pieces of knotted string, so that they could build replicas to the same dimensions for the benefit of those unable to make the long and dangerous journey across land and sea. These replicas were believed to convey the same blessings as their originals, and the Stations of the Cross, for example, grew out of a similar urge to provide the spiritual benefits of following the Via Dolorosa for the folks back home. So what distinguished the shrine at Walsingham from every other Marian shrine in the country, and helps explain why it became *the* leading English

shrine of Our Lady, was that it was centred on a replica of the
Holy House of Nazareth, the location of the Annunciation and
the moment when, it was believed, the eternal Word of God took
human flesh in the womb of Mary.

For the shrine's first century or so pilgrim numbers remained
small, to judge by the poverty of the priory. What changed that
was the favour shown to Walsingham by the royal builder of
Westminster Abbey, Henry III. Starting in 1226, he made a dozen
pilgrimages to Walsingham and showered the shrine with lavish
benefactions, including, in 1241, the gift of wax for 3,000 tapers
to burn at the shrine on the feast of the Assumption. And where
the king led, courtiers and the fashionable followed, the 'press of
peers' mentioned in the Tudor lament. Edward I, Henry's son, was
even more devoted to the shrine than his father, and thereafter, till
the break with Rome, every English monarch except Richard III
made at least one pilgrimage to Walsingham. Signs of royal favour
accumulated, not least in Henry VIII's reign, when Catherine of
Aragon donated the triumphant English battle standards after the
Battle of Flodden. Though we have no way of measuring statistically,
by the early fifteenth century Walsingham's religious celebrity was
exceeded only by Becket's shrine at Canterbury, and perhaps not
even by that. The priory, throughout the twelfth century the poor
cousin of other Augustinian houses, had become one of the richest
monasteries in England, and the shrine itself gloriously decorated
not only with the usual wax ex-votos but also with the accumulated
wealth donated by grateful pilgrims – as Erasmus saw for himself
in 1511, 'you would say it was the abode of saints, so dazzling it
is with jewels, gold and silver'. All that came to an abrupt end
with the dissolution of the shrine in July 1538: the shrine image
was carted off to Thomas Cromwell's house at Chelsea and in all
probability burned alongside other famous images: Our Lady of
Worcester, Our Lady of Ipswich and Our Lady of Willesden. The
gold and silver ex-votos were dispatched to the king's jewel house,
and the priory unroofed.[5]

There is no way of measuring the psychic and emotional impact
of the sudden destruction of England's greatest Marian shrine,

though even before the shrine itself had been dismantled an abortive rising, the so-called Walsingham plot of 1537, led to the execution for treason of a number of Walsingham men, including the sub-prior of the monastery.[6] But resistance did not last. The memory of Walsingham's reputation as England's Nazareth, a 'Holy Land', lingered till the end of the century and is reflected in a cluster of (occasionally disreputable) Elizabethan love poems, including Ophelia's song in the mad scene in Hamlet.[7]

And then the shrine effectively disappears from English consciousness till the nineteenth century. An amateurish excavation of the priory grounds in 1854 correctly identified the site of the Holy House, but the first comprehensive discussion of the shrine did not appear till 1879, with the publication of the Roman Catholic antiquary Edmund Waterton's *Pietas Mariana Britannica*, an idealized evocation of medieval England as 'Mary's dowry'. Waterton's romantic medievalism had more than a touch of Ye Olde English Tea Shoppe about it – he insisted on spelling Our Lady's name and title with a terminal 'e': 'Marye', 'Ladye'. But he devoted 54 pages to a detailed account of the medieval shrine and its similarities to the more famous shrine of Loreto, with copious documentation from the priory's cartulary, from the Pynson ballad, from records of royal and aristocratic benefactions, from William of Worcester's measurements of the Holy House from 1479, from Erasmus's satirical account of his pilgrimage in 1511 and from the official records of the priory's dissolution.[8]

Pietas Mariana Britannica attracted a very wide readership, Anglican as well as Roman Catholic, and those readers included an outstanding Tractarian priest, Arthur Wagner, vicar for 50 years of St Paul's, Brighton. Wagner was an archetypal eminent Victorian, who used his considerable personal wealth to build housing for the poor of Brighton and founded a religious order for women working with charity schools and reformed prostitutes, and he built a series of vast and spectacular chapels of ease in the town, which all became flagships for advanced Anglo-Catholic ritual and teaching. Wagner was a voracious reader with a long-standing interest in Walsingham, which the publication of *Pietas Mariana Britannica* focused. In 1886 he built a church dedicated to the Virgin Mary on his country estate at Buxted in Sussex. Its Lady Chapel was built to the measurements of the Holy House at Loreto, and an internal screen marked off the dimensions of the Holy House at Walsingham as reported by William of Worcester. There was no statue, and no attempt to revive pilgrimage, but within a decade of its construction this Buxted Walsingham Chapel would exercise a decisive influence on the revival of Roman Catholic pilgrimage to Walsingham itself and, in the longer term, on the creation of the Anglican shrine.[9]

The link between Buxted and Walsingham was Fr Philip Fletcher. In the early 1870s Fletcher had been one of Wagner's curates at St Bartholomew's, Brighton, and though he soon after became a Roman Catholic, Fletcher remained grateful for all he had learned from Wagner, and he was interested in the creation of the Walsingham Chapel at Buxted. In 1887 Fletcher was one of the two co-founders of the Guild of Our Lady of Ransom, a Roman Catholic organization dedicated to the conversion of England, but which also offered financial aid to impoverished Roman Catholic parishes. In 1896 the Catholic priest at King's Lynn, George Wrigglesworth, issued a public appeal for funds to replace his ruinous Pugin church: on behalf of the guild, Fletcher went to see how they could help. King's Lynn had been one of the stopping points on the northern and overseas pilgrim route to Walsingham, and had a famous fourteenth-century chapel said to be associated with the shrine, Our Lady of the Mount. Fletcher suggested that the new church in Lynn should include a Lady Chapel built to the dimensions of the Holy House, like the chapel at Buxted. Wrigglesworth, who had made the pilgrimage to Loreto, eagerly took up this suggestion. In 1897 he obtained a papal rescript from Leo XIII re-establishing the ancient shrine of Our Lady of Walsingham: according to Fletcher, the Pope had declared that 'When England comes back to Walsingham, Mary will come back to England'. On 19 August that year a new statue of Our Lady of Walsingham, carved at Oberammergau, was processed through the streets from the railway station via the Chapel on the

Mount to the new church: a crowd of hundreds, led by 30 little girls dressed in white, sang an adaptation of the Lourdes hymn, and the preacher at benediction that afternoon underlined the significance of the re-established shrine for a resurgent Roman Catholicism in England: 'All past Christian glories are ours: renew them, create others. The future of the church in this land depends on the seeds which are now sown.'

The King's Lynn chapel was to remain the official Roman Catholic shrine to Our Lady of Walsingham for another 40 years. But both Wrigglesworth and Fletcher aspired to re-establish pilgrimage in the village itself. And the means to do so seemed providentially to hand. In 1894 another wealthy Anglo-Catholic philanthropist, Charlotte Boyd, had crossed the Tiber to become a Roman Catholic. One of her many Anglican enterprises had been the purchase of former monastic sites to return to charitable and religious purposes. In 1893 she had begun negotiations to buy a medieval wayside chapel in the village of Houghton, just outside Walsingham: tradition had it that this so-called Slipper Chapel, which till recently had served as a barn and cow byre, was the place where pilgrims shed their shoes to walk the last stony mile to the Holy House. By the time she actually got hold of the chapel, however, she had changed Churches, and was now eager to see the chapel become the base for a revived Roman Catholic pilgrimage. So the day after the enthronement of the new statue in the shrine in King's Lynn, Fr Fletcher, Fr Wrigglesworth, Miss Boyd and a party of 50 members of the Guild of Our Lady of Ransom took the train to Walsingham and processed from the railway station with cross and banners to the Slipper Chapel, singing the Litany of Loreto and the 'Ave maris stella', the first public pilgrimage to Walsingham itself since the Reformation.

But at this point Fletcher's and Boyd's residual Anglican romanticism came into head-on conflict with pastoral realities and the constrained finances and manpower of a struggling Roman Catholic diocese. There were no Roman Catholics in Walsingham, and very few in north Norfolk, which was part of the vast diocese of Northampton, under Bishop Arthur Riddell. Though not blind to the imaginative appeal of Walsingham, Riddell's priority was the provision of pastoral care for the larger centres of population in the region. He was willing to consider establishing a mission priest at the Slipper Chapel, as a basis for outreach to nearby towns such as Dereham, Fakenham and Wells. But Miss Boyd mistakenly believed that the Slipper Chapel had been run by Benedictine monks in the Middle Ages, and dreamed of re-establishing a monastic community there. An increasingly exasperated correspondence resulted in her offering the chapel to the diocese for the unrealistically large price of £2,000: on the bishop's refusal, she donated the chapel to Downside Abbey. Riddell, however, withheld permission for any public *cultus* at the chapel, including the celebration of Mass, and, when the priest of the Suffolk Benedictine parish of Beccles broached the possibility of organizing a parish pilgrimage to Walsingham, told him that 'There is only one pilgrimage approved by me, that to the Shrine of Our Lady of Walsingham at Lynn. I cannot approve of any other.' In fact, Bishop Riddell did not rule out the idea of a revived pilgrimage in Walsingham itself, but considered that 'The only reason to my mind for translating the Shrine from Lynn would be the recovery of the exact spot of the ancient shrine and the reconstruction of the old Loreto [...] We must wait patiently for better times in North Norfolk.'

In fact, the aspiration to get hold of the original site of the Holy House very nearly materialized: the heir presumptive to the Lee-Warner estates, which included the priory site, became a Roman Catholic in 1907 and made a solemn vow to restore the Holy House as a Roman Catholic shrine when he came into possession. In the event, however, the desperate finances of the estates meant that they passed instead into the hands of the Lee-Warners' bankers, the Gurney family, originally Quakers, and the dream of a restored Roman Catholic Holy House evaporated.[10]

It was at this point that Fr Alfred Hope Patten entered the story.[11] Hope Patten was a charismatic but complex character, who has always divided opinion. Dogged by recurrent bouts of ill health, real or imagined, and quite probably dyslexic, Hope Patten had a phobia about examinations, left school at 16 and never went to university. Though he subsequently acquired a remarkable stock of specialist ecclesiastical learning, like many autodidacts his mind was narrowly focused, and he found it almost impossible to see other people's points of view. But he was handsome, charming, austerely devout and, when enthused, hugely energetic, and his charm, energy and single-mindedness enabled the creation and preservation of the Anglican shrine.

Hope Patten was that rare and exotic creature, an Anglican papalist.[12] Raised in the advanced ritualism of Brighton's Anglo-Catholic churches, he came to believe that the Church of England was neither an autonomous body nor a distinct branch of the universal Church but an integral part of Western Christendom, owing obedience to the Pope though sadly separated by tragic historical circumstance from visible communion with the Holy See – he preferred to speak of the provinces of Canterbury and York rather than the Church of England. Anglican clergy were therefore obliged to obey the laws and liturgical norms of the broader Western Church, including celibacy of the clergy, and any local canons, formularies or episcopal diktats in conflict with those wider norms could and should be ignored or circumvented. Some Anglo-papalist clergy followed the logic of this and used the entire Roman liturgy in Latin, and after 1912 most probably used the English Missal, a translation of the Roman Missal into Tudor-style prose, with a few modifications to permit the inclusion of some elements of the Book of Common Prayer. Anglo-papalists dismissed more genteel, self-consciously English forms of high-churchmanship as 'British Museum religion', and favoured fiddle-backed vestments, birettas and Baroque church architecture. They were militant, self-consciously transgressive and opposition-minded, effectively congregationalist in their ecclesiology and constitutionally suspicious of bishops, whom they were prone to view as troublesome, dubiously Christian agents of the secular state.

Travels in France and Belgium gave Hope Patten a vision of what English parish churches might have looked like if there had been no Reformation, and models for how they ought to look now. A series of curacies in Anglo-Catholic parishes, including a year at Buxted, consolidated all this. He discovered a lifelong fascination with relics, developed a strong Eucharistic piety and, at Buxted in particular, fell in love with the idea of Walsingham. Public devotion to the Blessed Virgin had never been a dominant feature of mainstream Tractarianism, but the Angelus, rosary and litany of Loreto featured large in Anglo-papalist piety, alongside the service of Benediction with the Blessed Sacrament, for most other high-churchmen a bridge too far along the road to Rome, and in the late 1910s and 1920s a particular red rag to the majority of the episcopate.

In 1921 Hope Patten was offered the post of vicar of Walsingham, an impoverished living with three churches, which, after months of indecision, he accepted with an explicit determination to restore the pilgrimage and, with it, devotion to the Blessed Virgin within the Anglican Church. Within a year of his arrival he had found in the British Museum a seal depicting the medieval shrine image, and commissioned a replica (carved by a Roman Catholic Carmelite nun) which was solemnly blessed and installed in the Lady Chapel of the parish church in July 1922, and the practice of daily recitation of the rosary before the statue was begun. The first pilgrimage was advertised through the Anglo-papalist League of Our Lady for late October the same year. It was a catastrophe: only two of the expected 40 pilgrims for whom food and accommodation had been provided turned up. With characteristic resourcefulness Hope Patten marched into the village rounding up anyone not bed-bound or out at work, formed them into a procession, and the pilgrimage went ahead as a parish event.

But soon a more successful pattern emerged, with several residential pilgrimages a year recruited initially from Anglo-papalist networks in London and the south coast, eventually extending to include parties from Anglo-Catholic parishes in the Midlands and north. These jamborees were soon given additional weight by the presence of Mowbray Stephen O'Rorke, former bishop of Accra, who became rector of nearby Blakeney in 1924, and who (despite remonstrations from the bishop of Norwich) cheerfully presided at High Mass and solemn pontifical Vespers and Benediction as part of the pilgrimage liturgy, wearing a mitre a good deal taller and more impressive than the Pope's. Houses in the village were acquired to serve as pilgrim hostels, nuns recruited from Yorkshire to assist the pilgrims, an association of priests formed to promote interest in Anglo-Catholic parishes and a journal, *Our Lady's Mirror*, created to inform and promote the growing network of supporters. Gradually the parish church was transformed into an ever more appropriate setting for pilgrimage, as it filled up with statues, lamps, reliquaries and side-altars.

Remarkably, Hope Patten seems to have managed all this without alienating his conservative Norfolk parishioners, at least in his early years in Walsingham: a steady stream of local lads was recruited as altar boys, attendance at the Sunday High Mass was regularly in three figures and stolid north Norfolkers even queued for the confessional, though Eustace Gurney, the local squire and owner of the priory grounds, remained hostile.

All this eventually aroused the vigilance of the bishop of Norwich, Bertram Pollock, a conservative low-churchman who viewed the promotion of Mariolatry in his diocese with a distaste amounting to horror. In 1930 he came to see what was going on for himself and was aghast at the confessional in the north aisle, tabernacle and reliquaries in the Lady Chapel and, worst of all, the candle stand before the statue of Our Lady of Walsingham under its canopy: it was all much worse than he had feared. Bishop Pollock asked Hope Patten to replace the statue with a picture or icon, and the vicar meekly agreed to remove it from the parish church altogether. But this was not the victory the bishop might have imagined, for Hope Patten had already acquired a plot of land near the priory grounds on the Holt Road, and now determined to build a separate shrine chapel there. Quite apart from the symbolic significance of the restoration of the Holy House, a shrine based in private property would be less vulnerable to interference, far more likely to endure. And to ensure that, Hope Patten founded a college of lay and clerical guardians under a master to govern the shrine, and insulate it against episcopal meddling or change of incumbent in the parish.

Though the site of the original Holy House had been established by the excavation of 1854, Hope Patten convinced himself that this new building was in fact on the exact site of the original, a conviction cemented when a sealed-up Saxon well was discovered in the course of digging the foundations. Walsingham, like Lourdes, would have its own healing waters. From this point on he would insist on the absolute continuity between the old buildings and the new. The robed and crowned statue was solemnly processed to its new home by a crowd of hundreds led by white-clad maidens on 15 October 1931. The preacher that day was one of Hope Patten's mentors, the uncompromising Anglo-papalist Fr Alban Baverstock, whose sentiments on the occasion were apocalyptic:

> On all sides attacks are being made on traditional Christian doctrine and morals […] And too often the Anglican trumpeter gives an uncertain note, or even seems to sound on behalf of the Enemy. We learn to our sorrow that our Bishops cannot be depended upon to defend Christian doctrine or even Christian morals. But we must not lose heart on this account. Put not your trust in princes, not even in princes Ecclesiastical. The Enemy is coming in like a flood. But surely here in Walsingham, with the re-erection of England's Nazareth, with its shrine to the Incarnation, the Spirit of the Lord is lifting up a banner. Faith will rally in those whose hearts are His round this banner. And where there is faith in the Holy Incarnation, faith in the Word made flesh of Mary's flesh, there victory is assured. This is the victory that overcometh the world, even our faith.[13]

Though the 1920s and '30s were in fact the heyday of Anglo-Catholicism, there is a defiantly beleaguered air to the sermon, and those most involved with the shrine in those years undoubtedly shared Baverstock's sense of belonging to an enlightened but embattled remnant. There are accounts of some of the pilgrims in those years sallying out in small groups to recite the rosary in some of the more conventional parish churches in the Walsingham area, buoyed up by the sense that in doing so they were striking a blow for the full faith. But while Hope Patten himself shared all that, he did also see the shrine as a powerhouse for the rest of the Church of England, an instrument of the Anglo-papalist project of reunion with the Holy See by transforming Anglican practice Romewards from the grassroots up. And he was anything but apologetic about his papalism. The Latin inscription on the dedication stone of the shrine chapel read:

> This Shrine, founded in the year 1061 at the will of the Blessed Virgin Mother of God in honour of the mystery of the sacred Incarnation [...] and afterwards utterly overthrown by the King who raged with the most foul love of gain (on whose soul may God have mercy) now for the first time in the year 1931 and the ninth year of the pontificate of our most holy Lord Pius XI. P.M. was restored, Bertram Bishop of the Church of Norwich, and Hope Patten parish priest of Walsingham holding office. A.M.D.G.[14]

Bishop Pollock was not amused and insisted his name be removed from what became known as the 'stone of offence', despite Hope Patten's explanation that the inscription was intended

> as a witness to the claim of Anglicans, which claim our English Roman 'friends' will not allow, namely that we (the donors) believe that in this year of grace 1931 the rightful parish priest of Walsingham is Hope Patten, *not* Fr Grey of Fakenham – and that the true bishop of the diocese is Dr Pollock and not the Bishop of Northampton.[15]

The paradox was, of course, that, devoted as he was to Roman ways, and from the late 1930s incorporating more and more of those ways directly into the shrine's worship, he never in fact much liked English Roman Catholics, 'our brethren of the Italian mission' – and, it must be admitted, with some reason. In 1925 the abbot of Downside had refused permission for Anglicans to recite the rosary in the Slipper Chapel, and when in 1932 Hope Patten asked the

monks of Prinknash to print some prayer cards for the shrine, he
had been rebuffed by the abbot, who wrote, insufferably:

> You see, dear Sir, we Catholics naturally feel that the
> Pre-Reformation Shrine should be in our hands, from which
> it was torn at the Reformation. While we rejoice sincerely at
> the revival of devotion to the Blessed Mother of God among
> Anglicans, we feel that her official cultus belongs to us.[16]

And by the mid-1930s the brethren of the Italian mission had arrived
on Hope Patten's own doorstep. In 1931 Downside Abbey, discouraged by the continuing episcopal prohibition of public worship at
the Slipper Chapel, donated it to the diocese of Northampton. But
in 1933 Laurence Youens, a former Anglican enthusiastic about
the idea of a Roman Catholic presence at Walsingham, became
bishop of Northampton, and immediately set about restoring the
Slipper Chapel. A statue modelled, like the Anglican one, on the
Walsingham Priory seal was installed there under a painted canopy,
and on 19 August 1934 Cardinal Bourne, a sick man with only
months to live, accompanied by eight of the bishops of England
and Wales, led a huge open-air pilgrimage of 12,000 people in
the meadow beside the Slipper Chapel, and designated the chapel
England's national shrine of Our Lady. In the following year
Youens appointed a newly ordained priest, Bruno Scott James, as
custodian of the shrine. A former Anglican monk, Scott James had
in fact spent some time living under Hope Patten's tutelage, and
had made his decision to become a Roman Catholic at the deserted
Slipper Chapel itself. He now began an unconventional and, to
Hope Patten's eyes, provocative ministry at the Slipper Chapel.[17]

Despite the huge numbers at the inauguration in 1934, Roman
Catholic pilgrimage to Walsingham was slow to build: rank-and-
file Catholic devotion to Mary was more likely to express itself
at European shrines such as Lourdes or Fatima than in a remote
village in north Norfolk. But Scott James's charismatic personality
soon made its mark: from the middle of 1935 numbers began to
build, and he took to preaching in the open air from the steps of

the Slipper Chapel, sometimes up to eight times a day, often with his elegant Siamese cat perched on his shoulder. He also exercised a powerful ministry to students and working men through the confessional, and by 1938 he estimated that at least 50,000 pilgrims were coming to the Slipper Chapel annually, though numbers that year must have been boosted by a 10,000-strong National Youth Pilgrimage of Reparation led by Cardinal Hinsley, to commemorate the fourth centenary of the destruction of the original shrine. These kinds of numbers, significantly larger than those who could be attracted from the much smaller constituency available to the Anglican shrine, made expansion at the Slipper Chapel necessary. Scott James bought the meadow next door and built an open-air altar for large events, and added a new sacristy and chapel of the Holy Spirit, as well as a lavatory block. These signs of Roman Catholic temerity were resented, and letters of protest flowed in, including a remonstrance from the dean of Norwich, to which Scott James replied sweetly that he quite understood that when the Slipper Chapel had been in Anglican hands, and used for animals and crops, no building work had been needed, but now that it was in Catholic hands and once again being used for worship 'some development was necessary'.[18]

For both shrines the years leading up to the Second World War were a boom time, and both were enlarged to accommodate expanding numbers, and the Anglican shrine took on its present rather exotic appearance. But the outbreak of war put an end to any expansion: Walsingham, surrounded by Battle of Britain airfields, was in a high-security zone and effectively closed to pilgrims. So both shrines had to start again in 1945.

The story of Walsingham since the end of the Second World War is a story of a slow broadening, and emergence from different kinds of ghetto. Both shrines, like their medieval predecessor, had been founded to bear witness to the foundational doctrine of Christianity, that the word was made flesh and dwelt among us. The Holy House and the Slipper Chapel were each meant to be images of that larger house of God in which the whole of humanity is invited to find its home. But, being the product of human fallibility, they were both also fortresses of exclusion – outposts on the hostile front line between the two Churches and, in the case of the Anglican shrine, of divisions within a single Church, a badge of party.

And the Anglican shrine experienced a period of drift immediately after the war. Fr Hope Patten was ageing, and many of his projects, such as the creation of a college of canons at the shrine following the Augustinian rule, were to end in failure. And although the number of parishes linked to the Anglican shrine continued to grow, the shrine's appeal was still very much confined to a self-defining constituency of advanced Anglo-Catholics, easily dismissed as high camp, the resort of the gin, lace and biretta brigade – that is how it is affectionately satirized as 'the Walsingham Way' in Andrew Wilson's blackly comic novel *The Healing Art*.[19]

But the very foundations of the Anglo-papal movement which had given birth to the shrine were about to be shaken. Roman Catholic Mariology reached its high point in the decade after the war, with the definition of the doctrine of the Assumption in 1950 and the Marian Year of 1954, when the apostolic delegate came to Walsingham and crowned a new statue for the Slipper Chapel before a crowd of 20,000 pilgrims in the grounds of the priory. But already there were signs of thaw in the apparently immovable iceberg of Roman Catholic teaching and practice. This was manifested liturgically in the 1950s in the revival of the Easter Vigil, and papal encouragement of dialogue and evening Masses. This trickle of change would turn into a tidal wave with the calling of the Second Vatican Council and its much more drastic reforms. Hope Patten did not live to see that, but he strongly disapproved even of Pius XII's modest reforms, and put a notice up in the shrine church forbidding congregations to make the responses at Mass.

The fact was that the revolution that was Vatican II cut the ground from under the whole Anglo-papalist project, which had been to prepare the Church of England for reunion with Rome by bringing Anglican theology and practice into exact conformity with ultramontane Catholicism, which seemed beyond any possibility of change. But now the Catholic Church itself seemed to be turning its back on the theological and liturgical flagpoles to which Anglo-papalism had nailed its colours. I recall my own callow amusement when, in the late 1960s, after the introduction of the stripped-down *missa normativa* of Paul VI, the Anglo-papalist vicar of St Clement's Church in Cambridge put a notice up in his porch: 'The Bishop of Rome is no longer prayed for in this Church.' Had the Anglican shrine at Walsingham remained similarly entrenched in the old ways, it would surely have withered.

But both shrines were about to experience transformation. Hope Patten died, dramatically, in 1958, immediately after officiating at benediction in the shrine church. His successor, Colin Stephenson, a more ebullient personality and a brilliant communicator, saw the need to integrate the shrine more firmly within the Norwich diocese and the wider Church of England, and he brought a more open and less beleaguered ethos to the shrine.[20] That integration was assisted by the fact that many aspects of Anglo-Catholic practice had been assimilated into mainstream Anglican worship, and by the growing number of appointments of Anglo-Catholic clergy to bishoprics. A high point in that process came in 1985 when David Hope, master of the College of Guardians and a former principal of St Stephen's House and vicar of All Saints, Margaret Street, was appointed archbishop of York. A wider range of parishes was affiliating with the shrine, and a larger and more mixed constituency turned up for the annual pilgrimages. In 1980 Robert Runcie, archbishop of Canterbury, preached at the annual pilgrimage, a precedent followed by all his successors.

The Roman Catholic shrine underwent equally profound change. One of the consequences of the conciliar changes was a significant diminishment of the dominant place of Mary in Catholic piety, a move towards a more Eucharistic focus. That may well turn out to have been a temporary swing of the pendulum. It has affected western European and British Catholics much more than Churches in Africa and Asia: it's significant that in recent years ethnically based pilgrimages to the Slipper Chapel by Tamil and Filipino Catholics resident in Britain form its largest groups, coming sometimes up to 20,000 at a time.

But unquestionably the most remarkable and momentous development has been the transformation of Anglican–Roman-Catholic relationships in Walsingham. Down to the end of the 1950s, Roman Catholics had resolutely refused any *communicatio in sacris* with Anglicans or Protestants – hence the prohibition on Anglican prayer in the Catholic shrine. The more open ecclesiology and active commitment to ecumenism of the Church after Vatican II meant that Catholics, in most cases with a huge sigh of relief, came down off the barricades and began to pray with and learn from their Christian brethren. This was facilitated by the move of the post-conciliar Church towards a different kind of Mariology, away from the exclusive emphasis on Mary's uniqueness and privileges, which in the pontificate of Pius XII had seemed likely to culminate in a theologically suspect and ecumenically disastrous definition of Mary as Mediatrix of all graces. Instead, the council proposed a Mariology of inclusiveness, in which Mary is understood as a 'Type', or symbolic embodiment, of the church and pattern of discipleship, concepts far more easily appropriated within the churches of the Reformation.

All this brought about a drastic transformation of relations between the two shrines. In 1968 the newly founded Ecumenical Society of the Blessed Virgin Mary hosted a joint meeting of Anglicans and Roman Catholics associated with Walsingham, including the two shrine administrators and the future bishop of East Anglia, Alan Clarke. They pledged themselves to encourage joint pilgrimages, to regular shared worship in both shrines, to promote each other's shrines in their literature and to establish a permanent forum for co-operation. Bishop Clark and the Anglican suffragan bishop of Lynn led the first ecumenical pilgrimage in 1970, and from then on collaboration has built steadily, a process that culminated in 2018 in the ecumenical covenant signed by the custodians of both shrines.

There were notable landmarks along this road. When in 1982 Pope John Paul II celebrated Mass in Wembley stadium, the custodians of the Anglican and Catholic shrines together carried the image of Our Lady of Walsingham to the altar. The year before, when the Anglican shrine celebrated its jubilee, the director of the Catholic shrine had preached, recognizing Hope Patten as a prophet, an instrument of unity in God's hand, and in the hand of Mary, who is the archetype of the listening disciple:

> She is here to heal those wounds of sin and divisions. She has used Fr Patten and indeed many other faithful workers. She has taught us to listen, to understand, to tolerate and to grow in love [...] Our future seems to point towards ever-closer unity. We must learn not only to pray together, which we do regularly [...] but to accept each other's differences and work together for a united future. We pray that we may be instruments in Mary's hands.[21]

It has to be said that, when these words were first spoken, the possibility of institutional unity between the Roman Catholic and Anglican Churches seemed closer to realization than it does today. The ordination of women, and differing approaches to issues of human sexuality and gender, marriage and the family – issues that exist in both Churches but which are more overt and insistent within Anglicanism – have created new and not easily resolvable barriers between the two communions. Within the Anglican communion the same issues pose difficult problems for Anglo-Catholics, and one controversial outcome of those difficulties was the creation of the ordinariate of Our Lady of Walsingham.

And the growing openness in the culture at large to material and more sacramental forms of religious expression such as pilgrimage comes at a price. It has been accompanied and perhaps enabled by a corresponding haziness about the precise meaning of such forms of expression: pilgrimage may work for more people because it is much more loosely integrated into the Catholic and Anglican orthodoxies that it once articulated. Make of it what you will, but Mgr John Armitage, Custodian of the Roman Catholic shrine, reports that the Slipper Chapel is now quite possibly the largest venue for Hindu pilgrimage in Britain, and that gifts of gold from Hindu pilgrims will help pay for new mosaic work there.[22]

But when all that has been said, there remains the unlikely fact that the wracks of Walsingham have been rebuilt: the English door into the household of Nazareth opened nine centuries ago by Richeldis is open once more, and welcoming pilgrims from every nation, tribe, tongue and, it would now seem, creed. An unhealthy zeal to collect the scalps of other Christians has been transformed to a more generous spirit, in which both shrines seek to witness to the message of the Christian doctrine of the Incarnation – the human heart of God open for human salvation, and the nurturing care of his Mother.

Writing the Reformation: Fiction and Faction

The quincentenary commemorations of the Protestant Reformation in 2017 culminated on Halloween, 31 October, the date on which Martin Luther posted his 95 Theses on the door of the castle church in Wittenberg in 1517. Except, of course, that he didn't. The story of the posting of the theses is a constructed memory, first mentioned a generation after it is alleged to have happened, a convenient mythical shorthand for processes that were in fact a good deal more complicated and long-drawn-out.[1] England, too, has its own Reformation myths. The memory of the break with Rome and all that flowed from it is inextricably associated with the Tudor dynasty, and in particular the reign of Henry VIII, a king who was already being given larger-than-life mythic status in his own lifetime, not least by Holbein's unforgettable portraits, their many versions and many derivatives. And the multiple forms of Tudor mythology remain big business. Tudor historical fiction is routinely near the top of the bookseller's charts, from C. J. Sansom's sombre whodunnits to Jean Plaidy's, Philippa Gregory's or Alison Weir's romantic romps.[2] TV audiences a few years back lapped up three series of Michael Hirst's preposterous bodice-ripping soap *The Tudors*, even though the series cast an ageless and gorgeously fey Irishman as the gross and ghastly Henry VIII, and appeared to construct its scripts by taking some of the facts and all of the fallacies about the period, adding a generous serving of sex, shaking them all up in a box and rearranging them into episode-length entertainments.[3]

Altogether more seriously, Hilary Mantel's *Wolf Hall* and *Bring Up the Bodies*, the first two volumes of the trilogy now completed by *The Mirror and the Light*, an epic based on the career of Thomas Cromwell, have both won the Booker Prize, an unprecedented feat by any author.[4] Dramatized by Mike Poulton for the National Theatre and hugely successful West End productions that moved on to Broadway, the first two books were then turned into a riveting six-part TV series starring Mark Rylance. So the key players in the struggle for the soul of early Reformation England – Cardinal Wolsey and Thomas Cranmer, Thomas Cromwell and Thomas More, and of course Henry VIII and Ann Boleyn – seem almost as familiar as the stars of *East Enders* or *Coronation Street*.

This fascination, of course, is not new: the Tudor past has always loomed in the English imagination, because the momentous repudiation of the Catholic past by three of the five Tudor monarchs was to be the determining fact of English politics for the next three centuries, feeding an emerging sense of British identity that came to understand Catholicism as intrinsically alien – conveniently, of course, forgetting that Alfred the Great, Henry V and Geoffrey Chaucer were all Catholics or that the national shrine and seat of coronations, Westminster Abbey, was built by Henry III to house the tomb of a papally canonized English king and as a shrine for a crusader relic of Christ's Holy Blood.

Commemoration is always as much about the present as the past: we mark some events and forget others, depending on how those events contribute to our own priorities and sense of identity. Catholics remember the Reformation, I suppose, mainly for what it destroyed – 'bare ruined choirs where late the sweet birds sang' – Protestants for the benefits it brought: above all, perhaps, an open Bible, symbolizing universal access to the truth without the intervention of priests, and quite possibly the single most important influence on the development of the language. And in

England Protestants have traditionally remembered too the cost of Reformation, and the sins perpetrated by its enemies. The memory of the reign of the Catholic Queen Mary, 'Bloody Mary', when the founding fathers of the Anglican Church were exiled or executed by burning alive along with almost 300 humbler Protestant men and women, would become one of the building blocks of English national consciousness. As Charles Dickens insisted in his *Child's History of England*, attempts by Catholic apologists to present Queen Mary as 'quite an amiable and cheerful sovereign' were utterly specious – 'The stake and the fire were the fruits of this reign, and you shall judge the Queen by nothing else'.[5] And, as the role of the Democratic Unionist Party in the balance of power at Westminster during Theresa May's premiership reminded us, the atavistic memories then created continue to play a role even in our increasingly secular age.

And the fact is that, as soon as the history of the Tudor age began to be written, it was not only already being shaped by the struggle between Catholicism and Protestantism but also being fictionalized in the interests of one or the other. Which version of fact and fiction you subscribed to depended on the religious preconceptions of those who both wrote and read it. John Foxe's *Actes and Monuments*, usually known as 'Foxe's Book of Martyrs', with its stirring portrayal of Protestant heroism in the face of Catholic savagery, set the agenda for all subsequent Protestant retellings of the Tudor story. Down to the Victorian era, most of the major historians of Tudor England followed Foxe's admiring portraits of Ann Boleyn, Thomas Cranmer and especially Thomas Cromwell, all of whom Foxe thought were the heroes of the early Protestant cause.[6] In a secularized form that line was also followed by the great Victorian historian of Tudor England, James Anthony Froude, who saw the Tudor age not so much as the dawning of the Gospel light but rather as laying the groundwork for the British Empire. So Froude justified even the most egregious of Cromwell's and Henry VIII's acts of tyranny in the name not of the Gospel but of national progress. It was indeed a pity that Fisher and More had to be executed but, sadly, they were backward-looking obstacles to national progress, and so Henry had done what he had to do. No omelettes without broken eggs.[7]

All of this, of course, found expression in literature and drama – Victorian readers in their hundreds of thousands eagerly lapped up fictional retellings of the glories of the Reformation and the triumph of the Protestant nation against an alien Catholicism, whose fundamentally treacherous character was revealed in the Armada – what Tennyson called 'those Inquisition dogs and the devildoms of Spain', fictionalized in novels such as Charles Kingsley's *Westward Ho!*[8] And for the Victorians the reign of Queen Mary, and the burnings of hundreds of Protestants, had special fascination, reflected in both fiction and drama. So Harrison Ainsworth's clunky novel *The Tower of London* was one of the best-sellers of the 1840s. Drawing sensational detail from *A Reading on the Use of Torture in the Criminal Law of England* (1837), by the legal historian David Jardine, Ainsworth's novel focused on Protestant resistance to the regime of Mary Tudor, on Wyatt's rebellion and on the execution of the teenage Protestant nine-day queen, Lady Jane Grey, whose decapitation, in the ludicrously exaggerated final words of the novel, removed 'one of the fairest and wisest heads that ever sat on human shoulders'.[9]

A rather more interesting product of the 1840s was Aubrey de Vere's posthumously published verse drama *Mary Tudor*, in which Queen Mary and Cardinal Pole are portrayed as reluctant persecutors, coerced into savagery by Mary's blood-thirsty and ultra-orthodox Spanish husband, and egged on by cynical and Machiavellian turncoats such as Bishop Stephen Gardiner.[10] So far as I know, the play was never produced on stage, but in 1876 Henry Irving and Ellen Terry took the lead roles as Philip and Mary in Alfred Tennyson's sub-Shakespearean verse drama *Queen Mary*. This relied for its history on Froude, and was intended, as Hallam Tennyson explained, to dramatize 'the final downfall of Roman Catholicism in England, and the dawning of a new age: for after the era of priestly domination comes the era of the freedom of the individual'.[11]

While Victorian Protestant novelists and dramatists drew on the long anti-Catholic historiographical tradition that stretched from

Froude back to Foxe, from the 1860s and 1870s onwards Catholic historians such as the convert Redemptorist T. E. Bridgett, the Jesuit John Morris and the Benedictines Aidan Gasquet and Bede Camm were producing what might be called alternative facts about the English Reformation.[12] They were backed by editions of documents and historical studies of 'the Troubles of our Catholic Forefathers', culminating in 1904 in the establishment of the Catholic Record Society and the subsequent publication of a steady stream of documents from the recusant period. Catholic novelists soon began to translate this rich material into fictional form. The key figure here is Fr Robert Hugh Benson, whose literary work is now a largely forgotten niche interest but who was in his lifetime one of the best-selling novelists of Edwardian England, and one of the most sought-after preachers in the English-speaking world.[13] He was the youngest son of Edward White Benson, archbishop of Canterbury, but converted to Catholicism in 1903 (an event that his family felt made him 'smug and insufferably pontifical'). Wildly eccentric and notoriously unkempt (he wore pyjamas under his cassock to a private audience with Pope Pius X), Benson immediately began a stream of entertaining but heavily didactic novels designed to present a Catholic corrective to Protestant fiction about the Tudor past. The first, published hot on his change of allegiance in 1904, *By What Authority?*, was a tale of persecution and heroic Catholic endurance set during the 1570s and 1580s. Next came *The King's Achievement*, set in the 1530s and dealing with the dissolution of the monasteries. The central character is Ralph Torridon, a young man corrupted by service to Thomas Cromwell, who turns his own monk brother out of Lewes Priory: the book is notable for an idealized portrayal of Thomas More's household in Chelsea. In 1906 Benson published *The Queen's Tragedy*, which dealt with the reign of Mary I.

The best of Benson's historical novels is *Come Rack!, Come Rope!*, published in 1912, a complicated romance set against the background of the mission of St Edmund Campion and the plot led by Anthony Babington to overthrow Elizabeth and put Mary, Queen of Scots, on the throne. Robin Audrey and Marjorie Manners, the star-crossed Catholic lovers at the centre of the book, are the children of Derbyshire recusant families, betrothed since childhood. But in the face of mounting persecution Robin feels a call to the priesthood. Marjorie heroically relinquishes her lover to his vocation, toys with the idea of going abroad herself to join a convent but eventually turns her home into a safe-house for fugitive priests, complete with a priest hole constructed by the Jesuit carpenter St Nicholas Owen. Robin departs for Rheims, is ordained and returns to a clandestine ministry in England, in the course of which he visits Mary, Queen of Scots, at Fotheringhay. He is eventually arrested by his own father, who has conformed to Anglicanism out of cowardice. Robin is tortured by the sadistic pursuivant Richard Topcliffe, condemned for treason and hanged, drawn and quartered at Derby. On the scaffold his final act is to absolve his now penitent and grief-stricken father, who has been brought to witness his son's martyrdom by the ever faithful Marjorie.

Come Rack!, Come Rope! was blatant sectarian propaganda, like most of the works I've been discussing so far. Benson's Protestant villains are hiss-boo bad, his Catholic heroes and heroines sweetly virtuous. Altogether more interesting was the almost contemporary trilogy of romances by another Catholic convert, dealing with the relationship between Henry VIII and his fifth wife, Katherine Howard, the first two volumes of which were set in the last year of Thomas Cromwell's life. Ford Madox Ford's *Fifth Queen* trilogy explored the relationship between Katherine, presented as an earnest, energetic, simple idealist, a devout Catholic committed to 'the Old Faith in the Old way', and the ageing and disillusioned Henry, who represents the world of power, force and moral compromise.[14] Behind Henry stands Thomas Cromwell, arrogant, ruthless, a devout disciple of Machiavelli, employing 700 spies, universally feared and hated, but genuinely devoted to 'kingcraft' and seeking through Henry to establish a rational and secular political order, whatever human casualties that might entail along the way. As he himself declares: 'before all creeds, and before all desires, and before all women, and before all men, standeth the good of this commonwealth, and state, and King, whose servant

I be.' These three are surrounded by vividly drawn supporting characters: Nicholas Udall, the Lady Mary's humanist tutor, a spy for Cromwell and a dedicated lecher, whose self-seeking lies drive much of the plot; Mary Tudor herself, gaunt, embittered and consumed with hatred of her father; Thomas Culpeper, Katherine's besotted cousin, whose relationship with her, unconsummated in the trilogy, ultimately led to his and her executions.

Ford's Cromwell has most of the characteristics of the Machiavellian brute of established Catholic historiography, though Ford allows him the pursuit of his own kind of ideal – a peaceful secular order, maintained by the exercise of power. Ford's bookish, austerely idealist Katherine is very remote indeed from the cheerful, flirtatious, luxury-loving teenager who emerges from the historical sources. In the trilogy she marries Henry (and is even prepared to become his 'leman' or mistress, at the cost of her own salvation) because she believes she can lead him back to the Catholic faith, convinced that, for all his ferocity, he shares the nobility of the heroes of her classical education. And Henry, who before he meets her is a 'grey and heavy king', oppressed by age and infirmity, persuaded that 'he lived among traitors and had no God to pray to', is won over by her idealism and is ready to repudiate his past – to 'sue for peace with the Pope, and set up a chapel to Kat's (Catherine of Aragon's) memory' – if only Katherine will 'wed me to keep me in the right way'.

It is not, of course, to be, and in the final volume of the trilogy Katherine acknowledges her disillusionment:

> I came to you for that you might give this realm again to God. Now I see you will not, for not ever will you do it if it must abate you a jot of your sovereignty [...] I was of the opinion that in the end right must win through. I think now that it never shall, or not for many ages – till our Saviour again come upon this earth with a great glory.[15]

The *Fifth Queen* trilogy – 'slow, intense, pictorial, and operatic', as William Gass characterized it[16] – has had distinguished admirers,

among them Joseph Conrad, who called it 'a noble conception
[...] the swan-song of historical romance', and Graham Greene,
who described it as 'a magnificent bravura piece'.[17] Ford's use in the
trilogy of a modernized version of Tudor diction has been praised,
though twenty-first-century readers are likely to be daunted by its
archaism: nobody eats bread by the loaf in these books, but always by
the 'manchett', and characters are prone to remarks like 'twas a small
talzie – a score of starved yeomen here and there': the cod-medievalism
of William Morris's prose romances hovers somewhere in the
background. And, though all its leading characters were real people,
the trilogy plays fast and loose with the facts of history. As Ford's
most recent biographer has observed, he displays 'a provocative
freedom with fact', a freedom Ford justified on the grounds that 'The
accuracies I deal in are the accuracies of my impressions'. Graham
Greene pointed to the extraordinary visual impression of scene after
scene in the novels, such as that in which we first encounter Cromwell,
standing gazing into the icy dark of the Thames under the light of a
guttering cresset as his barge moves down river in the wake of the
king's disastrous first meeting with Anne of Cleves. 'Has a novel ever
before been lit as carefully as a stage production?' The theatrical or
cinematic technique, Greene suggested, pervades the trilogy: 'Nicolas
Udall's lies, which play so important a part in the first volume, take
their substance from the lighting: they are monstrously elongated or
suddenly shrivel: one can believe anything by torchlight.'

The Fifth Queen represents the high point of Victorian and
Edwardian fictionalizations of the Tudor reformations: the 1950s
would see the creation of two versions of the Henrician Reformation
that were even less equivocal masterpieces. The better-known of these
two is Robert Bolt's A Man for all Seasons, which began life in 1954 as a
radio play, was adapted in 1957 for television, moved to the West End
as a stage play in 1960 and finally became an Oscar-winning film in
1966, directed by Fred Zinnemann, and with a spectacular ensemble
cast: Paul Scofield as Thomas More, Robert Shaw as Henry VIII and
Leo McKern as Cromwell. Bolt's play followed a long tradition in
which More was idolized as the wisest and best man of his age, the
urbane and kindly humanist whose home in Chelsea was a sunny idyll

of learning and civilized values. Originating in the vivid hagiographic memoir of More written by his son-in-law William Roper, that image of More had been given new academic respectability by the Anglican literary scholar R. W. Chambers in a beautiful but equally hagiographical biography of More published in 1935, the year of More's canonization. Bolt drew heavily on Chambers's work, but put his own distinctive spin on it. Bolt's More is not a martyr for religious truth but an icon for the age of dictators and the McCarthyite witch hunts, a twentieth-century liberal born before his time, dying in defence of the rights of the individual against a coercive regime. Bolt's play and the film derived from it offered a seductive but radically misleading picture of More, as a liberal individualist concerned above all with personal integrity: at one point Bolt's More, challenged by the Duke of Norfolk for sacrificing everything for the mere 'theory' of papal supremacy, declares:

> Why, it's a theory yes … But what matters to me is not whether it's true or not but that I believe it to be true, or rather not that I *believe* it, but that *I* believe it … I trust I make myself obscure?[18]

The historical More emphatically did not place this kind of absolute value on the individual's integrity: as a good late medieval Catholic he insisted on the primacy of the objective truth, witnessed to by the community of the Church, whatever the individual did or didn't believe about it. That was why he was so implacably opposed to heresy, and why in the 1520s More, unusually for a layman, became the most active agent in Henry and Wolsey's campaign against heresy and banned books, a campaign that Bolt, like Chambers, ignores – of which more in due course.

But whatever its historical shortcomings, Bolt's brilliant picture of More as the advocate of individual conscience caught the public imagination, and the success of the film fed a striking revival of interest in More and his times. An international team of scholars launched a multi-volume scholarly project to produce critical editions of all More's writings, and in 1963 *Moreana*, a scholarly journal entirely devoted to the study of More, was founded by a group of scholars calling themselves, revealingly, the *Amici Thomae Mori*. The early issues of *Moreana* were full of references to Bolt's play and its film version, in which, despite the play's side-stepping and even distortion of More's religious motivation, the journal's founder, Fr Germain Marc'hadour, considered that 'the voice of Thomas More rings true, and is recognized by those familiar with his life and works'.[19]

More's Roman Catholic admirers ever since have been prone to appropriate Bolt's portrayal of the champion of the individual conscience as confirmation of Sir Thomas's sanctity. On 31 October in the Jubilee year 2000, Pope John Paul II proclaimed St Thomas More patron saint of statesmen and politicians. As was customary, the Pope preached a homily on the occasion, subsequently issued as an apostolic letter or *motu proprio*, which can be read on the Vatican website.[20] Some months before the event, the draft of this *motu proprio* was sent to me, via Cardinal Murphy O'Connor, for comment and correction. I was never told who had written this draft, but I assume that it wasn't the Pope, since I gather he is infallible, and this text had a fine crop of errors. The author was under the impression, for example, that More's favourite child and confidant had been his son John, rather than his beloved daughter Margaret. Factual howlers apart, however, the text laid heavy stress on More's belief in the sovereignty of conscience, very much in the manner of Bolt's play, and it said not a word about More's pursuit of heresy and heretics, both as a polemicist and, more immediately, as the Crown's chief law officer. I wrote an urgently phrased commentary on the draft, pointing out the errors and urging the inclusion somewhere in the text of a frank admission of these unpalatable aspects of More's activities as a hammer of heretics. The howlers duly disappeared and, although the section on conscience was not drastically remodelled, it did at least now include a diplomatically vague allusion to More's anti-heretical vigour, but in the form of a moral figleaf rather than a frank address of the craggier aspects of More's anti-heretical zeal. The text now read:

> it was precisely in defence of the rights of conscience that the example of Thomas More shone brightly. It can be said that he

demonstrated in a singular way the value of a moral conscience which is 'the witness of God himself, whose voice and judgment penetrate the depths of man's soul', *even if, in his actions against heretics, he reflected the limits of the culture of his time.*

The other great work of art dealing with the Reformation to appear in the 1950s is much less well known. This was a blockbuster 700-page novel *The Man on a Donkey*, published in two volumes in 1952, dealing with the dissolution of the monasteries and the series of rebellions in northern England that the dissolution helped trigger in 1536 and 1537, dubbed collectively the Pilgrimage of Grace.[21] It was the work of an Oxford-trained historian, Hilda Prescott, best known for a biography of Mary Tudor that had won the James Tait Black Prize in 1941. *The Man on Donkey* has been largely ignored in accounts of the modern English novel, but its recent reprinting led to some favourable discussion, and I'm by no means alone in believing it to be one of the greatest historical novels in English or any other language, on a par with the work of the nineteenth-century masters of the genre, Scott and Manzoni.

The novel is written in the form of a series of parallel chronicles, tracing the history of five key characters – some real historical personages, some invented – over the 30 years leading up to the outbreak of the Pilgrimage of Grace. At the heart of the book is the figure of Robert Aske, the ebullient one-eyed Yorkshire lawyer initially coerced into a leadership role in the Lincolnshire rising in 1536, but who became the Grand Captain of the Pilgrimage and was eventually excruciatingly executed in York by hanging from a church tower in chains till he died of exposure and starvation. Alongside Aske the novel has four other central characters. Thomas, Lord Darcy, is a devoutly conservative northern grandee who, like Aske, had become a reluctant participant in the Pilgrimage but who came to see it as a true crusade in defence of ancient decencies and who was beheaded in 1537. Christabel Cowper is another real historical character, but imaginatively fleshed out by Prescott as the worldly and scheming last prioress of the Benedictine priory at Marrick, near Richmond, whose struggles to save Marrick

Priory and her own dominant position there cleverly echo the larger ambitions of Cromwell and King Henry, in whom she misguidedly places her trust. Julian Savage, hopelessly in love with Aske, is one of two bastard daughters of Edward Stafford, Duke of Buckingham, executed by Henry VIII in 1519. Finally there is Gilbert or Gib Dawe, a Marrick peasant turned priest, whose angry embitterment at his own poverty leads him to embrace an apocalyptic and denunciatory version of the new Protestant Gospel. In addition, weaving through the story are the gnomic utterances of a mysterious female visionary, an idiot serving-woman named Malle, whose pacifist visions of Christ, the eponymous 'Man on a Donkey', glimpsed in and about Marrick and the surrounding dales, provide a mystical commentary on the violent upheavals that form the main thread of the story. And that story is framed, like an illuminated book of hours, by a series of lyrical descriptions of the changing seasons and the routine labours of the rural year, which set the doomed tragedy of the Pilgrimage in a grander and more hopeful natural context. Formally, the novel is genuinely innovative, written in hundreds of often very short sections that cut back and forth cinematically between the main characters: the pace of the story is immensely leisurely, character, place and event unfolding slowly, but inexorably weaving together towards the climax of the Pilgrimage and the novel's harrowing end.

Prescott was a professional historian, who attached a three-page bibliography of primary and secondary sources to her novel, and her portraits of historical characters such as Aske and Darcy stick close to the documented facts. She was also a devout Anglican and, like the Dodds sisters, whose two-volume study of the Pilgrimage, published in 1915, was her principal narrative source,[22] she entertained no illusions about the standard of Tudor monastic life – almost all the monks and nuns who appear in her book are, like Christabel Cowper, worldly and spiritually mediocre. But Prescott manages to convey the tragedy and betrayals of the dissolution without idealizing the institutions that were dissolved. Readers of Dom David Knowles's magisterial study of the dissolution, which appeared later the same decade, would have recognized the fundamental accuracy of Prescott's portrayal of Marrick Priory.[23] And despite her own Anglican convictions, Prescott explored the conservative religious convictions of the Catholics Aske and Darcy with profound sympathy and insight, even though one of the novel's themes is the incompatibility of resort to violence with the gospel of Christ, the novel's mysteriously glimpsed 'Man on a Donkey'. Prescott's novel has its flaws – the gnomic mystical utterances of the visionary Malle, such as 'there is darkness, and God moving nigh-hand in the darkness', are sometimes uncomfortably reminiscent of Stella Gibbons's *Cold Comfort Farm*, with its 'There's something nasty in the woodshed'. But in its combination of historical accuracy with vivid and complex characterization, cumulative narrative power and imaginative empathy, it represents a high point of fictional treatments of the Tudor reformations. Prescott's take on the history of the period was learned and accurate, but not revisionist. Her presentation of both King Henry and his chief minister, Thomas Cromwell, was conventionally negative and hostile. Cromwell in her book is highly able and superficially charming, but beneath the charm he is corrupt, greedy, cynical, ruthless and cruel. It's the picture of Cromwell's character that had been promoted in the standard biography published by the Harvard historian Roger Merriman in 1902,[24] and though handled much more three-dimensionally, in all essentials Prescott's Cromwell is barely distinguishable from Hugh Benson's version.

But, even as Prescott wrote, the framework of Tudor history was being revised in ways that would profoundly affect fictional portrayals of the period. From the early 1950s onwards the Cambridge historian Geoffrey Elton was turning out a series of groundbreaking studies of Henrician England which placed Cromwell centre-stage as a principled modernizer, intent on reforming both Church and state, an administrative genius who was the mastermind of a 'Tudor Revolution in Government'. And in 1959 the Hull-based religious historian Geoffrey Dickens published a short biography of Cromwell claiming him not only as a conscientious and patriotic administrator of genius but as a devoutly committed evangelical, protector and promoter of England's earliest Protestants, whose greatest and most enduring achievement would be the so-called Great Bible, issued in 1538. Dickens' and especially Elton's take on Cromwell quickly established itself. In 1968, in what is still the standard biography of Henry VIII, Elton's robustly Catholic pupil, Jack Scarisbrick, gave the king himself more agency in the religious revolution of the 1530s than his great teacher was willing to allow, but nevertheless endorsed the new consensus:

> Far from being the ruthless Machiavellian of legend, Cromwell was a man possessed of a high concept of the state and national sovereignty, and a deep concern for Parliament and the law; an administrative genius, one who may have lacked profound religious sense, though instinctively favourable to some sort of Erasmian Protestantism, but something of an idealist nonetheless. That the 1530s were a decisive decade in English history is due largely to his energy and vision.[25]

But Elton had not only prompted a rethink about Cromwell. Partly in reaction to Bolt's anachronistic secular canonization of More, Elton turned his formidable attention to a deconstruction of More's reputation. In a series of debunking essays spread over 30 years, he argued that More had spent four 'idiot years' trying to be a monk of the Charterhouse, and, having opted instead for marriage, spent the rest of his life struggling with a sense of religious and moral failure. Elton's More was a repressed 'sex-maniac', unable to shake off the conviction 'that he had failed to live up to what he regarded as God's ultimate demand on man', namely, celibacy. This was the explanation not only of what he considered More's morbid self-flagellation and hair shirt but also of the tone of More's writings against the Reformation, 'endless, nearly always tedious, passionate, devoid of humour and markedly obsessive', a display of 'helpless fury' rooted in More's own misanthropic pessimism, and above all in his unresolved and morbid sexuality. Few of his admirers, Elton insisted, 'have ventured to become acquainted with the relentless persecutor of religious dissidents, the savage polemicist, the teller of rather nasty tales about invariably shrewish women, the authoritarian servant of a dictatorial Church'. More, so regularly treated as transparently understandable, is for Elton one of the most complex and difficult characters in history.[26]

Elton's take on More drew support from a surprising quarter. In 1984 Richard Marius, one of the editors of the great Yale edition of More's writings, published a biography that offered a highly Freudian reading of More's activities against heresy. Marius portrayed More himself as a man tormented by 'a wearing battle to resolve the conflict between powerful sexual desire, and the guilty conviction that sexuality was tainted', who spent the last 15 years of his life in violent repudiation of his earlier humanist convictions.[27] It is important to grasp that this reading of More's character and motivation rests on a single casual, indeed joking, remark by Erasmus, that More had decided against becoming a monk because it was better to be a chaste husband than a lewd priest, and on a highly dubious Freudian interpretation of the rhetoric of his anti-heretical writings.[28] But the revisionism of Elton, Marius and those influenced by them provides the prospectus for the characters of Cromwell and More as they are presented in *Wolf Hall*. It's to Mantel's engrossing but historically troubling sequence of novels I want to turn now.

In the Living Hall of the Frick Collection in New York two great portraits face each other on either side of the fireplace, Hans Holbein's unique and unblinking analysis of the personalities of the two most famous laymen in early Tudor England: More, richly dressed but unshaven, sensitive, self-questioning, far-sighted, every inch what the art critic Waldemar Januszczak has called 'one of the most noble presences in the whole of British portraiture';[29] and Cromwell, the ultimate bureaucrat, cold, calculating, his expressionless pebble-eyes bleakly watchful, his hand tightly gripping one of the thousands of letters that consolidated his equally tight hold on power in the 1530s. Both portraits feature often in Mantel's trilogy, and she has published an intriguing meditation on the portrait of More in the form of an open letter to the man himself, and builds round it one of the themes of the trilogy, finding in his face signs of neurosis and inverted vanity.[30]

By contrast, for Mantel the portrait of Cromwell is 'an act of concealment', contrived between Holbein and the sitter himself, which is perhaps just as well, since Mantel's Cromwell admits that it makes him look 'like one of the fellows who chucks drunkards out of taverns', and even like a murderer.[31]

But the portrayal of the two men in *Wolf Hall* reverses the verdict implicit in Holbein's devastatingly revealing pictures. Though More's execution takes place at the end of *Wolf Hall*, he looms as a presence throughout the trilogy, a deliberate foil to the central character, almost a mirror image, reversing the roles traditionally assigned to the two men in other fiction about the reign. For the wise, kindly and fundamentally decent hero of the *Wolf Hall* trilogy is not Thomas More but Thomas Cromwell. The noble and sensitive face in the Holbein portrait of More is for Mantel in fact that of a religious fanatic and sadistic torturer. And emphasizing the role reversals, in Mark Rylance's TV portrayal Cromwell is even made to look like Holbein's refined More, not Holbein's thuggish Cromwell, while the More played by Anton Lesser is a sinister and joyless puritan, a man whose social charm is reported but never enacted on stage. Instead we see a man able to make 'twisted jokes, but not to take them', whose cruel humour masks self-loathing and a steely religious bigotry.[32] *Wolf Hall's* More is the polar opposite of Bolt's man for all seasons, a sneering misogynist who specializes in humiliating the women in his household, who are all afraid of him. He's a religious fanatic, flogging himself in a fear-driven piety, obsessively writing vitriolic and obscene polemical books, implacably hunting down defenceless Protestants, imprisoning and torturing them in his own cellars, relentlessly questioning them while they are racked, 'a master in the twin arts of stretching and compressing the servants of God' and sending his victims to the stake so broken by suffering that they have to be carried to their execution in chairs. The novels harp on More as the supposed torturer – the theme recurs seven times in *Wolf Hall* alone.[33] Mantel's Cromwell even appears to credit the ludicrous claim – first aired in 2003, on the basis of no evidence whatever, by the journalist Brian Moynahan – that More, while locked up in the Tower, with his income and assets sequestered and his wife reduced to writing begging letters, 'has a sticky web in Europe still, a web made of money' through which he orchestrates and pays for the arrest of William Tyndale, and so was ultimately to blame for Tyndale's burning – an event that took place more than a year after More's own execution. In the final book of the trilogy, Cromwell even blames More for the Pilgrimage of Grace, the rebellion that erupted in Lincolnshire a year and a half after his death: 'it all goes back to More.'[34]

In all this, Bolt's play is manifestly directly in Mantel's line of fire. Most historians agree that the evidence that finally led to More's execution for treason was perjured testimony by the despicable time-server Richard Riche, one of Cromwell's henchmen, and the incident gives rise to the best joke in *A Man for All Seasons*. Riche was rewarded for his testimony by being made attorney-general of Wales. During the trial More spots the Dragon of Wales on Riche's chain of office and remarks 'with pain and amusement', as the stage direction says, 'Why Richard, it profits a man nothing to give his soul for the whole world ... But for Wales!'[35] But in Mantel's version More really does let slip a treasonable utterance while talking to Riche in the Tower – he is betrayed into self-incrimination by his dismissive contempt for a man he thinks of no importance.[36] Even when he is being badgered by members of the Privy Council to make him abandon his belief in papal authority, it is More's face, not those of his tormentors, that becomes 'a mask of malice'.[37] Far from being the innocent victim of a cruel regime, the More of *Wolf Hall* is a calculating political schemer, treated better than he deserved. After his arrest his successor as Lord Chancellor, Thomas Audley (of all people!), assures More that he will not be tortured: 'we spare you the methods that you used on others.'[38]

All More's actions are interpreted negatively. When his first wife, Joan, died, More, a busy lawyer and rising politician, was left with five children all under the age of six. To provide them with the care they needed he married again within months, choosing the motherly widow of a city merchant several years older than himself. In *Wolf Hall* this pragmatic move becomes evidence of More's self-loathing inability to live without sex: 'When More's first wife died,' the voice of the narrator – Cromwell – records, 'her successor was in the house before the corpse was cold [...] human flesh called to him with its inconvenient demands [... but) if you are so lenient with yourself as to insist on living with a woman, then for the sake of your soul you should make it a woman you don't really like.'[39] And his refusal to accept that Henry, not the Pope, is the head of the Church arises not from principled conviction but because 'More is too proud to retreat from his position. He is afraid to lose his credibility with the scholars in Europe.'[40]

When all allowance is made for the conventions of fiction, it's pretty obvious that the writer of *Wolf Hall* intensely dislikes the historical More, though that perception is complicated by Hilary Mantel's open letter to More, which, while maintaining that 'we have to lie about you a little to like you', is by no means straightforwardly hostile. But Mantel's More is, first and last, a steely bigot: as she writes in that letter:

> Your later admirers have made you a liberal icon, a martyr for freedom of conscience. They see in you certain secular virtues that you would have despised as vices. You were not tolerant and would have thought it shameful to be so. You did not believe that a man's own conscience should act as his chief moral guide.[41]

Now certainly More's views on the limits of liberty of conscience are pretty difficult for any twenty-first-century person to understand or sympathize with. In the 1530s More wrote thousands of pages of ferocious polemic against the Reformation, books in which he defended the execution of stubborn or relapsed heretics, in language whose violence now makes even his most ardent admirers quail. He notoriously called Thomas Hitton, burned in 1530 for heresy, 'the devil's stinking martyr'; heretics were not men of conscience but 'a few myschevous persons' driven by 'desire of a large lybertye to an unbrydeled lewdness/ and [...] an hye devylesshe pryde cloked under pretexte of good zele and symplenes'. More believed that unrepentant heretics who went defiantly on preaching their errors were 'well burnt' and went straight from the temporal fire to the eternal. In keeping with those fierce sentiments, over the previous ten years More, recruited into Henry's and Wolsey's campaign against heresy, had led a series of nocturnal raids on London homes and warehouses to suppress the trade in banned Protestant books and, like other Tudor magistrates, he interrogated suspects in his house in Chelsea. *Wolf Hall* dramatizes the rumours current in More's own day that he had not only arrested but tortured these prisoners, and in a flashback in *Bring Up the Bodies* he is portrayed questioning the evangelical barrister James Rainham on the rack, a scene that duly made its way into the television adaptation. That More was a torturer is now widely believed to be true, mainly because of its prominence in Mantel's novels or their TV adaptations.

There is a real issue here. More's detestation of heresy was deep and vehement, and certainly incompatible with Bolt's picture of the martyr for the individual conscience. And yet we can be fairly certain that these claims that More used torture against heretics are false. Whatever else he was or wasn't, More was a truthful man. He was one of the very few Tudor Englishmen who refused to take the Oath of Succession, and he ultimately died rather than subscribe to it, because the oath implied that the king was the head of the Church. All but one of the Tudor bishops and most of the monks, priests and lay householders in England – even More's beloved daughter Meg – signed up to that claim. But More died for refusing it, because he would not swear to a lie. So we can believe him when in 1533 he solemnly swore, 'so help me God', that he had never tortured anyone. In the *Apology of Sir Thomas More*, published the year before his arrest, he specifically denied all the charges of torture and maltreatment of Protestant suspects that are dramatized in *Wolf Hall*.

> 'Of all that ever came into my hands for heresy', he insisted, 'as helpe me God, [...] never had any of them any stripe or stroke given them, so mych as a fylype on the forhed.'[42]

Yet the accusations More solemnly denied were recycled as fact by the Protestant martyrologist John Foxe, and passed from there into the Protestant historiographic tradition. More recently, and probably in conscious reaction to Bolt's play, they were given new currency in popular historical works such as Brian Moynahan's biography of More's *bête noire*, William Tyndale, and in Jasper Ridley's *The Statesman and the Fanatic*, a double 'biography' of Wolsey and More.[43]

The *Wolf Hall* trilogy, the most celebrated and widely read historical fiction for decades, is worlds away from such vulgar exercises in sectarian demonology. But the same accusations of cruelty are central to Mantel's characterization of More, and Mantel's formidable grasp of Tudor sources is deployed to heighten the picture, even where the torture theme is absent from the source itself. There is a particularly striking example towards the end of *Wolf Hall*. Early in May 1535 Cromwell visited More in the Tower to try to persuade him to accept, or appear to accept, the Supremacy. More sent a detailed account of the interview to his daughter Margaret, and Mantel draws effectively on More's letter for one of the most telling scenes in *Wolf Hall*. In the course of the conversation More famously declared to Cromwell, 'I do nobody harme, I say none harm, I thynke none harme, but wysh everybodye goode. And yf thys be not ynough to kepe a man alyve in good fayth I long not to lyve.'[44] As even Geoffrey Elton conceded, 'Cromwell was evidently impressed' by this eloquent declaration: he spoke to More 'full gently' and said he would report to the King and discover 'his gracious pleasure'.[45]

In Mantel's reworking of this scene, however, Cromwell's reaction is anything but gentle: he 'cuts in on him, incredulous':

You do nobody harm? What about Bainham, you remember Bainham? You forfeited his goods, committed his poor wife to prison, saw him racked with your own eyes [...] you had him back in your own house two days chained upright to a post [...] and still your spite was not exhausted: you sent him back to the Tower and had him racked again, so that finally his body was so broken that they had to carry him in a chair when they took him to Smithfield to be burned alive. And you say, Thomas More, that you do no harm?[46]

Here, in uncharacteristically awkward prose, the novelist writes against the grain of her source, to heighten the portrait of More the torturer. And here, as elsewhere, Mantel seems to have Bolt's *Man for All Seasons* firmly in her sights. Bolt drew on that same letter to Margaret for material for More's speech at the culmination of the trial scene in Act II: having been found guilty of treason, and immediately before Audley passes sentence of death on him, as the stage directions specify, More 'pauses, and launches, very quietly, ruminatively, into his final stock-taking':

> I am the King's true subject, and pray for him and all the realm […] I do none harm, I say none harm, I think none harm. And if this be not enough to keep a man alive, in good faith I long not to live […] I have, since I came into prison, been several times in such a case that I thought to die within the hour, and I thank Our Lord I was never sorry for it, but rather sorry when it passed. And therefore, my poor body is at the King's pleasure. Would God my death might do him some good.

Where Bolt follows his extract from the letter with that protestation of resignation and loyalty, Mantel punctures the pathos of 'I do none harm, I say none harm, I think none harm' with Cromwell's luridly vehement case for the moral prosecution.

By contrast, consider Mantel's handling of an equally well-known incident from another contemporary source, George Cavendish's *Life and Death of Cardinal Wolsey*, which has always been taken, and was certainly originally intended, to show Cromwell to disadvantage. On All Saints' day 1529 Wolsey's fall was nearing its nadir: he and his dwindling entourage were camping uncomfortably in the palace at Esher, and on All Saints' morning the cardinal's servant George Cavendish was amazed to discover his colleague Thomas Cromwell, whose evangelical sympathies and anticlericalism were already in evidence, 'leaning in the great window', holding, of all things, a book of hours, and reciting Matins of the Virgin Mary – the most Catholic form of prayer imaginable. Cromwell even wept while he prayed, which, as Cavendish remarks with ironic relish, 'had been a strange sight in him before'. When Cavendish enquired 'Why, Master Cromwell, what meaneth all this your sorrow? Is my lord [Wolsey] in any danger for whom ye lament thus?' Cromwell explained that his tears were for himself, not Wolsey: 'Nay, nay […] it is my unhappy adventure, which I am likely to lose all that I have travailed for all the days of my life for doing of my master true and diligent service.'[47]

Cavendish's slyly artful telling of this story suggests a more self-seeking and duplicitous Cromwell than suits Mantel's fiction. As Diarmaid MacCulloch points out, the sudden reversion to papistical modes of prayer in the face of disaster chimes with the religiously conservative will Cromwell made at this time, full of protestations of old-fashioned piety and provision for prayers for the dead, and very possibly a smoke-screen in case Wolsey's fall should expose his unprotected protégé to suspicions of heresy. But it is also possible that the recent death of his wife and daughters had made Cromwell more receptive to the value of prayers for the dead. MacCulloch therefore offers two possible explanations for these sudden and frankly improbable manifestations of old-time piety – 'the trimming of his convictions, or a genuine change of devotional mood'. Mantel rejects both these possibilities, and constructs instead an elaborate emotional back-story as a more benign reading of that tearful encounter in the great hall at Esher. In Mantel's version Cromwell is not praying to the Virgin, not praying at all. He is holding the book of hours because it had belonged to his recently dead wife, and his little daughter Grace, also recently dead, had loved its decorated margins and full-page illuminations. Gazing at its images of spring flowers and misty lines of trees, but also of death and loss, the infant victims of Herod's murderous rage in the Slaughter of the Innocents, Cromwell's tears fall because as he turns the pages he feels the hand of his dead daughter turn them with him. His crassly self-pitying reply to Cavendish's intrusive questioning, that he is weeping for his blighted prospects, is thus explained away as the ploy of a sensitive soul concealing an intimately private moment of emotional desolation: the blundering Cavendish 'cannot see his daughter's fingers touching the page, or his wife's hands holding the book'.[48]

This turning of the source on its head to convey a precisely opposite meaning is itself, of course, artfully done: the scene is one

of the most moving in *Wolf Hall*. But its spinning of the source in
a highly improbable direction is surely uncomfortably reminiscent
of Ford Madox Ford's 'provocative freedom with fact'. And spin
of this sort in Cromwell's favour pervades *Wolf Hall*: Mantel's
Cromwell is benignly omnicompetent, a social and religious
reformer, a sincere supporter of the Protestant Reformation who
nevertheless shies away from the fanatical enthusiasm of religious
zealots of every stamp: 'dear God' Cromwell says, 'More, Tyndale,
they deserve each other, these mules that pass for men.' Though
Cromwell throughout the trilogy is a Protestant by conviction, he
is credited with positive devotion only in the final volume of the
trilogy, *The Mirror and the Light*.

The prevailing impression, if anything heightened in the stage
and television adaptations, is of a kind of secular saint, whose
talents and humane attitudes foreshadow the twenty-first century
rather than his own. He is a financial and administrative wizard, a
Renaissance lover of books and visual arts, a polyglot linguist fluent
in French, Italian, German, Flemish, Spanish and Welsh, who
cannot be found on the afternoon that his wife dies of plague because
he is having a lesson in Polish, who quizzes a foreign ambassador
on the difficulties of learning Arabic and who, in his last weeks
in the Tower, seeks solace in the study of Hebrew grammar. He is
sensitive to the sufferings of the long-dead victims of medieval anti-
Semitism, he enquires of condemned prisoners to make sure they
are being properly fed. He is a conservationist *avant la lettre*, who
disapproves of hunting because it has driven 'the bear, and the wolf
and the wild boar' to extinction, and by 1540 he is actually planning
the reintroduction of beavers to England! He has even invented a
mechanical spit to make life easier in the kitchen. His fictional
household at Austin Friars outdoes More's household in Chelsea
for charm and civilization. It is a paradise of religious tolerance,
where European scholars of every persuasion find patronage and
shelter, a home for waifs rescued from the streets, whose kitchens
turn out industrial quantities of soup and sausage to feed hundreds
of paupers at the door; its rooms and passageways echo to music and
the laughter of charming flocks of 'merry children rescued from the

cloister'. Cromwell himself is not only a doting parent and foster-parent but also a benign local godfather, sorting out the parish's problems for the neighbours who flock to ask his help. In contrast to More's misogyny, he is always nice to women (with the notable exception of Ann Boleyn). Even his skin has almost supernatural qualities. When, at the start of the second volume of the trilogy, the entire court goes out hunting in the blazing sunshine, without their hats because the king has dispensed with his, everyone from the king down gets badly sunburned. Not Cromwell, whose sallow skin is mysteriously immune to such weakness.[49]

All's fair in fiction, and some of this has some warrant in the historical record, though the humanitarian and environmental virtues with which Mantel endows her hero seem more redolent of twenty-first-century Islington than sixteenth-century Putney. Certainly Cromwell's competence and political skills need no comment. His history before 1520 is largely unrecorded, but he was indeed a soldier of fortune in Italy, with a spell in the French army: he had worked for the Frescobaldi banking family in Venice and as a cloth merchant in the Low Countries. But the historical Cromwell was definitely not Mantel's benign neighbourhood Mr Nice. What evidence there is suggests that he was in fact the neighbour from hell, brazenly encroaching on his outraged neighbour's boundaries to enlarge his own property at Austin Friars. The London antiquary John Stow recorded that Cromwell had gone so far as to annex and put a wall round 'twenty-two foot of everyman's ground', and even set one inconvenient house in neighbouring Throgmorton Street on rollers, moving it without consultation those same twenty-two feet into Stow's father's garden.[50] In the final volume of the trilogy Mantel exonerates Cromwell from any blame in the matter, with a stroke of the pen: 'I know where my boundaries are.' So, Cromwell's servant Christophe remarks, Stow can 'go fuck himself'.[51]

The reader smiles at Stow's father's discomfiture, whatever the (unrecoverable) historical reality, but a more major theme in their paired characterization, Cromwell's fictionalized outrage at More's alleged cruelty, raises more serious issues and can't be squared with Cromwell's own actual political record. If we can be reasonably sure that More was not a torturer, we can be quite certain that Cromwell was. A recurrent theme of the three novels is Cromwell's horror at the burning of heretics. In fact, in his capacity as Vicegerent in Spirituals, Cromwell personally headed the commission that interrogated and condemned to death a cell of continental Anabaptists, up to 25 of whom were burned at the stake in London and neighbouring towns in May 1535. The co-ordination of these burnings was quite certainly Cromwell's, who personally assured the imperial ambassador that he would see them carried out. The episode constituted what Diarmaid MacCulloch has described as 'one of the most spectacular co-ordinated burnings of heretics in England in the whole century, outclassing any single set-piece of Queen Mary's reign twenty years later', and, by the same token, hugely surpassing More's direct involvement in just three cases of heresy ending in execution.[52]

Cromwell meted out greater savagery to defenders of the old faith. Among all the spiritual mediocrity of the religious orders that Cromwell dissolved, the English Carthusians stand out as exemplary exceptions, their houses filled with men living austere and devoted lives, which even Cromwell's commissioners could not fault: as MacCulloch shows, Cromwell himself seems to have attempted to shield them from dissolution. Unsurprisingly, however, it was the Carthusians who virtually alone among the monastic orders made a collective principled stand against the new doctrine of the king's spiritual supremacy. Cromwell saw to it that they were savagely punished. Three of their leaders, including John Houghton, prior of the London Charterhouse in which More had tried his vocation, were convicted of high treason by a reluctant London jury, under pressure from Cromwell. To the horror of Catholic Europe, they were hanged and disembowelled at Tyburn in May 1535, still wearing their monastic habits, the hangman prolonging their sufferings as a warning to others. Three more Charterhouse monks were butchered the following month.

Unsurprisingly, public reaction to this unprecedented treatment of exemplary clerics in their religious habits was unfavourable, and Cromwell decided not to repeat the experiment. But after two years of further harassment ten more members of the London Charterhouse still refusing the oath were sent to Newgate gaol without trial, chained upright to posts with their hands behind their backs and left to die. According to a romantic but probably basically reliable tradition preserved in the More circle, More's adopted daughter, Margaret Giggs, helped them by disguising herself as a milkmaid, cleaning the excrement from around them and feeding them with food smuggled into the gaol in a milk pail: she was discovered, and all but one of the ten died, reportedly of 'gaol fever'.[53]

The cruelty with which the Carthusians were treated was very probably attributable to King Henry's own relentless intolerance of opposition, and MacCulloch excuses Cromwell on the grounds that 'ultimately one cannot expect the chief minister of an angry and ruthless king to do much more than obey his will or face the consequences', though that amelioration might be pleaded for the agents of atrocity in any murderous regime.[54] But whoever ordered it, it was Cromwell who managed the process. And the appalling death of the disembowelled Carthusians is evoked with a chilling absence of sympathy in *Wolf Hall*, where Cromwell reflects with grim relish on the suffering they will endure – 'the most horrible of all deaths, pain and rage and humiliation swallowed to the dregs, before each one dies [...] he crawls like an animal round and round on the bloody boards'. But he excuses himself. These 'treacherous monks' deserve whatever they get. 'He has spoken gently,' Cromwell muses, speaking of himself in the third person: 'he has spoken bluntly, he has threatened and cajoled [...] It is all to no avail. Their response is, go away, go away, and leave me to my sanctified death.'[55] In other words, the monks' conscientious refusal of the oath is a perverse devotional indulgence, mere sanctimonious stubbornness: they have chosen this death for themselves, so are neither to be admired nor pitied. All they had to do to survive was swear an oath they did not believe, just as, Cromwell reflects in *The Mirror and the Light*, More could have freed himself at any moment – 'All he had to do was say some magic words.'[56]

Unsurprisingly, there is no mention of Cromwell's role in the Anabaptist burnings in *Wolf Hall*, but the final volume of the trilogy does in fact allow us a glimpse of Cromwell the torturer at work, one aspect of the slow deterioration that is one of the themes of *The Mirror and the Light*. In the spring of 1537 he is busy interrogating suspects in the wake of the Pilgrimage of Grace, wearily returning home each night from torturing the 'snivelling wrecks' in the Tower to deal with other business and reflecting, like the good man and king's servant he is, that he is 'willing to pinch a man with pains, if nothing else will work, though the threat will do more, and he regards it as a defeat if he has to call for chains and heated irons'.[57] Interrogation under torture is here softened to 'pinching with pains', and the chains and heated irons, we are invited to think, are the sad and reluctant necessities of a manager of men in Henry VIII's England. In the circumstances, Cromwell's reproach to More at the end of *Wolf Hall*, 'I would have left you, you know. To live out your life. To repent of your butcheries. If I were king', has, retrospectively, a very hollow ring.[58]

Mantel's extraordinary achievement in scooping the Booker Prize twice, together with the immense impact of the plays and television series based on her books, has given her fictional treatment of the Henrician reformation a distinctive kind of authority. She was the BBC's Reith lecturer in 2017, and took the relationship between historical truth and historical fiction as the theme of her lectures. Now it must be emphasized that she has been very clear that her version of the period is, in the end, imaginative fiction, and she has reminded her critics that a novelist is not on oath when writing about historical characters. The novelist, even the historical novelist, is allowed to make things up. She has also pointed out that almost all of the references to More's cruelty in the books are in reported speech – that is, they are what More's enemies said about him, and not necessarily what the novelist believes, though, given the unrelieved awfulness of More throughout the trilogy, this authorial distancing does not altogether convince.

A significant text here is the set of character notes Mantel provided for the published text of Mike Poulton's dramatizations, in which the usual Eltonian tropes about More appear – Thomas is a psychological mess who could 'keep a tribe of analysts in business for life', he 'seems vulnerable, even harmless', but inside his 'barriers are rigid and [his] core is frozen'. More is a man who 'can't live without sex', and the inner conflict this generates means he has to flagellate himself 'as a distraction'. More has 'a poisoned spring' inside him: his persecution of heretics is a means of releasing his inner violence instead of suppressing it, but his writings against heresy reveal that inner violence, because they are filled with 'an uncontrollable flood of scatological language'. Once again, we need to remind ourselves that this last claim is not borne out by the historical facts: there is no 'flood' of filth – More's 'scatology' is confined to a single Latin treatise, royally commissioned, of 1523, in riposte to an equally potty-mouthed text by Luther. More's English polemical writings are neither more nor less ribald than Chaucer or Shakespeare and a good deal milder than the comedy of his contemporary and fellow humanist Rabelais, and the sense of humour on display when More does deploy bawdy would have seemed tame in a Victorian music-hall.[59]

Mantel has indignantly repudiated any idea that her trilogy presents a 'Manichaean duel' between opposites, and points to the recurrence in the trilogy of 'Cromwell's long fascination with More, his often reluctant sympathy with him'. Nevertheless, in the trilogy More and Cromwell are repeatedly paired as opposites, and we are never permitted to see anything in More that might account for Cromwell's fascination or sympathy: More is never given even a momentary share in any of the decencies so lavishly bestowed on his fictional opposite, while Mantel's character notes on More suggest his deliberate casting as anti-hero.

Mantel's emphasis on her adherence to the sources and historiography of the period, which she certainly knows intimately, coupled with her insistence in the Reith lectures that historical fiction can offer valid insights into the motivation and character of the people of the past, raises difficult questions about the boundaries between fiction and 'faction'. Her choice of topic as Reith lecturer is itself evidence of the ambiguous claims – and impact on public perception – of her kind of writing. Her striking assertion that 'History is not the past, it is our way of organising our ignorance of the past' brings historical research and historical fiction disturbingly close together.

Mantel's sustained exploration of the most tumultuous years of Henry VIII's reign through the eyes of that reign's principal political fixer is a very remarkable imaginative feat, an exercise in historical presence and virtuosic ventriloquism that has become more assured with each successive volume. Her immersion in the historical sources, from the minutiae of Cromwell's political networking to the food, fashions and feel of the early Tudor court, gives the novels an extraordinary vividness and sense of authenticity. But their finest achievement is not in the questionable reversal of the roles of More and Cromwell, which is so prominent a part of the trilogy's structure but which, it seems to me, ultimately fails as fiction because it will not stand as history. The More of *Wolf Hall* is dangerously closer to a gargoyle than a portrait. The fictional More is just too unmitigatedly awful to be squared with what was thought and said about the historical More by his contemporaries, especially those who knew him most intimately – Erasmus, More's own close family and, not least, the unblinking eye of Holbein, those who, in Diarmaid MacCulloch's words, '*were there*'.[60] Interestingly, in the television version, Anton Lesser's poignant portrayal of More's final days in the Tower did convey both the dignity and the pathos of More's lonely stance and helped to give the character a three-dimensionality that the More character is not permitted in the novels themselves, though it's clear from Mantel's open letter to Sir Thomas that she herself is sensitive to both the dignity and the pathos of his courageous end.

The rapidity of the translation of Mantel's sequence into stage play and television series made it an international phenomenon but by the same token, of course, complicates any judgement about its ultimate status as art. Who can read the books without 'seeing' Mark Rylance as Cromwell or Mark Gatis in all his feline malevolence as Gardiner? But however the trilogy may look to posterity, in the long as well as the short run Mantel's greatest triumph of historical imagination will surely be judged to be her funny, insightful and touching tragicomic portrait of Cardinal Wolsey. Here too she takes some liberties with the historical record (once again, inevitably, to More's discredit). In *Wolf Hall* Wolsey is an urbanely tolerant man, who deplores More's fierce campaign against heretical books in the 1520s: the cardinal even tips Cromwell off about More's imminent raid on the house of the London evangelical Humphrey Monmouth, so that Cromwell can pass the word to dispose of incriminating evidence.

> 'Monmouth ... I am merely mentioning his name. Because ... Now why am I?' The Cardinal had closed his eyes. 'Because I am merely mentioning it.'[61]

The historical Wolsey undoubtedly preferred persuasion to coercion, but, as the great Cardinal's most authoritative modern biographer has insisted, More was acting in those raids not on his own initiative but as Wolsey's agent in what was Wolsey's campaign against Protestant books, and the arrested suspects were subsequently tried under the cardinal's legatine powers, overriding local episcopal jurisdiction and irritating More's close friend Cuthbert Tunstall, bishop of London, in the process.[62]

But Mantel's portrayal of the tender relationship between the cardinal and his most faithful servant, Thomas Cromwell, provides the connecting thread of the entire trilogy, even in the incident-crowded final volume, half-way through which Wolsey's ghost falls momentously silent. Mantel here shines a persuasive historical as well as fictional light on the careers of both men. One of the earliest biographies of More was Thomas Stapleton's *Tres Thomae*, 'The Three Thomases'.[63] Mantel's lavish trilogy offers its readers much more than a triple portrait, but it too is dominated by the imagined figures of three Thomases – Cromwell, Wolsey and More. And apart from Cromwell himself, whose inner voice pervades all three books, Wolsey is *Wolf Hall's* most vivid creation, just as Cromwell's loyalty to Wolsey is the force that drives the plot. Revenge against Wolsey's tormentors becomes the key to what Mantel allows us to see is Cromwell's otherwise morally loathsome destruction of Anne Boleyn and her supposed lovers, an interpretation giving imaginative flesh and blood to a plausible if only partial mitigation of Cromwell's relentless role in Anne's downfall.

This line of interpretation appears to have been Mantel's own, hardly if at all hinted at in the existing historiography about Cromwell, and her writing gave it an imaginative force that had a direct and beneficial impact on Diarmaid MacCulloch's magisterial biography of Cromwell, published in 2018. As Peter Marshall has remarked, MacCulloch takes this idea of Cromwell's abiding loyalty to the memory of the cardinal and explores it 'more thoroughly and seriously than any previous historian'. Marshall rightly attributed this focus to Mantel's novels, and characterized the influence of her books on MacCulloch's biography as 'a rare and interesting example of how an exercise of historical imagination can act as a spur to serious scholarly investigation'.[64]

But the trilogy's very brilliance as fiction presents a corresponding historical problem. In her Reith lectures Mantel defended historical fiction against those who

> say that by its nature it's misleading. But I argue, a reader knows the nature of the contract. When you choose a novel to tell you about the past, you are putting in brackets the historical accounts – which may or may not agree with each other – and actively requesting a subjective interpretation.[65]

In a sharp exchange with the editor of the journal *History Today* in 2015, she firmly rejected any suggestion that her novels have contributed to public misunderstanding of the Tudor past. 'Readers', she insisted, 'are not simple-minded. They can entertain ambiguities, appreciate complexity.'[66] It would be reassuring to think that that was always true. But the compulsiveness of Mantel's writing, her insistence on her faithfulness to contemporary Tudor sources and *Wolf Hall*'s prime-time exposure on TV have combined to ensure that fiction has been taken for fact, and the necessary distinctions blurred. The most judicious recent writer about Thomas More, the Cambridge historian Professor John Guy, complained during the 2017 Hay Festival about interviewing candidates for places to read history at Cambridge, eager to air their expertise on Thomas Cromwell, but whose 'knowledge', it emerged, had been derived from watching *Wolf Hall*.[67] David Starkey has been, characteristically, more dismissive: 'We really should stop taking historical novelists seriously as historians,' he has said.

> The idea that they have authority is ludicrous. They are very good at imagining character: that's why the novels sell. They have no authority when it comes to the handling of historical sources. Full stop ... I wouldn't dream of commenting on Hilary Mantel as a novelist, frankly I'd be grateful if she stayed off my patch as a historian.[68]

One does not need to take quite so proprietorial an attitude to the Tudor past to regret that Mantel's take on More and the causes he defended have indeed become gospel for a high proportion of the chattering classes, coincidentally chiming with a plunge in the Catholic Church's reputation because of sexual abuse scandals. One reviewer put the matter starkly: 'In the end, however wedded you are to subtle revisions and shades of grey, you cannot back Cromwell without spitting on More.'[69] The spitting has become widespread. At the height of the television serialization of *Wolf Hall* in 2015, the left-leaning celebrity Anglican cleric Dr Giles Fraser wondered in his regular *Guardian* column whether we shouldn't in fact think of More as a monster rather than a saint. After Mantel, 'gone is the More of heroic humanism popularized by Robert Bolt's *A Man for All Seasons*.' Instead, 'she reminds us that More was persecutor-in-chief towards those who struggled to see the Bible translated into English [...] personally responsible for the burning of a number of men who dared question the ultimate authority of the Roman Church.' He went on to describe More's alleged torture of the evangelical lawyer James Bainham, whom More 'had burnt at the stake' for his refusal to recant. And Dr Fraser cited as his source for these assertions – that week's episode of *Wolf Hall*.[70]

Such fatuity is by no means confined to the historically unschooled. In the week before the publication of *The Mirror and the Light*, the BBC's *Today* programme ran an interview with the historian and curator Tracy Borman, who had been inspired by reading

Wolf Hall to write a popular biography of Cromwell. Questioned by the interviewer on Mantel's contribution to historical knowledge, Borman singled out the trilogy's highlighting of the 'brutal tortures' More had wreaked on his Protestant victims.[71]

The caveats of historians seldom shape popular opinion. Even the most popular of the novels considered in the first half of this essay by and large followed and reflected contemporary historical assumptions about their period: none of them, not even Prescott's masterly fictionalizing of the Pilgrimage of Grace, can be said to have altered popular thinking about the period they portrayed. But Mantel's trilogy *has* reconfigured perception of Tudor England for the early twenty-first century, just as surely as, and even more pervasively than, Bolt's *Man for All Seasons* did for the last decades of the twentieth. And for all her insistence that she is, after all, simply a writer of fiction, Mantel may have had some such outcome in mind: there is an evident iconoclastic urge at work in her portrait of More, a conscious desire to dethrone the hero of Bolt's play.

No one is obliged to think Thomas More a saint: his world view was not ours, and his actions against heresy certainly require interpretation to a culture ill equipped to understand, much less approve, them. But even those who destroyed him thought him a great man. In making the arrangements for More's execution, the real Cromwell, in MacCulloch's words, 'could not bring himself' even to name so revered a victim – 'When Master Fisher shall go to execution, *and also the other.*'[72] More was remembered with admiration in Elizabethan London as virtuous, witty and wise, an upholder of the rule of law and, interestingly, a martyr for the rights of conscience against an overweening state.[73] He was emphatically not a monster. Whatever her intentions, it is hard to put down Mantel's learned and darkly witty fiction without regret, and some puzzlement, at her trilogy's unmitigated construction of a vain, cruel and mean-spirited Thomas More.

Notes

CHAPTER I

This essay is also included in Dee Dyas and John Jenkins (eds), *Pilgrimage and England's Cathedrals: Past, Present, and Future* (London, 2020).

1   Lubin, Helen, *The Worcester Pilgrim* (Worcester, 1990); Webb, Diana, *Pilgrimage in Medieval England* (London and New York, 2000), pp. 210–13. For other observations about the significance of the Worcester pilgrim burial see Duffy, Eamon, *Royal Books and Holy Bones: Essays in Medieval Christianity* (London, 2018), pp. 205–6.

2   Weaver, F. W. (ed.), *Somerset Medieval Wills*, Third Series, Somerset Record Society vol. 21 (1905), p. 14.

3   Northeast, Peter (ed.), *Wills of the Archdeaconry of Sudbury, 1439–1474, Part 1,* Suffolk Records Society, vol. 44 (Woodbridge, 2010), no. 489.

4   Ibid., no. 1207.

5   Weaver, F. W. (ed.), *Somerset Medieval Wills*, Second Series, Somerset Record Society, vol. 19 (1903), p. 30: Webb, *Pilgrimage in Medieval England*, p. 199. For the cult of Edmund Lacy, see Orme, N., 'Two saint-bishops of Exeter: James Berkeley and Edmund Lacy', *Analecta Bolandiana*, vol. 104 (1986), pp. 403–18; Radford, U. M., 'The wax images found in Exeter Cathedral', *Antiquaries Journal*, vol. 29 (1949), pp. 164–8.

6   Duggan, Anne, 'The cult of St Thomas Becket in the thirteenth century', in Meryl Jancey (ed.), *St Thomas Cantilupe, Bishop of Hereford. Essays in His Honour* (Hereford, 1982), pp. 21–44.

7   Townsend, Eleanor, 'Pilgrimage', in Richard Marks, Paul Williamson and Eleanor Townsend (eds), *Gothic, Art for England 1400–1547* (London, 2003), pp. 424–35, at pp. 428–9. The fullest account of the changing appearance of Becket's shrine, and of pilgrim access to it, is now John Jenkins, 'Modelling the Cult of Thomas Becket in Canterbury Cathedral' (2020), published online by the *Journal of the British Archaeological Association*, DOI: 10.1080/00681288.2020.1771897. On the impact of Becket's cult in

other Cathedrals: John Jenkins, 'Replication or rivalry? The "Becketization" of pilgrimage in English Cathedrals', *Religion*, vol. 49.1 (2019), pp. 24–47.

8   Binski, Paul, *Becket's Crown: Art and Imagination in Gothic England, 1170–1300* (New Haven, CT, and London, 2004), pp. 84–7 (on the vigour and persistence of the cult of St Etheldreda), 123–46. Death and canonization dates are from Farmer, David Hugh, *The Oxford Dictionary of Saints*, 3rd edn (Oxford, 1992).

9   Crook, John, *English Medieval Shrines* (Woodbridge, 2011), pp. 160–2: Farmer, *Oxford Dictionary of Saints*, pp. 506–7.

10 Binski, *Becket's Crown*, p. 126.

11 Shinners, John, 'The veneration of saints at Norwich Cathedral in the fourteenth century', *Norfolk Archaeology*, vol. 40.2 (1988), pp. 133–44, at p. 137.

12 Crook, *English Medieval Shrines*, p. 252: Cole, R. E. G., 'Proceedings relative to the canonisation of Robert Grosseteste, bishop of Lincoln', *Associated Architectural Societies' Reports and Papers*, vol. 33 (1915–16), pp. 1–34.

13 Malden, A. R. (ed.), *The Canonization of St Osmund, from the Manuscript Record in the Muniment Room of Salisbury Cathedral* (Salisbury, 1905).

14 Raine, James (ed.), *The Fabric Rolls of York Minster,* Surtees Society, vol. 35 (Durham, 1859), pp. 225–6.

15 Crook, *English Medieval Shrines*, passim.

16 Ibid., pp. 235–9.

17 Ibid., pp. 230–4, 220–6, 244–6, 260–2.

18 Ibid., pp. 280–1.

19 For a good discussion of the issues round visibility, 'shrine vistas' and the impact of screens and reredoses, see Nilson, Ben, *Cathedral Shrines of Medieval England* (Woodbridge, 1998), pp. 81–91.

20 Draper, Peter, 'Enclosures and entrances in medieval cathedrals', in Janet Backhouse (ed.), *The Medieval English Cathedral: Papers in Honour of Pamela Tudor-Craig* (Donington, 2003), pp. 76–88, at pp. 80–1.

21 Translation from the Canterbury Customary, BL Add Ms 59616, by John Jenkins, slightly modified. I am grateful to Dr Jenkins for permission to quote from his forthcoming edition and translation.

22 Fowler, J. T. (ed.), *Rites of Durham*, Surtees Society, vol. 107 (1902), p. 94.

23 Erasmus, 'A pilgrimage for religion's sake', in Craig R. Thompson (ed. and trans.), *Ten Colloquies* (Indianapolis, IN, 1957), pp. 83–7.

24 'In which time the feretrarian called the *temporal* will open the doors of the church and by three rings of the bell gives notice to the people that it is the time to assemble for the mass of St Thomas, summoning and assembling pilgrims and travellers, if there are any.' From the Canterbury Customary, BL Add. MS 59616, see note 21 above.

25 Crook, *English Medieval Shrines*, pp. 218–20, 264–6.

26 Ibid., pp. 218–20.

27 Thacker, Alan, 'The cult of the saints and the liturgy in the middle ages', in Derek Keene, Arthur Burns and Andrew Saint (eds), *St Paul's, the Cathedral Church of London, 604–2004* (New Haven, CT, and London, 2004), pp. 113–122, at p. 121.

28 Fowler, *Rites of Durham*, p. 30.

29 Ibid., p. 38.

30 Ibid., pp. 44–5; for the exclusion of women from Cuthbert's shrine, but access for women to the Galilee Chapel and its altars, see ibid., pp. 35, 42–51. Brown, David (ed.), *Durham Cathedral, History, Fabric and Culture* (New Haven, CT, and London, 2015), pp. 64, 172.

31 For two lists of the relics and other treasures at St Cuthbert's shrine in the fourteenth century, see Shinners, John (ed.), *Medieval Popular Religion, 1000–1500* (Peterborough, Ont., 1999), pp. 195– 200.

32 Fowler, *Rites of Durham*, p. 5.

33 Nilsen, *Cathedral Shrines of Medieval England*, p. 52.

34 Legg, J. Wickham, and Hope, W. H. St John (eds), *Inventories of Christchurch Canterbury* (London, 1902), pp. 80–94.

35 The reference to dining 'after' is an allusion to the fact that pilgrims were encouraged to make their visit to the shrine fasting.

36 Bowers, John M. (ed.), 'The Canterbury Interlude and Merchant's Tale of Beryn', in *The Canterbury Tales: Fifteenth-Century Continuations and Additions* (Kalamazoo, MI, 1992), lines 130–204, available online at http://d.lib.rochester.edu/teams/text/bowers-canterbury-tales-fifteenth-century-interlude-and-marchants-tale-of-beryn

37 Bowers, Roger, 'The liturgy of the cathedral and its music', in Patrick Collinson, Nigel Ramsay and Margaret Sparks (eds), *A History of Canterbury Cathedral* (Oxford, 1995), pp. 408–50, at pp. 419–23.

38 Spencer, Brian, 'Medieval pilgrim badges', in J. G. N. Renaud (ed.), *Rotterdam Papers: A Contribution to Medieval Archaeology* (Rotterdam, 1968), pp. 137–53; Spencer, Brian (ed.), *Salisbury Museum Medieval Catalogue,* Part 2, *Pilgrim Souvenirs and Secular Badges* (Salisbury, 1990).

39 Duffy, E., 'Monasticism and the religion of the people: Crowland Abbey', in *Royal Books and Holy Bones* (London, 2018), p. 269.

40 Townsend, 'Pilgrimage', pp. 430–1.

41 James, M. R. (ed.), 'Lives of St Walstan', *Proceedings of the Norfolk and Norwich Archaeological Society*, vol. 19 (1917), pp. 238–67. The brass plate from Glastonbury is illustrated in Webb, *Pilgrimage*, p. 87.

42 Webb, *Pilgrimage in Medieval England*, pp. 63–91; Oates, J. C. T., 'Richard Pynson and the Holy Blood of Hayles', *The Library*, 5th series, 13 (1958), pp. 269–77. The Walsingham legend is printed in J. C. Dickinson, *The Shrine of Our Lady of Walsingham* (Cambridge, 1956),

pp. 124–30. Robinson, J. A., *Two Glastonbury Legends* (Cambridge, 1926); Traherne, R. F., *The Glastonbury Legends* (London, 1967). A critical edition of Henry Bradshaw's Life of St Werburge is available online at http://www.medievalchester.ac.uk/texts/introbradshaw.html. For Lydgate's life of St Edmund, see Marks, Williamson and Townsend (eds), *Gothic, Art for England*, p. 429.

43 The Henry VI miracle book is printed in Paul Grosjean (ed.), *Henrici VI Angliae regis miracula postuma ex codice musei britannici regio 13. C. VIII* (Brussels, 1835).

44 Malden, *Canonization of St Osmund*, pp. 56–90.

45 Ibid., p. 57–9.

46 Ibid., pp. 59–60.

47 Ibid., p. 63.

48 Ibid., pp. 68–9.

49 Ibid., pp. 59, 77. Both miracles are said to have occurred 40 years earlier; despite the difference in names, it is possible that the two accounts represent muddled recollections of the same incident.

50 Ibid., p. 63.

51 Ibid., pp. 76–7.

52 Ibid., pp. 78–9.

53 Ibid., p. 67.

54 Ibid., p. 63.

55 Ibid., p. 66.

56 Ibid., pp. 71–2.

57 Ibid., pp. 80–1.

58 What follows is based on a transcript of Durham Dean and Chapter Muniments Misc. Chart 7159*, kindly supplied by Dr John Jenkins.

59 Duffy, 'St Erkenwald', in Duffy, *Royal Books and Holy Bones*, pp. 165–86, especially pp. 168–70; Barron, Caroline, and Rousseau, Marie-Hélène, 'Cathedral, city and state 1300–1540', in Burns and Saint, *St Paul's*, p. 40.

60 I am indebted to unpublished research by my former student Fr Nikolaos Vernezos for these details of bequests to St Hugh's head.

61 Nilsen, *Cathedral Shrines of Medieval England*, pp. 144–82 (discussion), 210–42 (tables and graphs).

62 Canterbury figures set out in Nilsen, *Cathedral Shrines*, pp. 211–15.

63 For a discussion of the issue of locality and convenience versus distance and difficulty, see Duffy, *Royal Books and Holy Bones*, pp. 205–20.

64 Canterbury customary, BL Add. MS 59616, see above, note 21.

65 Shinners, 'The veneration of saints at Norwich Cathedral', pp. 134–7: Nilsen, *English Cathedral Shrines* p. 238, graph 9. Nilsen's discussion on pp. 156–8, based on Shinner, post-dates the Peltiers' adoption of

St William by a century! For a discussion of the origins of the cult of William of Norwich, see Duffy, *Royal Books and Holy Bones*, pp. 125–35.

66   Shinners, 'The veneration of saints at Norwich Cathedral', pp. 139–40.

67   See the will of Thomas Peckerell, cited above, note 4.

68   Swanson, Robert, *Indulgences in Late Medieval England* (Cambridge, 2007), pp. 357–8.

69   Ibid., p. 361 (Norwich).

70   Wriothesley, Charles, *A Chronicle of England*, 2 vols, Chetham Society, new series, vols 11 and 20 (1875, 1877), vol. 1, p. 31. But the bones may simply have been reburied, as St Cuthbert's were at Durham: see Butler, John, *The Quest for Becket's Bones* (New Haven, CT, and London, 1995). Fowler, *Rites*, p. 103.

71   On which see Marshall, Peter, 'Forgery and miracles in the reign of Henry VIII', *Past and Present*, no. 178 (February 2003), pp. 39–73.

CHAPTER 2

This essay originated as a lecture given in Ely Cathedral, 18 November 2019.

1   Stevenson, William, *A Supplement to the Second Edition of Mr Bentham's History and Antiquities of the Cathedral and Conventual Church of Ely* (Norwich, 1817), pp. 55–6. The original deed of surrender is lost, but a copy by the cathedral historian James Bentham is in Cambridge University Library, CUL MS Add. 2957, fols 166*v*–168*r*.

2   For the early history of the community, see Keynes, Simon, 'Ely Abbey 672–1109', in Peter Meadows and Nigel Ramsay (eds), *A History of Ely Cathedral* (Woodbridge, 2003), pp. 3–58.

3   Crook, John, *English Medieval Shrines* (Woodbridge, 2011), pp. 59–61.

4   For a discussion of Norman attitudes to Saxon saints, see ibid., pp. 107–32.

5   Owen, Dorothy, 'Ely 1109–1539: priory, community and town', in Meadows and Ramsay (eds), *History*, pp. 59–76.

6   Summaries of the architectural development of the cathedral in the chapters by Eric Fernie for the Norman period, and John Maddison for the Gothic cathedral, in Meadows and Ramsay (eds), *History*, pp. 95–142; for the transformation of the cathedral buildings in the fourteenth century, and the ideas behind it, see Binski, Paul, *Gothic Wonder: Art, Architecture and the Decorated Style 1290–1350* (New Haven, CT, and London, 2014), pp. 187–279.

7   Binski, *Gothic Wonder*, pp. 193, 196.

8   Boyd, Beverly, *The Middle English Miracles of the Virgin* (San Marino, CA, 1965); Williams Boyarin, Adrienne, *Miracles of the Virgin in Medieval England: Law and Jewishness in Marian Legends* (Woodbridge,

2010); Morgan, Nigel, 'Texts and images of Marian devotion in English twelfth-century monasticism', in Benjamin Thompson (ed.), *Monasticism and Society*, Harlaxton Medieval Studies (Stamford, 1999), pp. 117–36; Morgan, Nigel, 'Texts and images of Marian devotion in thirteenth-century England', in W. M. Ormrud (ed.), *England in the Thirteenth Century*, Harlaxton Medieval Studies (Stamford, 1991), pp. 69–103; Morgan, Nigel, 'Texts and images of Marian devotion in fourteenth-century England', in N. Rogers (ed.), *England in the Fourteenth Century*, Harlaxton Medieval Studies (Stamford, 1992), pp. 34–57.

9   The fullest attempt to identify the subjects of the ruined sculptures is by M. R. James, *The Sculptures in the Lady Chapel at Ely* (London, 1895).

10   Meadows and Ramsay, *History*, p. 71.

11   Ibid., pp. 86–8.

12   Lefferts, Peter, 'Cantilena and antiphons: music for Marian services in late medieval England', in P. Lefferts and B. Seirup (eds), *Current Musicology*, 45–7 (1990), pp. 247–82; Morgan, Nigel, 'Marian liturgy in Salisbury Cathedral', in J. Backhouse (ed.), *The English Cathedral*, Harlaxton Medieval Studies (Stamford, 2002), pp. 91–113.

13   Meadows and Ramsay, *History*, p. 177.

14   Maddison, John, 'The Gothic cathedral', in Meadows and Ramsay, *History*, at p. 124.

15   Figures taken from the Ely sacrist's and feretrar's rolls, reproduced in Ben Nilson, *Cathedral Shrines of Medieval England* (Woodbridge, 1998), pp. 216–18.

16   Nilson, *Cathedral Shrines*, p. 156.

17   Binski, *Gothic Wonder*, pp. 209–14.

18   Greatrex, Joan, 'Benedictine observance at Ely', in Meadows and Ramsay, *History*, pp. 77–93.

19   Greatrex, Joan, 'Rabbits and eels at high table: monks of Ely at the university of Cambridge, c.1337–1539', in Thompson, Benjamin (ed.), *Monasteries and Society in Medieval Britain: Proceedings of the 1994 Harlaxton Symposium* (Stamford, 1999), pp. 312–28.

20   The classic account is by Dom David Knowles, in *The Religious Orders in England*, vol. 3, *The Tudor Age* (Cambridge, 1959). There is an overview with documents in Joyce Youings, *The Dissolution of the Monasteries* (London, 1971). The case for a genuinely reforming rather than economic motivation for the dissolutions is argued by G. W. Bernard in 'The dissolution of the monasteries', *History*, vol. 96, no. 4 (324) (October 2011), pp. 390–409, and in *The King's Reformation: Henry VIII and the Remaking of the English Church* (New Haven, CT, and London, 2005), pp. 243–76. Bernard discusses the final phase of the dissolutions (during which Ely was suppressed) in *The King's Reformation*, pp. 433–74. For

Wolsey's attitude to monasticism, see Gwynn, Peter, *The King's Cardinal* (London, 1990), pp. 469–79.

21 The Act is printed in J. R. Tanner (ed.), *Tudor Constitutional Documents A.D. 1485–1603* (Cambridge, 1940), pp. 59–63.

22 Frere, Walter Howard, and Kennedy, William McClure (eds), *Visitation Articles and Injunctions of the Period of the Reformation*, vol. 2, *1536–1558* (London, 1910), p. 5.

23 Dodds, Madeleine Hope, and Dodds, Ruth, *The Pilgrimage of Grace 1536–7 and the Exeter Conspiracy 1538* (Cambridge, 1915), despite its age, remains indispensable: the best modern account is by Richard Hoyle, *The Pilgrimage of Grace and the Politics of the 1530s* (Oxford, 2001).

24 Bush, M. L., *The Pilgrimage of Grace: A Study of the Rebel Armies of October 1536* (Manchester, 1996), p. 343

25 Tanner, *Tudor Constitutional Documents*, p. 64.

26 *Letters and Papers, Foreign and Domestic of the Reign of Henry VIII: Preserved in the Public Record Office, the British Museum and Elsewhere in England* (London, 1864–1932), vol. 13, part 1 (1538), pp. 144–5, item 67.

27 Butler, John R., *The Quest for Becket's Bones* (New Haven, CT, and London, 1995), Chapter 7.

28 Frere and Kennedy, *Visitation Articles*, p. 38.

29 Atherton, Ian, 'The dean and chapter, reformation and restoration: 1541–1660', in Meadows and Ramsay, *History*, at pp. 169–71.

30 Knowles, *Religious Orders*, vol. 3, pp. 376–82.

31 Meadows and Ramsay, *History*, pp. 172–4.

32 For Goodrich's career, see the *Oxford Dictionary of National Biography* article, by Felicity Heal, available at https://www.oxforddnb.com/search? q=Goodrich%2C+Thomas&searchBtn=Search&isQuickSearch=true

33 Frere and Kennedy, *Visitation Articles,* pp. 67–9.

34 Meadows and Ramsay, *History,* pp. 172–3.

35 For Boxall, see the article in the *Oxford Dictionary of National Biography* by C. S. Knighton, available at https://www.oxforddnb.com/view/10.1093/ ref:odnb/9780198614128.001.0001/odnb-9780198614128-e-3094? rskey=gBIvc5&result=1 and Duffy, Eamon, *Fires of Faith: Catholic England under Mary Tudor* (New Haven, CT, and London, 2009), pp. 69, 196.

36 Law, Ceri, *Contested Reformations in the University of Cambridge, 1535– 1584* (Woodbridge, 2018), p. 58.

37 For Thirlby, see the article in the *Oxford Dictionary of National Biography* by C. S. Knighton, available at https://www.oxforddnb.com/view/10.1093/ ref:odnb/9780198614128.001.0001/odnb-9780198614128-e-27184 ?rskey=Y781Sj&result=1. For Thirlby's role in Cranmer's ritual disgrading, see MacCulloch, Diarmaid, *Thomas Cranmer, a Life* (New Haven, CT, and London, 1996), pp. 590–93.

38 For Perne's remarkable career, see Collinson, Patrick, McKitterick, David, and Leedham-Green, Elizabeth, *Andrew Perne: Quatercentenary Studies*, Cambridge Bibliographical Society Monographs no. 11 (Cambridge, 1991). Collinson's essay 'Perne the turncoat' was reprinted in his *Elizabethan Essays* (London, 1994), pp. 179–217; see also Collinson's article on Perne in the *Oxford Dictionary of National Biography*, available at https://www.oxforddnb.com/view/10.1093/ref:odnb/9780198614128.001.0001/odnb-9780198614128-e-21975

39 Wenig, Scott, 'The Reformation in the diocese of Ely during the episcopate of Richard Cox, 1559–77', *The Sixteenth Century Journal*, vol. 33, no. 1 (Spring 2002), pp. 151–80.

40 Payne, Ian, 'Music and liturgy to 1644', in Meadows and Ramsay, *History*, esp. pp. 226–9.

41 For the situation in early Reformation Durham, see essay 3 in this volume, 'A People's Tragedy', pp. 50–2.

42 Frere, W. H., and Douglas, C. E. (eds), *Puritan Manifestoes* (London, 1907), p. 32.

CHAPTER 3

This essay originated as a lecture given as part of Durham University's '1569 Rebellion Anniversary Conference', 2019.

1 Sharp, Sir Cuthbert, *The Rising in the North ... being a reprint of the Memorials of the Rebellion of the Earls of Northumberland and Westmoreland edited by Sir Cuthbert Sharp 1840*, facsimile reprint (Shotton, 1975), pp. 36–7 [hereafter Sharp, *Memorials*].

2 See the discussion in Kesselring, K., *The Northern Rebellion of 1569: Faith, Politics, and Protest in Elizabethan England* (London, 2007), pp. 61ff. Kesselring's book is the most thorough and persuasive modern account of the rebellion as a whole, and I have broadly accepted his analysis of the motivation of the rank and file.

3 Sharp, *Memorials*, p. 45.

4 Ibid., pp. 56, 83; Fletcher, Anthony, and McCulloch, Diarmaid, *Tudor Rebellions*, 4th edn (London, 1997), p. 151.

5 As argued by Fletcher and MacCulloch in *Tudor Rebellions*, p. 102.

6 Sharp, *Memorials*, pp. 41–2.

7 Fowler, J. T. (ed.), *Rites of Durham; being a Description or Brief Declaration of all the Ancient Monuments, Rites and Customs belonging or being within the Monastical Church of Durham before the Suppression, written 1593*, Surtees Society, 107 (1902), p. 27.

8 Marcombe, David, '" A Rude and Heady People": the local community and the rebellion of the northern earls', in David Marcombe (ed.), *The*

Last Principality: Politics, Religion, and Society in the Bishopric of Durham, 1494–1660 (Nottingham, 1997), p. 134. Dr Marcombe's 1973 Durham PhD thesis, 'The Dean and Chapter of Durham, 1558–1603', is the best study of the promotion of Protestantism in the diocese in Elizabeth's reign.

9   Raine, James (ed.), *Depositions and Other Ecclesiastical Proceeding from 1311 to the Reign of Elizabeth*, Surtees Society, 21 (London, 1846) p. 119.

10   Marcombe, 'A Rude and Heady People', pp. 139–40.

11   Ibid., pp. 138–9: Kesselring, *Northern Rebellion*, p. 71: Raine, *Depositions*, pp. 110–11, 184–8.

12   Sharp, *Memorials*, p. 52.

13   Raine, *Depositions*, p. 166.

14   Ibid., pp. 185–93.

15   Ibid., p. 131 and passim.

16   Ibid., pp. 136–7 (testimony of Prebendary Cliffe).

17   Ibid., p. 144.

18   Ibid., pp. 137, 148.

19   Sharp, *Memorials*, pp. 212–13.

20   Raine, *Depositions*, pp. 174–5.

21   Ibid., p. 180: the parish church in question appears to have been Auckland St Andrew.

22   Ibid., pp. 144, 159, 160, 174–5, 198.

23   Ibid., p. 164.

24   Ibid., pp. 139–42.

25   Ibid., pp. 162, 165–6.

26   Ibid., p. 167.

27   Ibid., p. 170.

28   Ibid., pp. 172–3.

29   Ibid., p. 160.

30   Ibid., p. 137.

31   Ibid., p. 149. For Brimley's career, see the Durham doctoral thesis by Brian Crosby, *The Choral Foundation of Durham Cathedral c. 1350-1650*, available at http://etheses.dur.ac.uk/769/.

32   Sharp, *Memorials*, pp. 73–4.

33   Ibid., p. 121.

34   Ibid., p. 135.

35   Ibid., p. 130.

36   Ibid., p. 141.

37   Ibid. p. 163.

38   Ibid., p. 173.

39   Raine, *Depositions*, pp. 168–9.

40   Sharp, *Memorials*, p. 188.

41   Raine, *Depositions*, p. 149.

CHAPTER 4

An earlier version of this essay was given as a lecture at the symposium 'Memory, Martyrs and Mission: Aspects of Priestly Formation for England and Wales, 1118–2018', organized by the Venerable English College in Rome in May 2018.

1   Guilday, Peter, *The English Catholic Refugees on the Continent, 1558–1795* (London, 1914), pp. 65–6.

2   Cardon, George, *La Fondation de l'université de Douai* (Paris, 1892), p. 145.

3   For the background, see Cardon, *Fondation*, and Löwe, J. Andreas, 'Richard Smyth and the foundation of the University of Douai', *Nederlands archief voor kerkgeschiedenis / Dutch Review of Church History*, vol. 79, no. 2 (1999), pp. 142–69.

4   Löwe, 'Richard Smyth and the foundation of the University of Douai', pp. 142–69.

5   Possoz, Alexis, *Mgr Jean Vendeville, évêque de Tournai, 1587–1592* (Paris, 1862), p. 28.

6   Knox, T. F. (ed.), *The First and Second Diaries of the English College, Douay, and an appendix of unpublished documents* (London, 1878), p. xxviii; Knox, T. F. (ed.), *The Letters and Memorials of William Cardinal Allen* (London, 1882), p. 22.

7   The phrase is Thomas Stapleton's, applied to Bishop William Barlow of Chichester, who had deprived him of his Chichester prebend in 1563; O'Connell, Marvin R., *Thomas Stapleton and the Counter-Reformation* (New Haven, CT, and London, 1964), p. 28.

8   Stapleton, Thomas, *A Counterblast to M. Hornes vayne blaste against M. Fekenham Wherein is set forthe: a ful reply to M. Hornes Answer, and to euery part therof made, against the declaration of my L. Abbat of Westminster, M. Fekenham, touching, the othe of the Supremacy* (Louvain, 1567), p. 19.

9   Knox, *First and Second Diaries*, pp. xxxix, xliii; Knox, *Letters and Memorials*, pp. 62, 67.

10 Knox, *First and Second Diaries*, p. xlii; Deutscher, Thomas, 'Seminaries and the education of Novarese parish priests, 1593–1627', *Journal of Ecclesiastical History* (July 1981), pp. 303–19, at p. 313.

11 A similar picture obtained in Fiesole two generations on: Comerford, Kathleen M., 'The influence of the Jesuits on the curriculum of the diocesan seminary of Fiesole, 1636–1646', *The Catholic Historical Review*, vol. 84, no. 4 (October 1998), pp. 662–80.

12 On the Jesuits, the *Ratio studiorum* and St Thomas, see Broderick, James, *The Life and Work of Blessed Robert Francis Cardinal Bellarmine* (London, 1928), vol. 1, pp. 374–84. An annotated translation of the 1599 *Ratio* is available online at http://www.bc.edu/sites/libraries/ratio/ratio1599.pdf

13 Duffy, Eamon, *Reformation Divided: Catholics, Protestants and the Conversion of England* (London, 2017), p. 172.

14 Allen's own account of the syllabus is in Knox, *Letters and Memorials*, pp. 62–7, translated in Knox, *First and Second Diaries*, pp. xxxviii–xliii. It is closely followed by Gregory Martin in G. B. Parks (ed.), *Roma sancta* (Rome, 1969), pp. 114–19. Martin's text was written soon after Allen's letter, and no doubt drew directly on it.

15 Martin's preface to the Rheims New Testament (slightly abbreviated) is conveniently printed in Pollard, Alfred W., *Records of the English Bible* (Oxford, 1911), pp. 301–13 (quotation at p. 308).

16 The most thorough discussion of all these issues is Carleton, James B., *The Part of Rheims in the Making of the English Bible* (Oxford, 1902). See also Westcott, Brooke Foss, *A General View of the History of the English Bible*, rev. William Aldis Wright (London, 1905), pp. 105–8, 256–65.

17 Martin, *Roma sancta*, p. 116.

18 Allison, A. F., and Rogers, D. M., *The Contemporary Printed Literature of the English Counter-Reformation between 1558 and 1640*, vol. 1, *Works in Languages Other than English* (Aldershot, 1989), no. 1210. See the valuable discussion by Bill Sheils, 'The gospel, liturgy and controversy in the 1590s: Thomas Stapleton's *Promptuaria*', in James Kelly and Susan Royal (eds), *Early Modern English Catholicism, Identity, Memory and Counter-Reformation* (Leiden, 2017), pp. 189–205.

19 Martin, *Roma sancta*, p. 117.

20 *The New Testament of Iesus Christ, translated faithfully into English out of the authentical Latin* [...] *in the English College of Rhemes* (Rheims, 1582), p. 8.

21 Stapleton, Thomas, *Promptuarium catholicum* (Augsburg, 1622), pp. 11–16.

22 Knox, *Letters and Memorials*, pp. 32–3.

23 Frick, David A., 'Anglo-Polonica: the Rheims New Testament of 1582 and the making of the Polish Catholic Bible', *The Polish Review*, vol. 36, no. 1 (1991), pp. 47–67.

CHAPTER 5

This essay originated as a lecture delivered in various locations to celebrate the fourth centenary of the publication of the King James Bible in 2011.

1 Listed in Norton, David, *The King James Bible: A Short History from Tyndale to Today* (Cambridge, 2011), pp. 55–60.

2 Campbell, Gordon, *Bible: The Story of the King James Version* (Oxford, 2010), p. 265.

3 https://www.youtube.com/watch?v=EJtCqjUUHGo

4 See the discussion of 'AVolatry' in David Norton, *A History of the English Bible as Literature* (Cambridge, 2000), pp. 400–04.

5   *The Guardian* (10 January 2013).

6   For a much wider list, see the 'Index of expressions' in David Crystal, *Begat: The King James Bible and the English Language* (Oxford, 2010), pp. 303–10.

7   McGrath, Alistair, *In the Beginning: The Story of the King James Bible and How It Changed a Nation, a Language, and a Culture* (London, 2001), p. 305.

8   The most recent discussion of King James's intentions is Ken Fincham, 'The King James Bible, crown, church and people', *Journal of Ecclesiastical History*, vol. 71, no. 1 (January 2020), pp. 77–97.

9   There is a useful brief survey in Norton, *Bible as Literature*, pp. 10–26. For a large-scale modern biography see David Daniell, *William Tyndale: A Biography* (New Haven, CT, and London, 1994). Daniell produced a modern spelling edition of the 1534 text as *Tyndale's New Testament* (New Haven, CT, and London, 1989), and of Tyndale's incomplete *Old Testament* (New Haven, CT, and London, 1992).

10 For Coverdale, see: Norton, *Bible as Literature*, pp. 29–34; Daniell, David, *The Bible in English* (New Haven, CT, and London, 2003), pp. 173–89; and Mozley, J. F., *Coverdale and His Bibles* (London, 1953).

11 Berry, Lloyd E., *The Geneva Bible, A Facsimile of the 1560 Edition: With an Introduction* (Madison, MI, 1969). All Geneva citations are from this edition. Daniell, *Bible in English*, pp. 275–319.

12 Daniell, *Bible in English*, pp. 338–47.

13 Some of the Geneva annotations likely to have offended James are discussed by McGrath, *In the Beginning*, pp. 141–8.

14 There is a vivid if highly coloured account in Adam Nicolson, *Power and Glory: Jacobean England and the Making of the King James Bible* (London, 2003), pp. 42–61.

15 Nicolson, *Power and Glory*, p. 54.

16 Norton, *King James Bible*, pp. 55–60.

17 Daniell, *Bible in English*, p. 439.

18 See the discussion of the process of translation in Norton, *King James Bible*, pp. 81–110; Daniell, *Bible in English*, pp. 438–56.

19 There is a good discussion of these and other stylistic aspects in McGrath, *In the Beginning*, pp. 253–76.

20 Norton, *Bible as Literature*, pp. 56–60.

21 Quoted in Dod, Albert B., *Essays, Theological and Miscellaneous, Reprinted from the Princeton Review: Second Series*, Part 4 (New York and London, 1847), p. 522.

22 Norton, *Bible as Literature*, pp. 107–10.

23 Ibid., pp. 211–12: Norton, *King James Bible*, pp. 164–9.

24 Norton, *Bible as Literature*, pp. 307–9.

25 Eliot, T. S., 'Religion and Literature', in John Hayward (ed.), *T.S. Eliot, Selected Prose* (Harmondsworth, 1953), pp. 31–42, discussed in Martin Warner, 'Reading the Bible "as the report of the Word of God": the case of T. S. Eliot', *Christianity and Literature*, vol. 61, no. 4 (Summer 2012), pp. 543–64.

26 The text of Auden's letter is reproduced at https://www.patheos.com/blogs/geneveith/2012/05/auden-on-modern-liturgies/ Auden wrote a number of letters in the same vein to episcopalian clergy.

27 Lewis's introduction to Phillips, J. B. (trans.), *Letters to Young Churches* (London, 1947), pp. vii–x. Discussion of Lewis's views in Norton, *Bible as Literature*, pp. 411–17: Lewis, C. S., *The Literary Impact of the Authorised Version: The Ethel M. Wood Lecture Delivered before the University of London on 20 March 1950* (London, 1950).

CHAPTER 6

This is a revised version of the 2011 Kidderminster Richard Baxter Quinquennial Lecture, and was therefore written before the publication of the five-volume critical edition of the *Reliquiae* by a team of scholars headed by Professor Neil Keeble – *Richard Baxter: 'Reliquiæ Baxterianæ', or, Mr Richard Baxter's Narrative of the Most Memorable Passages of his Life and Times*, ed. N. H. Keeble, John Coffey, Tim Cooper and Tom Charlton (Oxford, 2020).

1 Montaigne, Michel de, *Complete Works,* ed. Donald M. Frame (New York, London and Toronto 2003).

2 Evelyn, John, *The Diary of John Evelyn,* ed. E. S. de Beer, 6 vols (Oxford, 1955). There is also a one-volume selection edited by de Beer (Oxford, 1959) as well as many subsequent editions. Pepys, Samuel, *The Diary of Samuel Pepys: A New and Complete Transcription*, ed. Robert Latham and William Matthews, 11 vols (London, 1970–83). There is also a one-volume selection by Latham, published as *The Shorter Pepys* (Harmondsworth, 1987).

3 Nuttall, P. Austin (ed.), *The History of the Worthies of England: A New Edition*, 3 vols (New York, 1965); one-volume selection, *Fuller's Worthies, Selected from the Worthies of England* (London, 1987). Macray, W. Dunn (ed.), *The History of the Rebellion and Civil Wars in England Begun in the year 1641* (Oxford, 1888); one-volume selection by G. Huehns (Oxford, 1955) and many reprints.

4 Bunyan, John, *Grace Abounding to the Chief of Sinners*, ed. Roger Sharrock (Oxford, 1963); paperback edn, *John Bunyan: Grace Abounding to the Chief of Sinners*, ed. W. R. Owens (Harmondsworth, 1987). Penney,

Norman (ed.), *The Journal of George Fox*, 2 vols (Cambridge, 1911), with original spelling, is the best edition. There are single-volume modernized editions by Henry J. Cadbury, with a valuable introduction by G. F. Nuttall, *The Journal of George Fox: A Revised Edition* (London, 1975), and by Nigel Smith: *George Fox, the Journal* (Harmondsworth, 1998). See also Watkins, Owen C., *The Puritan Experience* (London, 1972).

5   Bennett, Kate (ed.), *John Aubrey: Brief Lives with an Apparatus for the Lives of our English Mathematical Writers*, 2 vols (Oxford, 2015); there is also a one-volume selection, ed. O. S. Dick, available in many editions.

6   Significantly, Baxter's *Reliquiae* is not discussed in Michelle M. Dowd and Julie A. Eckerle, 'Recent studies in early modern English life writing', *English Literary Renaissance*, vol. 40 (2010), pp. 132–62, or in Andrew Cambers, 'Reading, the godly, and self-writing in England, circa 1580–1720', *Journal of British Studies*, vol. 46 (2007), pp. 796–825.

7   Sylvester, Matthew (ed.), *Reliquiae Baxterianae: or, Mr. Richard Baxter's Narrative of the Most Memorable Passages of his Life and Times* (London, 1696); Nuttall, Geoffrey, 'The MS of *Reliquiae Baxterianae* (1696)', *Journal of Ecclesiastical History*, vol. 6 (1955), pp. 73–9. This essay was written before the publication of Neil Keeble, '*Reliquiae Baxterianae* and the shaping of the seventeenth century', in Edward Jones (ed.), *A Concise Companion to the Study of Manuscripts, Printed Books and the production of Early Modern Texts* (Chichester, 2015), pp. 229–48, but see the helpful introduction by Professor Keeble to the 1974 Everyman reissue of J. Lloyd Thomas's selection from the *Reliquiae: The Autobiography of Richard Baxter*. On Baxter's writing in general, see Keeble's superbly sensitive *Richard Baxter, Puritan Man of Letters* (Oxford, 1982).

8   Sylvester (ed.), *Reliquiae*, Part 1, p. 124.

9   *The Certainty of the World of Spirits* (London, 1691).

10 Sylvester (ed.), *Reliquiae*, Part 1 p. 7.

11 Baxter, Richard, *Poetical Fragments, Heart-Imployment with God and It Self: The Concordant Discord of A Broken-Healed Heart* (London, 1681), pp. 14–15.

12 Sylvester (ed.), *Reliquiae*, Part 1, p. 7.

13 Nuttall, 'MS of *Reliquiae*', p. 73.

14 Powicke, F. J., *A Life of the Reverend Richard Baxter, 1615–1691* (London, 1924); Powicke, F. J., *The Reverend Richard Baxter under the Cross (1662–1691)* (London, 1927); Nuttall, G. F., *Richard Baxter* (London, 1965).

15 Sylvester (ed.), *Reliquiae*, Part 3, p. 179.

16 *The Nonconformist's Memorial: Being an Account of the Ministers, Who Were Ejected or Silenced After the Restoration, Particularly by the Act of Uniformity, Which Took Place on Bartholomew-Day, Aug. 24, 1662*, 2 vols (London, 1775).

17   Lloyd Thomas, J. (ed.), *The Autobiography of Richard Baxter* (London, 1925).

18   Sylvester (ed.), *Reliquiae*, Part 1, p. 43.

19   *Confirmation and restauration the necessary means of reformation, and reconciliation; for the healing of the corruptions and divisions of the churches: submissively, but earnestly tendered to the consideration of the soveraigne powers, magistrates, ministers, and people, that they may awake, and be up and doing in the execution of so much, as appeareth to be necessary as they are true to Christ, his Church and Gospel, and to their own and others souls, and to the peace and wellfare of the nations; and as they will answer the neglect to Christ, at their peril. / By Richard Baxter, an unworthy minister of Christ, that longeth to see the healing of the churches* (London, 1658).

20   Sylvester (ed.), *Reliquiae*, Part 2, p. 303.

21   Ibid., Part 2, p. 47.

22   Ibid.

23   Aubrey, *Brief Lives*, Project Gutenberg edition, available at https://www.gutenberg.org/files/47787/47787-h/47787-h.htm, note 869.

24   *A Breviate of the Life of Margaret* [...] *Baxter* (London, 1681), pp. 93–4.

25   Sylvester (ed.), *Reliquiae*, Part 1, pp. 2–3.

26   Ibid., Part 1, p. 4.

27   Ibid., Part 3, pp. 16–17.

CHAPTER 7

An earlier version of this essay was given as a plenary lecture at the annual conference of the Catholic Theological Association of Great Britain in 2017, published as part of the conference proceedings in *New Blackfriars*, vol. 99, issue 1080 (March 2018), pp. 147–62.

1   Luther, Martin, *Table Talk*, ed. Theodore G. Tappert (Philadelphia, PA, 1967), vol. 54 of *Luther's Works*, gen. ed. Helmut T. Lehmann, no.4487, p. 346.

2   Text available at http://en.radiovaticana.va/news/2016/10/31/pope_and_president_of_lwf_sign_joint_statement/1269150

3   Text available at https://www.elca.org/Declaration-on-the-Way

4   Text available at http://www.vatican.va/roman_curia/pontifical_councils/chrstuni/lutheran-fed-docs/rc_pc_chrstuni_doc_2013_dal-conflitto-alla-comunione_en.html

5   http://liturgy.co.nz/pope-francis-to-make-martin-luther-a-saint-on-october-31

6   English text available at http://www.papalencyclicals.net/leo10/l10exdom.htm

7   *Commentaria de actis et scriptis Martini Lutheri Saxonis chronographice ex ordine ab anno Domini 1517 usque ad annum 1546 inclusive fideliter conscripta* (Mainz, 1549).

8   Denifle, H., and Weiss, A. M., *Luther und Lutherthum in der ersten Entwickelung quellenmässig dargestellt* (Mainz, 1904).

9   Smith, Preserved, review of Denifle in *The American Historical Review*, vol. 15, no. 2 (January 1910), pp. 367–9.

10 Rupp, Gordon, *The Righteousness of God* (London, 1953), p. 23.

11 English text available at https://archive.org/details/grisarsluther01grisuoft

12 Smolinsky, Heribert, *Die Erforschung der Kirchengeschichte: Leben, Werk und Bedeutung von Hubert Jedin (1900–1980)* (Münster, 2001). Lortz, Joseph, *The Reformation in Germany*, trans. by Ronald Walls (London and New York, 1968).

13 Heinrich Denzinger's *Enchiridion symbolorum et definitionum, quae de rebus fidei et morum a conciliis oecumenicis et summis pontificibus emanarunt* presented key extracts from conciliar, synodical and papal documents, to provide a concise distillation of fundamental Catholic teaching. Till the Second Vatican Council it was a standard reference work in seminaries and Catholic universities, in the process encouraging a narrowly propositional understanding of the nature of Catholic doctrine.

14 Lortz, Joseph, 'The basic elements of Luther's intellectual style', in Jared Wicks (ed.), *Catholic Scholars Dialogue with Luther* (Chicago, IL, 1970), pp. 3–33, at p. 32.

15 Iserloh, Erwin, *Luther zwischen Reform und Reformation: Der Thesenanschlag fand nicht statt* (Münster, 1966); trans. as *The Theses Were Not Posted: Luther between Reform and Reformation* (London, 1968).

16 Rupp, Gordon, review of Iserloh in *Journal of Theological Studies*, new series, vol. 19, no. 1 (April 1968), pp. 360–69.

17 Todd, John, *Martin Luther: A Biographical Study* (London, 1964).

18 Bagchee, Joydeep, and Adluri, Vishwa P., 'The passion of Paul Hacker: Indology, orientalism and evangelism', in Joanne Miyang Cho, Eric Kurlander and Douglas T. McGetchin (eds), *Transcultural Encounters between Germany and India: Kindred Spirits in the Nineteenth Century* (New York, 2013), pp. 215–29.

19 Hacker, Paul, *Das Ich im Glauben bei Martin Luther: der Ursprung der anthropozentrichen Religion* (Graz, Vienna and Cologne, 1966), trans. as *The Ego in Faith: Martin Luther and the Origin of Anthropocentric Religion* (Chicago, IL, 1970).

20 Hacker provided a convenient distillation of his main contentions in his essay 'Martin Luther's notion of faith' in Wicks (ed.), *Catholic Scholars Dialogue with Luther*, pp. 85–105, from which the quotations in the text have been drawn.

21 'Luther and the unity of the churches', *Communio*, vol. 11 (Fall 1984), pp. 210–26, available online at http://www.communio-icr.com/files/ratzinger11-3.pdf from which the following quotations are taken.

22 Scribner, R. W., 'Incombustible Luther: the image of the reformer in early modern Germany', *Past & Present*, vol. 110, issue 1 (1 February 1986), pp. 38–68.

23 For a useful overview, see Marshall, Peter, '(Re)defining the English Reformation', *Journal of British Studies*, 48 (July 2009), pp. 564–86.

24 Both David Batchi's *Luther's Earliest Opponents* (Minneapolis, 1991) and John Frymire's *The Primacy of the Postils: Catholics, Protestants and the Dissemination of Ideas in Early Modern Germany* (Leiden, 2010) suggest that a more extensive re-evaluation of the theology and pastoral effectiveness of the Church in pre-Reformation Germany might challenge the received narrative.

25 Stanford, Peter, *Martin Luther, Catholic Dissident* (London, 2017).

26 Rex, Richard, *The Making of Martin Luther* (Princeton, NJ, 2017), p. 223.

27 Ibid,, p. 218.

28 Ibid., p. 226.

29 Ibid., pp. 228–9.

CHAPTER 8

This essay first appeared as the introduction to *J. A. Froude's The Reign of Mary Tudor*. (London, 2009). It was written before the appearance of Ciaran Brady's magisterial biography *James Anthony Froude: An Intellectual Biography of a Victorian Prophet* (Oxford, 2014), now the indispensable first point of reference on Froude.

1 I have used the standard edition, *History of England from the Fall of Wolsey to the Defeat of the Spanish Armada* (London, 1879).

2 For Froude's career, in addition to the *Oxford Dictionary of National Biography* article by A. F. Pollard and William Thomas, see Paul, Herbert, *The Life of Froude* (London, 1905), and also Dunn, Hilary, *James Anthony Froude: A Biography*, 2 vols (Oxford, 1961–3). For appraisals of his work as a Tudor historian see, in ascending order of usefulness: Rowse, A. L., *Froude the Historian, Victorian Man of Letters* (Gloucester, 1987); Elton, G. R., 'J. A. Froude and his *History of England*', in *Studies in Tudor and Stuart Politics and Government:* vol. 3, *Papers and Reviews, 1973–1981* (Cambridge, 2003); and Burrow, J. W., *A Liberal Descent: Victorian Historians and the English Past* (Cambridge, 1981), pp. 231–85.

3 Froude, James Anthony, *Short Studies of Great Subjects*, second series (London, 1900), p. 101.

4   Froude's religious odyssey is described in Basil Willey's *More Nineteenth Century Studies: A Group of Honest Doubters* (London, 1963), pp. 106–36.

5   'Hallam's Constitutional History', in *Lord Macaulay's Essays and Lays of Ancient Rome* (London, 1909), p. 57.

6   Froude, Hurrell, *Remains of the late Reverend Richard Hurrell Froude* (London, 1838), vol. 1, p. 433. The Newman quotation is from Peter Knockles, *The Oxford Movement in Context: Anglican High Churchmanship, 1760–1857* (Cambridge, 1994), p. 124.

7   For a sometimes overenthusiastic assessment of Lingard's originality as a historian, see Jones, Edwin, *John Lingard and the Pursuit of Historical Truth* (Brighton, 2001).

8   See also Dunn, *Froude*, vol. 1, p. 174.

9   Paul, *The Life of Froude*, pp. 117–18.

10   Dunn, *Froude*, vol. 2 (1963), pp. 287–94.

11   Paul, *Froude*, pp. 192–8.

12   Froude, *History*, vol. 4, p. 239.

13   On Froude's intellectual indebtedness to Carlyle, see Burrow, *Liberal Descent*, pp. 252–6.

14   Dunn, *Froude*, vol. 1, p. 202.

15   Froude, *History*, vol. 2, pp. 215–17.

16   Ibid., pp. 248–55.

17   Dunn, *Froude*, vol. 2, p. 464.

18   Froude, *History*, vol. 1 preface (unpaginated).

19   Ibid., vol. 4, p. 240.

20   Ibid., vol. 4, p. 242.

21   Ibid., vol. 5, p. 203.

22   Ibid.

23   Ibid., vol. 5, p. 257.

24   Ibid., vol. 5, pp. 30–31.

25   Ibid., vol. 5, p. 411.

26   Ibid., vol. 5, p. 521.

27   Ibid., vol. 6, pp. 99–100.

28   Ibid., vol. 5, p. 217. Compare his striking summary of Elizabeth's religious scepticism at the conclusion of the History: 'To Elizabeth the speculations of so-called divines were but as ropes of sand and sea-slime leading to the moon, and the doctrines for which they were rending each other to pieces a dream of fools or enthusiasts [...] She saw through the emptiness of the forms in which religion presented itself to the world.' *History*, vol. 12, p. 506.

29   Ibid., vol. 5, p. 226.

30   Ibid., vol. 5, pp. 444–5.

31 Ibid., vol. 5, p. 410.

32 Ibid., vol. 5, pp. 523, 558, 560.

33 Tennyson, Alfred, Lord, *Queen Mary* (London, 1875); Tennyson, Hallam, *Alfred Lord Tennyson: A Memoir by His Son* (London, 1899), pp. 562–72.

34 For the revived emphasis on the centrality of Henry, see G. W. Bernard, *The King's Reformation* (London, 2005).

35 For example, Loades, David, *Mary Tudor: The Tragical History of the First Queen of England* (London, 2006).

36 Dickens, A. G., *The English Reformation* (London, 1989): for a treatment of Mary's reign which challenges the interpretation laid down by Froude, see Duffy, Eamon, *Fires of Faith: Catholic England under Mary Tudor* (New Haven, CT, and London, 2009).

37 Froude, *History*, vol. 5, pp. 246–7.

CHAPTER 9

This essay first appeared in *Historical Research*, vol. 77 (February 2004), pp. 98–110.

1 Dickens, A. G. (ed.), *The Register or Chronicle of Butley Priory, Suffolk, 1510–35* (Winchester, 1951), repr. in Dickens, A. G., *Late Monasticism and the Reformation* (London, 1994), pp. ix–xiv, 1–84.

2 Knowles, M. D., *The Monastic Order in England: A History of its Development from the Times of St Dunstan to the Fourth Lateran Council, 943–1216* (Cambridge, 1940); Knowles, M. D., *The Religious Orders in England*, 3 vols (Cambridge, 1948–59); Pantin, W. A., *The English Church in the 14th Century* (Cambridge, 1955).

3 The conflict between Gasquet and Coulton was sensitively treated in Dom David Knowles's 1956 Creighton lecture, 'Cardinal Gasquet as an Historian' (1957): For Coulton see Christianson, Gerald, 'G. G. Coulton: The Medieval Historian as Controversialist', *The Catholic Historical Review* Vol. 57, No. 3 (Oct., 1971), pp. 421–41; Gasquet, F. A., *Henry VIII and the English Monasteries: An Attempt to Illustrate the History of their Suppression*, 2 vols (1888–9); Gasquet, F. A., *The Old English Bible and Other Essays* (1897); Gasquet, F. A., *The Eve of the Reformation: Studies in the Religious Life and Thought of the English People* (1900); Gasquet, F. A., *Parish Life in Mediaeval England* (1906); Bishop, E., and Gasquet, F. A., *Edward VI and the Book of Common Prayer* (1890).

4 Coulton, G. G., *Ten Medieval Studies* (1930; Boston, 1959), pp. 198–9.

5 Coulton, G. G., *Friar's Lantern* (London, 1906).

6   Dickens, A. G., *The East Riding of Yorkshire with Hull and York: A Portrait* (Hull, 1955), pp. 62–3, 66.
7   Dickens, *East Riding*, pp. 111–12.
8   Coulton, *Friar's Lantern*, pp. 13, 15–16.
9   Dickens, A. G., *The English Reformation*, 1st edn (London, 1964), p. 10.
10   Dickens, A. G., *The English Reformation*, rev. edn (London, 1967), pp. 34, 37.
11   Ibid., pp. 13–16, 20.
12   Ibid., p. 444.
13   Ibid., pp. 21–2.
14   Ibid., p. 21 (my italics). Dickens's essay on Parkyn was reprinted and is most accessible in his collection *Late Monasticism and the Reformation* (London, 1994).
15   Chibi, Andrew Allan, *Henry VIII's Bishops: Diplomats, Administrators, Scholars and Shepherds* (Cambridge, 2003).
16   Dickens, *English Reformation* (1967), pp. 31, 33–4, 38–9, 444–5; Thompson, S., 'The pastoral work of the English and Welsh bishops, 1500–58', D.Phil. thesis, University of Oxford, 1984; Heath, P., *The English Parish Clergy on the Eve of the Reformation* (London, 1969); Knowles, *Religious Orders*, vol. 3, p. 126.
17   Dickens, *Register of Butley Priory*, p. 23; Knowles, *Religious Orders*, iii. 129.
18   Dickens, A. G., 'A municipal dissolution of chantries at York, 1536', *Yorkshire Archaeological Journal*, vol. xxxvi (1947), pp. 164–73, repr. in his *Reformation Studies*, pp. 47–56, at p. 51.
19   Ibid., p. 47; Dobson, R. B., *Church and Society in the Medieval North of England* (London, 1996), p. 263.
20   Dickens, A. G., *English Reformation*, 2nd edn (1989), p. 13.

CHAPTER 10

This essay originated as a lecture given in Westminster Abbey on 4 May 2019, as part of a day of events organised by the Anglican Shrine of Our Lady of Walsingham.

1   Text from Jones, Emrys (ed.), *The New Oxford Book of Sixteenth Century Verse* (Oxford, 2009), pp. 550–51.
2   Shell, Alison, *Oral Culture and Catholicism in Early Modern England* (Cambridge, 2007), pp. 89–90; Hackett, Helen, *Virgin Mother, Maiden Queen: Elizabeth I and the Cult of the Virgin Mary* (London, 1994), p. 159.
3   The documented facts about the early history of the shrine are set out in J. C. Dickinson, *The Shrine of Our Lady of Walsingham* (Cambridge, 1956), pp. 3–23.

4   The ballad is printed in Dickinson, *Shrine*, pp. 124–30.
5   Dickinson, *Shrine*, pp. 24–68; for Erasmus's account of his pilgrimage to Walsingham, see Thompson, Craig R. (ed.), *Erasmus, Ten Colloquies* (Indianapolis, IN, 1957), pp. 56–79.
6   Moreton, C. E., 'The Walsingham conspiracy of 1537', *Bulletin of the Institute of Historical Research*, vol. 63 (1990), pp. 29–43; Waller, Gary, *Walsingham and the English Imagination* (Farnham, 2011), pp. 65–90.
7   Morrison, Susan Signe, 'Waste space: pilgrim badges, Ophelia, and Walsingham remembered', in Dominic Janes and Gary Waller (eds), *Walsingham in Literature and Culture from the Middle Ages to Modernity* (Farnham, 2010), pp. 49–66.
8   Waterton, Edmund, *Pietas Mariana Britannica* (London, 1879); Waller, *Walsingham and the English Imagination*, pp. 162–8.
9   Brief biography by Nigel Yates in *Oxford Dictionary of National Biography*.
10 Rear, Michael, *Walsingham: Pilgrims and Pilgrimage* (Leominster, 2019), pp. 179–90. Fr Rear's book is the best history of both shrines.
11 For what follows, see Yelton, Michael, *Alfred Hope Patten and the Shrine of Our Lady of Walsingham* (Norwich, 2006), passim, and Rear, *Walsingham*, pp. 196–221.
12 Yelton, Michael, *Anglican Papalism: An Illustrated History, 1900–1960* (Norwich, 2005).
13 Baverstock's sermon is printed in Peter Cobb (ed.), *Walsingham* (Bristol, 1990), pp. 35–6.
14 Rear, *Walsingham*, p. 215.
15 Yelton, *Hope Patten*, p. 97.
16 Ibid., p. 262.
17 For Scott James's own account, see Scott James, Bruno, *Asking for Trouble* (London, 1962).
18 Rear, *Walsingham*, pp. 221–4.
19 Wilson, A. N., *The Healing Art* (London, 1980).
20 For his own account, see Stephenson, Colin, *Walsingham Way* (London, 1970).
21 Rear, *Walsingham*, p. 267.
22 Private communication to the author.

CHAPTER 11

Earlier versions of this essay were given as the 2017 Ebor Lecture in York Minster and the 2018 Friends of the British Library Lecture. I am indebted to the friends and colleagues who have commented on those earlier versions – Colin Burrow, Brian Cummings, David Hoyle, Peter Marshall, Melanie

McDonagh, Richard Rex and Alec Ryrie – who are, however, in no way to blame for whatever lapses of fact, taste and emphasis remain.

1   Iserloh, Erwin, *The Theses Were Not Posted: Luther between Reform and Reformation* (London, 1968), and my essay 'Luther through Catholic Eyes' above, pp. 125–42.

2   The first two of Sansom's 'Shardlake' novels, in which Cromwell features directly, are *Dissolution* (London, 2003) and *Dark Fire* (London, 2004). On Jean Plaidy, Philippa Gregory and Alison Weir see Megan Hickerson, '"Anne taught him how to be cruel": Henry VIII in modern historical fiction', in Thomas Betteridge and Thomas Freeman (eds), *Henry VIII and History* (Farnham, 2012), pp. 223–40.

3   The first of the four series of *The Tudors* was televised in 2007. At the time of writing (March 2020) all four series are still available in the UK on Amazon Prime.

4   *Wolf Hall* (London, 2009), *Bring Up the Bodies* (London, 2012) and *The Mirror and the Light* (London, 2020). The text of Nick Poulton's stage version of the first two books was published by Nick Hern Books in 2014. The TV series starring Mark Rylance is at the time of writing still available on Britbox.

5   Quoted in Freeman, Thomas, 'Inventing Bloody Mary', in Susan Doran and Thomas Freeman (eds) *Mary Tudor, Old and New Perspectives* (London, 2011), p. 93.

6   Duffy, Eamon, *The Reformation and the Grand Narrative*, Eoin MacNeill Lecture, Irish Manuscripts Commission (Dublin, 2013).

7   For Froude, see my essay 'James Anthony Froude and the Reign of Queen Mary' above and Ciaran Brady's magisterial *James Anthony Froude: An Intellectual Biography of a Victorian Prophet* (Oxford, 2014).

8   Morris, Kevin, 'John Bull and the scarlet woman: Charles Kingsley and anti-Catholicism in Victorian literature', *British Catholic History*, vol. 23 (1996), pp. 190–218.

9   Ligocki, Llewellyn, 'Ainsworth's historical accuracy reconsidered', *Albion: A Quarterly Journal Concerned with British Studies*, IV (1972), pp. 23–8.

10 de Vere, Aubrey, *Mary Tudor: An Historical Drama in Two Parts* (London, 1884).

11 Tennyson, Hallam, *Alfred Lord Tennyson: A Memoir* (London, 1897), vol. 2, p. 173.

12 For Bridgett, see the *Oxford Dictionary of National Biography* entry by Pollard, revised by Rosemary Mitchell. Bridgett wrote hagiographic but well-researched and pioneering biographies of John Fisher and Thomas More – the latter, according to Richard Marius, being 'the first and best

of the modern biographies': Marius, Richard, *Thomas More* (London, 1993), p. xix. For John Morris, see Pollen, J. H. *The Life and Letters of Father John Morris SJ* (London, 1896). Morris was born into an East India Company family, wrote a significant biography of Thomas Becket and was the postulator for the cause of the English martyrs, but his major work was the three volumes of edited documents, *The Troubles of Our Catholic Forefathers, Related by Themselves* (London, 1872–7). On Aidan Gasquet, see Knowles, David, *Cardinal Gasquet as an Historian*, The Creighton Lecture in History, 1956 (London, 1957); repr. in *The Historian and Character and Other Essays* (Cambridge, 1963), pp. 240–63. On Bede Camm, see Bellenger, Aidan, 'Dom Bede Camm (1864–1942), monastic martyrologist', in *Studies in Church History*, vol. 30 (Martyrs and Martyrologies) (Cambridge, 1993), pp. 371–81.

13 Martindale, C. C., *The Life of Mgr Robert Hugh Benson*, 2 vols (London, 1917); Grayson, Janet, *Robert Hugh Benson: Life and Works* (Lanham, MD, 1998).

14 *The Fifth Queen* (London, 1906), *Privy Seal* (1907) and *The Fifth Queen Crowned* (1908).

15 Mizener, Arthur, 'The historical romance and twentieth-century sensibility: Ford's *Fifth Queen*', *Sewanee Review*, vol. 78, no. 4 (Autumn 1970), pp. 563–77.

16 Gass, William 'The neglect of the *Fifth Queen*', in Sondra Strang (ed.), *The Presence of Ford Madox Ford* (Philadelphia, PA, 1981), p. 27.

17 Graham Greene, from the Introduction to *The Bodley Head Ford Madox Ford* (London, 1962); repr. in Strang, *Presence*, p. 5.

18 Bolt, Robert, *A Man for All Seasons*, in Tom Maschler (ed.), *New English Dramatists*, vol. 6 (Harmondsworth, 1963), p. 74.

19 Quoted by Peter Marshall in 'Saints in Cinema: *A Man for All Seasons*', in Susan Doran and Thomas S. Freeman (eds), *Tudors and Stuarts on Film: Historical Perspectives* (Basingstoke and New York, 2009), pp. 46–59, at p. 53.

20 http://www.vatican.va/content/john-paul-ii/en/motu_proprio/documents/hf_jp-ii_motu-proprio_20001031_thomas-more.html

21 Prescott, H. F. M., *The Man on a Donkey*, 2 vols (London, 1952). I have used the one-volume edition of 1953: the novel is currently (2020) available in a paperback reissue by Phoenix Press of the Ballantine Books edition of 1967, and on Kindle.

22 Dodds, Madeleine Hope, and Dodds, Ruth, *The Pilgrimage of Grace, 1536–7, and the Exeter Conspiracy, 1538*, 2 vols (Cambridge, 1915).

23 Knowles, David, *The Religious Orders in England*, vol. 3 (Cambridge, 1959); subsequently reissued in an abbreviated form as a standalone

book, *Bare Ruined Choirs: The Dissolution of the English Monasteries* (Cambridge, 1976).

24 Merriman, Roger Biglow, *Life and Letters of Thomas Cromwell*, 2 vols (Oxford, 1902).

25 Scarisbrick, J. J., *Henry VIII* (New Haven, CT, and London, 2011), p. 303.

26 Elton, G. R., 'The myth of Thomas More', *New York Review of Books* (3 February 1983), a review of Alistair Fox's *Thomas More: History and Providence* (New Haven, CT, and London, 1982).

27 Marius, Richard, *Thomas More* (London, 1993), quotation at p. xxi.

28 For some recent attempts to put More's attitudes and activities in relation to heresy in their proper context, see: Duffy, Eamon, *Reformation Divided: Catholics, Protestants and the Conversion of England* (London, 2017), pp. 19–95; Guy, John, *Thomas More* (London, 2000), pp. 106–25; and Rex, Richard, 'More and the heretics: statesman or fanatic?', in George M. Logan (ed.), *The Cambridge Companion to Thomas More* (Cambridge, 2011), pp. 93–115. On the specific claims that a key to More's character lies in deep-seated sexual neuroses, see the eminently sensible comments by Guy, *Thomas More*, pp. 32–6.

29 http://waldemar.tv/2015/01/the-true-face-of-the-tudors/

30 Mantel, Hilary, and Salomon, Xavier F., *Holbein's Sir Thomas More* (New York and London, 2018), pp. 11–17.

31 *Wolf Hall*, p. 527; *The Mirror and the Light*, pp. 257, 273.

32 *Wolf Hall*, p. 459.

33 Ibid., pp. 125, 298, 335, 348, 459, 628–9, 639–40.

34 Ibid., p. 590; *The Mirror and the Light,* pp. 429–30.

35 Bolt, *A Man for All Seasons*, p. 113.

36 *Wolf Hall*, pp. 632–3.

37 Ibid., p. 565.

38 Ibid., p. 628.

39 Ibid., p. 123.

40 Ibid., p. 515.

41 See above, note 20.

42 Trapp, J. B. (ed.), *The Apology of Sir Thomas More*, in *Complete Works of St Thomas More*, vol. 9 (New Haven, CT, and London, 1979), p. 118.

43 Moynihan, Brian, *If God Spare My Life* (London, 2003) (published in the USA as *God's Bestseller*); Ridley, Jasper, *The Statesman and the Fanatic: Thomas Wolsey and Thomas More* (London, 1982). Amusingly, Ridley's publishers, conscious of the impact of Bolt's play and anxious lest the title dissuade buyers, insisted on a change of title for the American market: in the USA Ridley's book appeared as *The Statesman and the Saint!*

44 Rogers, Elizabeth Frances, *The Correspondence of Sir Thomas More* (Princeton, NJ, 1947), p. 553.

45 Elton, G. R., *Policy and Police: The Enforcement of the Reformation in the Age of Thomas Cromwell* (Cambridge, 1972), p. 405.

46 *Wolf Hall*, p. 629.

47 Sylvester, Richard S., and Harding, Davis P. (eds), *Two Early Tudor Lives* (New Haven, CT, and London, 1962), p. 108, although I have accepted the text of Cavendish's remark suggested in MacCulloch, Diarmaid, *Thomas Cromwell: A Life* (London, 2018), pp. 88–9.

48 *Wolf Hall*, pp. 155–6.

49 *Bring Up the Bodies*, p. 4.

50 Kingsford, C. L. (ed.), *A Survey of London by John Stow* (Oxford, 1908), vol. 1, p. 179.

51 *The Mirror and the Light*, p. 292.

52 MacCulloch, *Thomas Cromwell*, p. 287. I owe the comparison between Cromwell's and More's involvements in burnings to Peter Marshall – see his *Heretics and Believers: A History of the English Reformation* (New Haven, CT, and London, 2017), p. 222.

53 For the tradition about Margaret Giggs, see Morris, *Troubles of Our Catholic Forefathers* (London, 1871), vol. 1, pp. 3–24.

54 MacCulloch calls it 'the King's savagery': *Cromwell*, pp. 280, 284.

55 *Wolf Hall*, pp. 622–3.

56 *The Mirror and the Light*, p. 812.

57 Ibid., p. 451.

58 *Wolf Hall*, p. 636.

59 *Wolf Hall and Bring Up the Bodies, adapted for the stage by Michael Poulton* (London, 2014), pp. 27–9. The claim that More's polemical writings are morbidly and revealingly foul-mouthed is insisted on both by Elton and Marius, and taken by them as evidence of More's diseased subconscious. In fact, however, More's use of scatological language occurs exclusively in the *Responsio ad Lutherum*, the 1523 Latin treatise – formally, a humanist 'diatribe' – probably commissioned by the Court for a learned European audience in defence of Henry VIII against the 'violently abusive derision' of Martin Luther; there is nothing 'uncontrolled' about it. More's expertise in the Latin classics is here at its most deliberate, and his deployment of sometimes brutal scatology, cloaked as it is in the decent obscurity of a learned language, is manifestly a considered riposte in kind to Luther's similarly potty-mouthed abuse of Henry, a literary tit-for-tat, not an unconscious giveaway of mental and moral chaos in More's buried psyche. As Richard Rex has remarked, it is curious that a culture in which four-letter words pass unremarked in TV and the cinema, and

other people's unwelcome ideas are routinely dismissed as 'crap', should make so much of a minor aspect of More's arcane Latin treatise. Professor Rex's remark occurs in a lecture given to the Iona Institute in Dublin, available at https://ionainstitute.ie/thomas-more-thomas-cromwell-and-wolf-hall/

60 MacCulloch, *Cromwell,* p. 4 (my emphasis).

61 *Wolf Hall,* p. 125.

62 Gwynn, Peter, *The King's Cardinal: The Rise and Fall of Thomas Wolsey* (London, 1990), p. 488.

63 For which see Sheils, W., 'Polemic as piety: Thomas Stapleton's *Tres Thomae* and Catholic controversy in the 1580s', *Journal of Ecclesiastical History,* vol. 60 (2009), pp. 74–94. The 'three Thomases' in Stapleton's treatise were the Apostle St Thomas, St Thomas Becket and, by implication, 'St' Thomas More.

64 The review, which appeared in the *Literary Review,* is available online at https://literaryreview.co.uk/king-henrys-henchman

65 Mantel's first Reith lecture, available at http://downloads.bbc.co.uk/radio4/reith2017/reith_2017_hilary_mantel_lecture1.pdf

66 Mantel, letter to *History Today* (1 July 2015).

67 As reported in *The Guardian* (31 May 2017).

68 As reported in the *Daily Telegraph* (11 May 2013).

69 *Daily Telegraph* (22 January 2015).

70 *The Guardian* (8 February 2015).

71 *Today,* BBC Radio 4 (25 February 2020).

72 MacCulloch, *Cromwell,* p. 280.

73 In the collaborative play of Sir Thomas More: see Jowett, John (ed.), *Sir Thomas More,* Arden Shakespeare, 3rd series (London, 2011).

Index